Laws of Creation

Laws of Creation

PROPERTY RIGHTS IN
THE WORLD OF IDEAS

Ronald A. Cass and Keith N. Hylton

HARVARD UNIVERSITY PRESS

Cambridge, Massachusetts, and London, England · 2013

Library of Congress Cataloging-in-Publication Data

Cass, Ronald A.
    Laws of creation : property rights in the world of ideas / Ronald A. Cass and Keith N.
    Hylton.
        p. cm.
    Includes bibliographical references and index.
    ISBN 978-0-674-06645-8
    1. Intellectual property.   2. Copyright.   I. Hylton, Keith N.   II. Title.
K1401.C375 2013
346.04'8—dc23
2012011488

For Suzie and Maria

Contents

Laws of Creation

1

Ideas, Property, and Prosperity

Ideas

Ideas are the engines of progress and prosperity. The first man to realize how to make fire and to use it to cook and provide warmth, the first to domesticate animals, the first to use a wheel to move loads across space, gave their societies an advantage in the race to survive.

Hoary examples make ready reminders of the power of ideas, but modern life abounds in illustrations of the way ideas change our world. Consider, for example, that life expectancy at the end of the twentieth century was more than one-and-a-half times what it was at that century's outset.[1] Why? In no small measure, that change reflects the contributions of penicillin and other antibiotics; vaccines to combat smallpox, measles, mumps, polio, and a myriad of other diseases; and advances in agriculture, food preservation, and transportation. Along with the sea change in medical care, better understanding of hygiene, better tools for controlling insects that carry malaria and encephalitis, widespread pasteurization of milk, and refrigeration of food took us from a U.S. childhood mortality rate of thirty per thousand in 1900 to a childhood mortality rate of less than two per thousand in 2000.[2]

Progress hasn't been limited to matters of health. Another example is the revolution in the way we communicate, in its speed, cost, and reliability. Communication that was uncertain a century ago has become reliable and instantaneous, allowing people to work together across great distances, the cornerstone on which much of international commerce rests. Where letters traveling by ship and train or pony once took weeks or months to arrive (frequently reaching their destination after the events they were addressing had passed), now discussions can be had across the globe in "real time."

The ability to speak at a distance in real time, of course, isn't so new. Alexander Graham Bell spoke to his assistant, Thomas Watson, over his invention, the telephone, and filed his patent in February 1876.[3] Yet this nineteenth-century invention still was a rare item for most of the world's population three-quarters of the way through the twentieth century. Even though satellites and undersea cables provided connections across long distances, the high cost of stringing wires to end-users kept basic telephone service from more than half the people on the planet as late as the 1980s.[4] But the development and diffusion of cellular telephone technologies and of Internet telephony (along with the more common keyboard communication over the Internet) at the end of the twentieth and beginning of the twenty-first century dramatically altered the landscape. Today, people in China can talk over the Internet to people in Chartres or Chicago, whenever they want and at virtually no cost.

Promoting Ideas

The ideas that tacked an extra thirty years onto our lives in the past one hundred years, that have made it possible to get more goods and services more cheaply and to share information and experiences instantly, did not come to everyone on equal terms. Some societies generate more ideas and receive the fruits of those ideas more readily than others. Legal origins and existing legal institutions may have played a role in this.

The role of law in encouraging development, diffusion, and exploitation of ideas is the core focus of this book. How legal institutions (i.e., law and its enforcement) encourage the development of ideas, their dissemination, and their best use are topics that could each take an entire volume. Our goal is not to provide an exhaustive treatment of any one of these matters, but to give readers an overview of the field. In the short compass we have, we describe the basic understanding on these issues, the legal rules that exist, the arguments about them, and the policies we think best serve society's interests.

Property Rights

We start with a concept that is implicated in almost any endeavor that involves an investment of ingenuity, time, and energy in creating something or in regulating its use. It is the concept of property. As we explain later, this is a controversial starting point for the world of ideas.

Property has been part of the bedrock of civilization from ancient times. Respect for property is demanded by ancient religious commandments, social compacts, and constitutions. Its importance to our lives and to progress is expounded by philosophers, economists, and social historians. John Locke famously proposed a theory of property as a natural right that has given rise to a cottage industry in scholarly discourse.[5]

The case for property rights also has an instrumental base. Casual observers of the human condition long have noted the difference secure property rights make in motivating individual initiative. Contemporaneous with the drafting of the American Constitution, an Englishman, Arthur Young, reflecting on his travels in France declared:

> Give a man the secure possession of a bleak rock, and he will turn it into a garden; give him a nine years' lease of a garden, and he will convert it into a desert. . . . The magic of property turns sand into gold.[6]

Yet recognition of the central role of property in our lives has coexisted with ongoing skepticism about the value and even the legitimacy of the concept of private property. The most extreme example of that skepticism was Proudhon's assertion that "property is theft."[7] That sentiment in some measure is shared by an array of academicians and pundits.[8] Although virtually everyone in Western democracies—and most other societies as well—today acknowledges the central role of property, academic and public policy discourse typically makes the acknowledgment a qualified one.

Three distinct themes run through the skepticism about private property: moral desert, egalitarianism, and socialist or welfarist instrumentalism. The first of these themes urges that possessors of property often have no moral claim to the property, having inherited it through no work of their own or having gained it by virtue of luck rather than because the possessor was especially clever or industrious.[9] The second theme is that, no matter what explains how people obtain property in the first place, there is a substantial value to be served by distributing it equally across a population.[10] The third theme is that as a practical matter centralized institutions can develop resources and direct them to their best—socially preferred—uses better than the market forces that are corollaries of private property rights.[11]

While these themes reflect personal value judgments, they also build on empirical assumptions. That is especially true of the third, instrumentalist, theme, which runs headlong into the instrumentalist case for property rights. One of the arguments for property rights is the assertion that the complex of activities associated with property—giving individuals control over property, letting them determine what uses are best, letting individuals exchange rights to use and control property in line with their own estimations of value—increases society's overall wealth and individuals' overall well-being. That is an empirical assertion, and it is at odds with assumptions behind the instrumentalist objection to property rights.

The empirical assumptions entwined in the instrumentalist challenge to private property rights encompass the supposition that central planning, scientifically informed, can avoid the costly errors that markets generate.[12] Evidence of such market errors is found in stock market crashes and "wasteful competition" that spends resources on production that cannot be sold for what it costs and that brings about frequent bankruptcy of businesses. The stock market crash of 2008 has generated a fresh round of arguments that markets driven by individual decisions typically fail.[13] For some writers, this evidence points to the superiority of a system in which the government would direct resources to their best uses instead of relying on individual decision-making.

The claim that central planning enjoys an instrumental advantage over private property and individual decision-making can be supported by references to deep-seated human inclinations to advance self-interest. One key concept in the litany of behaviors motivated by self-interest is "free riding," the instinct to get something for nothing by taking advantage of the investments of others, or by not investing where investment is necessary to maintain a resource.[14] Some of the best-known illustrations of the free-riding phenomenon travel under the label "the tragedy of the commons." These writings explore the ways in which commonly held resources—resources without well-defined individual property rights—tend to be overexploited.[15] Consider two prototypical examples: overgrazing and overfishing. Allowing cattle to roam freely across pastures provides no incentive to replenish the pastures and thereby ensure a sufficient food supply to sustain the population of cattle. Similarly, overfishing depletes stocks of fish in oceans and rivers beyond the point where the fish population is self-sustaining, ultimately putting all the fishermen out of business. Although everyone knows that failure to curb overgrazing or overfishing inevitably kills the proverbial golden goose, it happens repeatedly in settings where no one owns the goose.

Property Rights versus Collective Control

Different legal institutions offer the theoretical possibility of correcting problems such as overfishing. Perhaps no one institution is provably best, a priori, in all settings. That said, in an array of circumstances the property rights system (and market interactions based on those rights) dominates its primary alternative of collective decision-making through centralized authority.

The skeptical view[16] toward allocations generated under free markets and property rights often builds on visions of unbiased government decision-making and evidence that markets are imperfect. It downplays the evidence that casts doubt on the capacity of centralized institutions to access the information necessary to harness individuals' interests.[17]

After the fall of the Soviet Union, however, the consensus at the most abstract level is that private property rights and individual judgments executed through markets prove superior to central decision-making at promoting the development and preservation of property. Although there were many examples of the different incentives created by collective and private ownership, probably the single best illustration was a striking disparity in agricultural productivity: toward the end of the Soviet era, the small amount of land available for individual farmers to produce goods for their own account—less than three percent of the land used for agriculture—generated more than half the produce consumed in the nation.[18]

Of course, the conclusion that centralized ownership of resources is generally inferior to a system of private property and markets does not end the debate over property rights. Many writers who acknowledge some role for private property also see in numerous arenas a benefit to government regulation that has the hallmarks of central planning.[19] Commentators, for example, point to the plight of America's "unregulated" (by which they mean more open to competitive entry than was historically the case) passenger airline industry as an example of the problems that come with reliance on markets rather than regulation.[20] More recently, the standard reference for the risks of unregulated markets has been the financial industry, despite the fact that virtually all aspects of the industry are heavily regulated—and much of the responsibility for the 2008–09 financial crisis traces to regulation-induced mismatches in information and incentives.[21]

The more fine-grained arguments for government regulation in particular instances cannot be rejected on the same basis as the broader contentions in support of general collective ownership and control of property. As we explain in Chapter 2, instrumentalist arguments for private property rights do not establish any distinct set of rights as best for all circumstances, nor do they prove that no central authority can improve a society's lot by means that limit individual property owners' rights to do as they wish. Yet, in looking for starting points, not all-or-nothing conclusions, the basic case for property rights provides a presumptive origin or default position for analysis of specific interventions.

Intellectual Property

Among their other benefits, property rights provide the standard mechanism for aligning individual interests and incentives with social value. Because of this, some scholars and commentators assume that the same system that works for tangible property should provide the template for the world of ideas. We view this as a reasonable starting point, but it has become increasingly controversial.

Authors and inventors long have enjoyed property rights in their works, rights against the rest of the world to control the reproduction of creative expression and useful inventions. Although there are different histories for these rights and varied explanations for them, for at least two and a quarter centuries rights to control the fruits of an idea have been explained as serving the same instrumental ends as other property rights. Thus, for example, the U.S. Constitution expressly grounds these rights in the goal of promoting creative expression and invention. Article I, Section 8 of the Constitution empowers Congress "to promote the Progress of Science and useful Arts, by securing for limited Times to Authors and Inventors the exclusive right to their respective Writings and Discoveries."

The intuition behind the grant of such rights in the United States and other common-law nations[22] is simple: if property rights generally increase incentives to invest in discovering, caring for, and exploiting things, they should also increase the incentives to invest in discovering and using ideas. Admittedly, there is not a lot of rigorous learning about what prompts discoveries, especially the most important discoveries, or the creation of expressive works. Some scholars opine that money is not a prime motivation for creative energy, and some even suggest the possibility that the prospect of financial gain can reduce such investment.[23]

Acknowledging the limited state of our knowledge does not imply doubt about the soundness of the intuition behind intellectual property rights. Surely, money does not explain everything. The eccentric inventor, driven to invent and never thinking of personal gain, may have a "Eureka" moment, providing grist for storytelling. But the common human experience is that the prospect of increased wealth does, indeed, generate investment of time, energy, and creative thought. The pharmaceutical industry, which pours millions of dollars into research to produce new drugs, would not make the same investments if it faced the prospect of lower financial returns.[24]

While it may be true that some of the most successful inventors did not appear to be motivated by money, it is a mistake to conclude from that observation that there is no link between the prospect of financial reward and innovation. Probably the majority of researchers employed by pharmaceutical companies are not thinking about money when they go into their laboratories. But if there were no financial return to the products produced by their companies, how long do you think they would remain employed as researchers? Consider, for example, Maurice Hilleman, who developed nearly three dozen vaccines during his career at Merck, vaccines that save more than one million lives worldwide each year. Hilleman never showed an interest in financial rewards, and indeed the vaccine market has never been considered profitable in comparison to standard drugs.[25] Still, it was the stream of revenue secured by Merck's patents that allowed the firm to support Hilleman as he produced one life-saving vaccine after another. It is a profound mistake to think that simply because geniuses of Hilleman's stature often appear not to be motivated by financial reward that financial reward is not a crucial ingredient to creating the conditions under which their work can be accomplished.

The real question is not whether intellectual property rights, like other property rights, call forth investments that raise the stock of socially valuable inventions and creative expressions. On that margin, the world of ideas and the world of tangible things are the same. The serious question is what sort of rights will call forth the optimal amount and type of investment, and what price will be paid by society as a result. The answer in the physical world typically is that owners have rights to sell, rent, use, reshape, divide, or otherwise control the disposition of the things they own, subject only to regulations—such as nuisance law—designed to prevent owners from imposing on others.

Plainly, the world of ideas is not identical to the physical world. The fact that ideas are not physical means that staking claim to ideas is potentially more difficult than staking claim to property, as it cannot be secured through possession, a common mechanism for securing rights in an array of tangible things. This may be a reason to be cautious about creating property rights in ideas, as it alters the calculation of costs and benefits from such rights. The absence of a specific physical location for intangible property, however, turns out to be less important than it first seems, as ownership rights in many types of physical property are secured in ways quite similar to the means for securing rights for ideas.[26] Land ownership registration systems, for example, are more efficient mechanisms for determining rights in real property than physical examination of the land could be. The same holds true for automobile title systems and other record-keeping schemes that permit greater certainty and remote access to information about ownership of tangible goods. In many cases, similar impediments exist to determining ownership of tangible and intangible property, and similar mechanisms can be crafted to lower those hurdles.

A more important distinction is that possession of ideas is nonrivalrous. Unlike physical property, an idea can be possessed and used simultaneously by many people without its use by one person interfering with its use by another. Thomas Jefferson's observation on this point remains a classic statement:

> [An idea's] peculiar character . . . is that no one possesses the less, because every other possesses the whole of it. He who receives an idea from me, receives instruction himself without lessening mine; as he who lights his taper at mine, receives light without darkening me.[27]

The observation is, as a generality, sound, though there are some important qualifications. But what follows from it? Jefferson did not argue against property rights for ideas on the ground that ideas could be shared without the costs associated with attempts to use physical property simultaneously. He commented that rights to the fruits of one's ideas could indeed be supported as a spur to the pursuit of ideas, but he did not suppose that there could be a *natural right* to property in ideas. His remarks, in other words, went to the nature of the property right, not to its existence.

Other writers have gone where Jefferson would not, arguing that there is no case to be made for property rights in ideas at all. Richard Stallman urges that it is morally wrong to protect software as property, and more generally that intellectual property should be regarded as something quite different from—and not analogous to—tangible property.[28] He sees the award of intellectual property rights in ideas and their expression as inimical to freedom.[29] Stallman not only advocates reducing protection for intellectual property; he also favors compelling disclosure of information that is the basis for much intellectual property. For him, ideas are not merely nonrivalrous; at least within the realm he has focused on, ideas carry with them an imperative to be shared.[30]

More limited arguments against intellectual property rights (and against the analogy of such rights to other property rights) are offered by legal scholars such as Lawrence Lessig and David Post. Lessig, relying heavily on the nonrivalrous nature of ideas at the core of intellectual property, urges a reduction in protections for ideas and expression.[31] Lessig claims that cutting back on legal protections for authors and inventors would be beneficial in part because strong intellectual property rights actually do exactly the opposite of what is supposed by the instrumental case for them: stifling, rather than encouraging, creativity and suppressing, rather than promoting, progress. In the same vein, Post touts the flourishing of the Internet—which he calls essentially a copyright-free zone—as "the greatest outpouring of creative activity in a short span that the world has ever seen."[32]

Economists Michele Boldrin and David Levine provide a sophisticated economic defense for the anti-intellectual property viewpoint.[33] Their position, based on a strictly utilitarian framework, is that the costs of intellectual property far outweigh the benefits. Boldrin and Levine argue that the benefits of protection are exaggerated, since innovation would occur in a competitive economy without protection, and the availability of protection encourages an enormous waste of resources in obtaining it. They conclude that the current system of patent and copyright laws should be abolished.

In spite of the different perspectives offered from technologists, legal theorists, and economists, the question addressed implicitly or explicitly by opponents of intellectual property rights is whether the societal gains in additional creative or inventive production as a result of intellectual property rights are outweighed by the costs associated with the reduced use of protected intellectual products, including their use to create yet more such products. Although not the only issue relevant to the design of intellectual property rights, the trade-off between creation and exploitation of ideas is at the heart of the debate over intellectual property rights.

Lessig, Post, Boldrin, and Levine are among the most prominent of a chorus of writers offering arguments for cutting back on intellectual property protections in various ways. An even larger group of academics and commentators has inveighed against proposals to increase intellectual property protections or to expand their reach.

There is, at first blush, an odd sort of disconnect in the rising number of voices in opposition to intellectual property rights. At the same time as professorial voices questioning the underpinnings of the laws that protect intellectual property have multiplied, the demand for intellectual property courses in law schools has risen precipitously and the number of law teachers turning to this field has grown. The demand among students for intellectual property law courses reflects changes in the economy those students will engage after graduation. The past generation has seen an extraordinary change in the degree to which advanced economies depend on ideas to generate wealth. The common description is that we've moved from an agriculture-based economy, to a manufacturing-based economy, to a service-based economy, and now to an information-and-idea-based economy. If the shorthand description overstates the case, it nonetheless captures a change that has occurred in the United States, Western Europe, Japan, and other developed nations.

Parallel to the change in the importance of ideas to developed economies, there has been a sea change in the ease with which many ideas (or at least particular creative expressions of ideas) can be copied. The photocopier, digital photography, the computer, and other technological changes (e.g., the digital fabricator) have drastically reduced the cost of copying, even as the value of copying would seem to have expanded. The expected outcome would seem to be greater need for protection of the investment in creating and managing intellectual property. Of course, this returns us to the trade-off question just identified. The concrete problems confront us with increasing frequency. If pharmaceuticals and biologics hold the key to improved health, but copying them is increasingly easy once their pharmacology is disclosed, why should society not seek to secure the rewards of innovation to creators of these products? If software development boosts productivity across a wide swath of the economy but software is, thanks in large measure to the computing power it serves, more readily copied when its information is shared, would social interests be served by stronger enforcement of the protections for creators of software? If society increasingly values the product of entertainers and authors, but their work is more readily reproduced, should we enhance protection against unauthorized reproductions?

Roadmap

The book addresses these questions and provides a framework for evaluating the major controversies about intellectual property rights today. We start with the basic concept that underlies most of the rights we have today that are at issue in both academic debates and real-world conflicts: the right to own, use, control, and dispose of property. Chapter 2 explains the basic arguments over property rights and the theoretical underpinnings of modern rights. Chapter 3 turns to the application of these concepts to intellectual property. The chapter focuses particularly on the trade-offs between immediate costs of the rights and their benefits over time, a balance that is critical to understanding much of modern intellectual property law.

Chapters 4 through 7 review the contours of the four principal bodies of intellectual property law: patent, trade secret, copyright, and trademark. Each body has its own peculiar doctrines, but the problems associated with the trade-off between the short-term and the long-term costs of intellectual property run through all four chapters.

The final chapters address the edges of law and policy presented by the existence of discrete bodies of law both inside and outside the field of intellectual property, by the existence of different national and international legal regimes, and by changes in technology and economic organization. Chapter 8 takes up issues involving the application of intellectual property law in a complex, global world, where other bodies of law and other nations' respect for intellectual property can have dramatic impact on the effective protection afforded. That chapter takes up some of the proposals for changing intellectual property law as well as exploring the implications of those proposals. Chapter 9 discusses the interaction between intellectual property law and antitrust law, two parts of the legal framework governing modern economies that often are seen as sources of warring doctrines. We conclude in Chapter 10 with an optimistic view of the current legal doctrines governing intellectual property but also with a cautionary note about the direction in which the laws might now evolve.

2

Rights to Property

Property Rights: Starting Simply?

Although the concepts of "property" and "property rights" are ancient, they remain subjects of debate. The core of the debate traces to the nature of property itself.

It is common to think of property as something obvious. We have things; they are *our* things; those things are our property. What could be simpler? And if something is *my* property, then I must have the right to control it. After all, I don't think about whether I need to ask your permission to read a book in my home or to turn on my computer. The things in my possession are my property and property law confirms my dominion over those things.

The nature of property and of property rights seems intuitively obvious, and also invariant. We may regard other bodies of law as contingent on the winds of political fortune, but we tend to think of property law as fixed and unchanging, as consisting of clear rules that have been in existence since early civilization. What could be clearer and more necessary for the ordering of society than rules that say "this is mine" and "that is yours"? Settling such questions is a prerequisite to social order and progress. It also seems a fairly basic task, not one calling for complex judgments. The manifest necessity for property rules together with their seemingly commonsense nature makes it natural to think of property law as consisting of rules that are stable and fixed for all time.

Everyone who looks seriously at the concepts of property and property rights, however, quickly learns that nothing about them is as simple as they seem. Do I need to possess something for it to be my property? If I possess something, is that enough? Are there things that cannot be my property, even if I find someone willing to sell them to me?

What counts as property and what rights attach to ownership of property vary across time and place. Decisions on these matters respond to changing technological, social, and economic conditions. As with so much of our basic legal structure, for the most part new property rules have emerged where the benefits of the security they provide are greater than the costs. There are some glaring counterexamples to this, and various governance systems have assigned different weights to a given set of circumstances. But by and large the rules for property reflect a rudimentary calculus of social costs and benefits.

In this chapter, we review justifications for property rights generally, a topic that has received copious attention over the past several hundred years. Our aim is to identify different strands or types of argument, some treating property as contingent on economic conditions, and others not. Along the way we will make the case for a utilitarian—or, more simply, "cost-benefit"—approach to property rights. This approach is sensitive to empirical questions and changing conditions.

Property Rights and Social Order

In looking at the justifications for property rights, it is helpful to begin by emphasizing the variation in rights over time and place. What is treated as property, and how it is treated, has fluctuated considerably.

Some matters have become recognized as property over time, while others have been withdrawn from the set of matters regarded as subject to ownership. Indigenous Americans recognized tribal claims, but not individual claims, to land.[1] Rights to useful ideas—patents—were unrecognized until roughly the 1400s, a relatively short time ago on civilization's time scale. Some property rights have all but disappeared, most notably slavery, the right to own other humans. For a less dramatic example, consider the right to own space in the radio spectrum, which was recognized in the United States early in the twentieth century but was then negated when legislation was enacted prohibiting ownership of any rights to spectrum space.[2] More recently, the U.S. Congress reversed course again and authorized the sale of rights to parts of the radio spectrum.[3]

In an early effort to understand what forces influence the shape of property rights, Adam Smith posited that property rights had developed through four stages of civilization, with different property rights associated with each stage.[4] Smith's four civilization stages were: hunter-gatherer, pastoral, agricultural, and lastly commercial societies. In hunter-gatherer societies, Smith argued that there would be little need for complicated property laws, especially rules governing possession of land. Certainly there would be a need for rules governing the allocation of food that had been gathered or captured. A mother who had gone into the forest to pull an apple from a tree for her child could not be left to the mercy of anyone who might decide to take the apple from her once she returned from the forest. Leaving each hunter and gatherer to protect what he or she acquired would induce a series of costly actions to protect the fruits of individuals' labors. Property rules for the society could reduce the costs that would otherwise be incurred and allow greater investment of the society's resources in securing the food necessary for survival. Outside of rules recognizing possession as sufficient for establishing property rights, however, there would be little need for any other property laws in hunter-gatherer societies.[5]

As the economic structure of society evolved through the succeeding stages, the property rules societies adopted changed. In the pastoral societies that raised animals for consumption, the need for property rules would multiply in comparison to the hunter-gatherer society. In addition to the rules making possession equivalent to property, there would be a need for rules on straying livestock, and rules controlling the exploitation of food sources for these animals, such as grazing areas. Detailed rules governing property in land would first appear in the agricultural societies. And, finally, the commercial societies would generate additional property rules to deal with the various items of value in a more advanced economy.[6] Smith predicted that property rules would expand with the scope of commerce.[7]

One lesson suggested by Smith's account of the development of property is that there may be no persuasive case for a set of property laws that are good for all times and under all conditions. There is a strong case for a specific property rule when the benefits of the security it provides substantially exceed its costs,[8] and this will depend on social and economic conditions that may change over time, or may vary across societies. Smith opined that the response to social and economic conditions generally explained the evolution of property law.

That is not a complete explanation, to be sure, and Smith does not offer it as such. There are some property rules that may never have been socially desirable, but were adopted and persisted because the winners from those rules were stronger than the losers. Smith gave examples from feudal times: all wild animals were the property of the king; large fish were the property of the king; a treasure trove found buried on your property belonged to the king. (All of which explains why it was good to be king.) Of course, even in these cases we cannot know for sure whether these feudal property rules were designed to extract wealth from the weak or to serve socially desirable ends, such as preventing the overexploitation of common resources.

While Adam Smith's argument suggests that there is no strong case for a universal set of property rules, it also suggests that there cannot be a strong case *against* property rules per se. Further, Smith's argument indicates that the case for property rules, depending as it does on social and economic conditions, would have to grow stronger over time, as the value of property to society rises and the number and complexity of interactions regarding property increases. Since the domain of commerce has expanded over time, the need for new property rules has expanded too, as Smith's account intimates. A critic of expanded property rules, going against the historical trend, should be expected to meet a high burden of proof.

Like all property rights, intellectual property rights are socially desirable only under the right conditions. As we consider the case for secure intellectual property rights in this book, we will proceed with an awareness of the social and economic contingency of all property rights. And given the contingent nature of property rights, any argument for or against them should be sensitive to empirical evidence respecting their effects.

For now, we consider the general case for property rights as it has developed over time. Some theorists have offered strong arguments, in the sense of treating property rights as "good for all times"; others have offered weak arguments that find property rights desirable only if the right conditions are satisfied. We review these arguments to explore the different perspectives offered in justifying property rights and to compare the strengths and weaknesses of these perspectives. Although we come to this issue from the "weak argument" school, we recognize, as we hope to make clear below, that there are valuable features of the "strong argument" school that should not be discounted.

The Case for Property Rights: Locke and Labor

The strong case for property commonly is traced to the following passage from John Locke's Second Treatise on Government:

> Though the earth, and all inferior creatures, be common to all men, yet every man has a *property* in his own *person:* this no body has any right to but himself. The *labour* of his body, and the work of his hands, we may say, are properly his. Whatsoever then he removes out of the state that nature hath provided, and left it in, he hath mixed his *labour* with, and joined to it something that is his own, and thereby makes it his *property.*[9]

Locke continued his argument with the example of apples pulled from a tree:

> I ask then, when did they begin to be his? when he digested? or when he eat? Or when he boiled? or when he brought them home? or when he picked them up? and it is plain, if the first gathering made them not his, nothing else could. That *labour* put a distinction between them and common: and added something to them more than nature, the common mother of all, had done; and so they became his private right.[10]

Locke's "labor-mixing" theory—that one gains a property right by mixing one's labor with something in the commons—seems intuitive. If someone engages in an activity that yields a product—in the apple example, something to eat—we instinctively think of the product as belonging to the person whose activity produced it. Even if the individual's act was not all that was needed to produce the apple, ready to be eaten, the fact that the individual's effort contributed to that end and that no one else's effort was involved seems enough to confer a property right in the apple to its picker. And the same intuition suggests that other efforts that yield other products also should confer a property right in the product to the person whose effort made it useful.[11] The intuition for most people does not follow the philosophical course by which Locke arrived at his labor-mixing theory—the predicate that each person owns his own labor and hence, within a certain domain of moral and industrious acts, must own the fruits of that labor. Rather, for most people, the intuition is a simple, unreflective sense that if I engage in an action that yields a benefit, I have at least a presumptive right to that benefit.

Simple and widespread as this intuition is, Locke's theory has been criticized as overstated at best. Robert Nozick gave the example of opening up a can of tomato juice and pouring it into the ocean.[12] He asked if he could gain ownership of the ocean by mixing his labor with it in this fashion. If not, why should one gain a property right in an apple merely because he has gone through the effort of pulling it from a tree?

A fair question, to be sure, but Nozick's criticism distorts Locke by making the leap from moral, productive labor that produces something of value to any physical activity at all, even wasteful conduct.[13] Suppose I run my wagon into a tree to get one apple and end up with a damaged tree and dozens of apples on the ground; does that count as "labor"? Clearly, Locke's theory of labor implicitly assumes an activity that produces more in terms of value to society than it destroys.

The labor-mixing theory is an example of a type of "good for all times and under all conditions" argument for property rights, of which we expressed skepticism at the outset. If an object in the commons becomes your property simply because you expended some effort in obtaining possession of it, then this is true for any person, at any time. There is no sense in which property rights depend on social or economic conditions under the labor-mixing theory—nor, under Nozick's view of Locke, upon considerations of proportionality between the labor invested and the property claimed. This is both a strength and a weakness of Locke's theory.

The strength of the argument, for Locke, was largely strategic. Locke chose to make a "good for all times" argument because he wanted to contest Thomas Hobbes's view that property rights were in all instances dependent on the whim of the government.[14] Locke saw government as sufficiently prone to invasions of interests in property—and with those invasions, impositions on related forms of liberty—that he sought a theory that would make property prior to, not dependent on, government. An argument for property rights that is contingent on economic and social conditions (which Locke was surely capable of making) might have been tailored to show what particular property rules serve overall societal values and under what limited conditions government should be permitted to act in a manner at odds with such rules. It might, in other words, have provided a theoretical case against the abuses with which Locke was concerned.

An argument of that more modest, contingent type, however, would have been more difficult to deploy in debate against Hobbes's position. After all, if the desirability of property rights depends on economic and social conditions, then, a Hobbesian would argue, you need a government to tell you whether the conditions were appropriate for recognizing property rights. If not government, who is to be arbiter of the circumstances under which particular property rights should be accepted? The basic case for government is that without it people cannot agree on rules for living in harmony—in the Hobbesian state of nature, life is all contest and combat. A theory of property rights contingent on distinct circumstances requires the referee function that Hobbes argued government alone could perform. Moving away from a relatively sweeping theory such as Locke's, then, puts us right back in the position that Locke was trying to avoid.

The labor-mixing argument avoids that problem by claiming a natural law basis, prior in time and legitimacy to government, for property rights. Beyond its strategic value for the debate in Locke's own time, this claim provides a stronger bulwark against government intrusions on property interests than a more textured theory of property rights. So far as they are accepted, strong theories provide greater safeguards by setting a framework for analysis that—even if incorporating considerations quite similar to those embodied in weaker theories—starts from a presumption more favorable to protection of property.[15]

The weakness of the labor-mixing argument is that, as Nozick's example shows, it yields absurd results in any case where the proportionality of the claim is unrelated to the amount and nature of the investment made to produce the good at issue. Indeed, the labor-mixing theory runs into difficulty in virtually every case involving a claim to something that can't be used or eaten up by one person.

The extreme case for such a thing is something that not only can't be consumed by one person; it doesn't seem to be consumed at all, but instead can be enjoyed by any number of people without affecting the enjoyment of the person claiming dominion. These are the goods that an economist would call "nonrivalrous" in consumption. An apple can be eaten up by one person; even if I were willing to share my apple, no one else can enjoy the part I've eaten—indeed, it is unlikely that anyone else would want to enjoy any part I have *not* eaten, for that matter—so the apple is "rivalrous" in consumption. But consider goods that are less rivalrous, such as the air or the ocean. If I mix my labor with the ocean, do I gain ownership of the ocean? If I mix my labor with the air, do I gain ownership of the air? No one would take such an argument seriously.

So the labor-mixing theory seems intuitively plausible only within certain limits and under certain conditions. In other words, the labor-mixing theory is not so congruent with common intuitions as it at first blush appeared to be. Instead, the theory must overlap with some other approach and is plausible only in the subset of cases that fall within the overlap.

The Case for Property Rights: Utilitarian Theory

Another approach that was formulated not long after Locke's offers a better prospect of mirroring common intuitions across the general range of cases. Utilitarian theorists, such as Jeremy Bentham,[16] David Hume,[17] and Adam Smith,[18] focused not just on the investment in securing possession of property but also on the benefits and costs of providing security to the possessor. In the case of the person who grabs an apple from a tree in the forest, there is a straightforward cost-benefit argument for recognizing a property right for that person. Suppose the apple is up for grabs, under the law, even after the first mover has taken it from the commons. You could say to the first mover, "Oh well, just go back into the forest and get another apple." But why should he do that if he risks someone else taking the apple? The easier it is for anyone to go get an apple, the less reason there is for anyone to take the apple from its picker. The more difficult it is—the deeper into the woods one must go, the more dangerous the route, the more arduous the climb—the more reason there is to protect the claim of the person who picked it.

The utilitarian analysis looks a bit like the labor-mixing theory in its attention to the investment—which in the apple example, as in many cases, consists of labor—being made to secure a particular good. The best way to make sure that benefits of industry and effort are rewarded is to give people security in the fruits (literally, in this case) of their efforts. Here, if we focus solely on that criterion, there is no reason to give the right to the apple to anyone else but the person who picked it, as no one else has invested in any way in producing or procuring it. Given that society is better off with more apples to eat rather than fewer, the utilitarian calculus favors giving a property right to the picker, in order to induce more investment in picking apples.[19] Unlike the labor-mixing theory, however, the cost-benefit approach does not raise proportionality problems; it does not suggest that trivial investments (Nozick's tomato juice example) can support inflated ownership claims to the good.

Utility and Conditions

Although the utilitarian case for property rights looks like a reasonable alternative to Locke's theory, it has the less desirable feature, to some proponents of property rights, of being dependent on the circumstances. Given that the utilitarian case for property rights turns on the incentives for the individuals involved, the starting point generally will be asking when rights are unnecessary to induce the first mover to make the investment in finding, improving, or preserving property. So, for example, if we could find conditions under which the first mover's incentive to go after apples would not be diminished by the second mover's expropriation, then there would not be a strong case for giving security to the first mover.

Any theory that posits the prospect of conditions under which presumptive rights do not attach invites a search for such conditions. That search, in itself, has a cost. The cost consists of the effort to identify the conditions (the administrative cost), the inducement to individuals who can benefit from persuading the deciding authority that conditions exist for softening property rights (rent-seeking cost), and the diminution in incentive to potential first movers in producing the benefits associated with property rights (incentive costs). All three costs are important to the analysis of property rights. Indeed, as a general rule property rights are determined under a utilitarian analysis in a manner that minimizes the sum of the administrative costs of determining their scope, the rent-seeking costs, and the incentive costs. For the moment, we focus on the incentive cost.

The immediate question, then, is whether there are cases that fit the example posited above, where the second mover's expropriation does not affect incentives of the first mover. Imagine a world in which no one can distinguish between family members and strangers. A parent who goes into the commons to get an apple for a child would, in those circumstances, be indifferent between giving it to one child or having another run up and take the apple. In this case, there would not seem to be a strong utilitarian argument for granting a property right to the parent who goes into the commons to gather food for members of the tribe.[20]

However, even in this example we might worry about the incentive for adults to go into the forest to get apples. Sociobiologists document examples in nature of attenuated ties between parents and offspring as the number of offspring rises or as the clarity of the parental tie declines.[21] Although the example of a parent who cannot distinguish family from nonfamily may seem fanciful, one should note that its assumption of an enlightened man who does not put the welfare of his own kin above that of strangers is central to socialist theories.

In addition to the justification for providing security to possessions, the utilitarian argument for property rights implies that property rights encourage the efficient allocation of resources through trade. By "efficient allocation," we mean that goods are assigned to the individuals who value them the most. Secure property rights encourage people to bargain for, rather than take, the things owned by others that they would like to possess. To return to the apple example, if the second mover really does value the apple more highly than the first, secure property rights encourage the second mover to offer to purchase the apple by exchanging something else of value for it. If the parties reach an agreement, both will be better off than under the alternative outcomes in which either (a) the first mover keeps the apple unmolested, or (b) the second mover steals the apple from the first mover. Through such exchanges, society's wealth increases.

Exchange provides an additional motivation for the first mover to go into the commons to take an apple. If the first mover takes the apple for his own consumption, he will spend only so much effort as is justified by his desire to eat the apple. However, if the first mover knows that he can exchange the apple for something else that he values more highly from someone else, he will have an even greater incentive to expend effort in gathering apples from the commons. Those who are particularly good at gathering apples—say, because they are good climbers—will devote themselves to the task. Those who are good at other things, say making tools for apple pickers, will devote themselves to that task and trade their tools for apples. Property rights not only encourage industry and effort, they also encourage trade and the division of labor that supports it.[22]

The benefits of basing economies on voluntary exchange can be seen by tracing the rise in living standards in market-based, property-rights-based societies over the past two centuries. As discussed in Chapter 1, the benefits of property rights and voluntary exchanges can be seen as well in comparing the trajectory of command-and-control economies with market-based economies over the last half of the twentieth century. For less sweeping, but recurrent, examples of the reason to value voluntary exchanges rooted in property rights, look at places where widespread looting occurs, a forced rather than voluntary exchange of goods. After such incidents, stores close and no longer offer goods for sale in the areas subject to looting. So, too, societies where government commandeers agricultural production or expropriates farmland almost invariably see drastic reductions in production the following season, often to the point where famine results.[23] The instinct to extract wealth by fiat, rather than induce its creation through voluntary exchange, is common to government; but whatever its short-term political benefits, that instinct repeatedly has produced dire consequences for the societies that indulge it.[24]

In connecting voluntary exchange to increased societal value, we do not mean to elide the debate over measuring value strictly by willingness to pay. The simple version of the exchange story, as noted already, is that if you value something I have more highly than I do, you will buy it from me. This story depends on two conditions. First, we must have some mechanism that allows for exchange, some market that at low enough cost allows me to sell something to you.[25] Second, we must be able to reflect the value we place on the good being bought and sold in a medium—typically money—that is subject to exchange. If you simply tell me you really value the apple I've picked more than I do, that won't be enough.

The second condition has occupied a great deal of academic attention. Modern writers have explained that budget constraints, based on differences in wealth, can prevent someone with higher subjective value from exchanging money for a good owned by someone who values the good less.[26]

But this is a purely theoretical objection to property-based systems of voluntary exchange, for several reasons. First, in many cases there is no need to resort to measures of subjective value other than money, as the individuals who are potential buyers have sufficient budgets for the goods at issue. Second, there is no way to tell what subjective values are for the individuals who are not engaging in voluntary exchanges. Third, any system that attempted to match goods with stated subjective values would encourage people to exaggerate those values and at the same time diminish their incentive to work in order to be able to afford the goods.

In the main, the critics of construing voluntary exchanges as wealth enhancing for society are simply registering a footnote to the discussion of property and markets. The critics are correct that we cannot with certainty say that all exchanges that should take place to increase social value will take place. But we can say that the exchanges that do take place between informed parties leave both better off; and in most instances secure property rights with voluntary exchange provide the best prospect for enhancing wealth.

Utilitarian Theory and the Actual Allocation of Property Rights
Recall that in criticizing Locke's labor-mixing theory, we noted that it broke down when applied to goods that are nonrivalrous, in the sense that one person's consumption does not preclude another person from enjoying the good. For example, if one person breathes the air, or enjoys the sunlight, he can't prevent others from doing the same. The utilitarian theory does not suffer the same breakdown, as it generally would not suggest a basis for recognizing property rights to nonrivalrous goods. If the state were to grant ownership of the air to one individual, he would have a difficult time securing the benefits to himself. If he worked to clean the air for himself, he would also clean it for others. Since so much of the benefit would go to others, his incentive to clean the air would not be great. Nor could he make a market in air to sell to others—without being able to force others to pay. It follows that on utilitarian grounds, society would not have a strong interest in granting property rights to air. This example suggests that the utilitarian case provides a better fit with observed property rights than Locke's labor-mixing theory.

Although Locke's theory is inferior to the utilitarian approach in its ability to explain the actual allocation of property rights, we noted earlier that it served a strategic function. The greatest problem in the history of government is constraining it from taking predatory actions against the powerless—in other words, to constrain government to the "rule of law." Property rights are a key component of any system of laws that constrains government from predatory conduct. But to serve as an effective constraint, property rights must be defined independently of the government's own immediate desires. For if the government has the exclusive power to define and redefine property rights to suit its own instantaneous needs, then there is no effective constraint against predation.[27]

That a wary concern for predation was the most likely reason Locke settled on the labor-mixing theory of property rights suggests another utilitarian function of property rules, one we alluded to earlier: to reduce the costs of rent seeking. Predation is a game that private parties as well as the government can play. Weak property rights provide incentives for private parties to attempt to expropriate those rights. Even when property rights provide no incentive for investment, they at least provide a deterrent to costly expropriation efforts.

In order for property rules both to protect incentives to invest (or trade) and to deter efforts to expropriate, they must be reasonably clear—that is, they cannot be full of "ifs" and "maybes." This suggests property rules will be observed where the administrative costs of determining the scope of an entitlement are relatively low.[28] This is another reason, in addition to the incentive argument mentioned earlier, that we generally do not see property rights in nonrivalrous goods such as air. Suppose the state announced that you had a property right in the air over your land. It would be difficult to determine the scope or indeed the meaning of this right.

Although we have separated out nonrivalrous goods from the set of ordinary goods, we should be cautious about the separation of these categories. We should be especially cautious about extrapolating from the example of air ownership to other instances in which items have some appearance of nonrivalrous goods. Quite often, goods are nonrivalrous to some degree but also can be provided in ways that allow the provider to capture enough of the benefits—often by distributing benefits discretely to those who will pay—to induce investment in producing such goods. Ronald Coase has documented that many classic public goods (an older term in economics for nonrivalrous goods) have actually been provided privately, despite theoretical impediments to such provision.[29] Lighthouses, police forces, armies, navies, clean air, and clean water—all have been subject to private provision.

Utilitarian theory does not suggest that goods with some nonrivalrous aspects are necessarily ill suited to private provision or to treatment as private property. Instead, utilitarian theory asks in each instance whether the circumstances surrounding the good are such that it can be treated as property more cost effectively than not. Because collective control over resources

has its own peculiar problems, the relative costs and benefits of alternative structures for control over resources cannot be answered simply by
observing that a given resource has some attributes—even very substantial
attributes—of public goods.

Kantian Theory

Kantian theorists have now become the largest source of "good for all times"
arguments for property rights, though modern Kantians have lost sight of
the strategic rationale that led Locke to his position. Many Kantians today
think the utilitarian arguments are unpersuasive or inadequate because they
fail to take rights seriously, fail to respect the autonomy of the individual, or
are too indeterminate.[30] So, they conclude, a theory of property rights based
on cost-benefit arguments must be rejected.

In the place of cost-benefit arguments, Kantian theorists say that property
rights respect and augment the autonomy of the individual by allowing him
to realize and extend his desires and plans through property.[31] The argument is obvious and, at the same time, unclear.

The Kantian argument from autonomy is obvious in the sense that any
secure right makes it easier to plan and to control one's future. The connection of autonomy to property rights, as to *any* legal right, is sound. Strong
ownership rights, rights to use property as the owner chooses, augment
autonomy by enhancing the freedom of the owner. So, for instance, owning
a plot of land in a place where ownership confers secure use rights allows me
to plant a garden and to watch the flowers grow into an arrangement that I
planned on my own. In this obvious sense, property rights allow me to
realize my plans. The more secure a property right I have—the less it depends
on contingencies; the broader the right is to use, exchange, and dispose of
property as I wish—the freer I am to pursue goals that depend on using the
property or on exchanging it for money that will in turn allow me to engage
in other activities of my choosing.[32] It is hard to imagine anyone disputing
this aspect of the Kantian claim from autonomy.

At the same time, it is unclear whether property rights have some special
import for autonomy, different from the significance of other secure legal
rights. If autonomy means financial independence from others, security in
one's property is undoubtedly a substantial input. If autonomy means merely

the freedom to follow one's interests, property rights will still be important, albeit to a smaller subset of people. They would not be of much significance, for example, to one who chose to forgo worldly goods and become a monk. Yet it seems odd to say that his autonomy is any less than one with substantial property interests. We might speak of the monk's interest in remaining in a religious order and relying on the order's rules as a form of property right, but this expansive view of property threatens to subsume all rights and interests within the single classification of property rights. For many people, autonomy as freedom may turn heavily on secure rights to property, but for others those rights will be secondary.

The Kantian position that property rights are essential extensions of our autonomy, in this sense, is overstated. Indeed, the Kantian argument connecting property rights to autonomy seems to have it backwards. Although autonomy is augmented if property rights (like other rights) are secure rather than ambiguous, property rights are not best understood as allowing us to extend our plans, and our personalities, through the things we own. Property rights are not so much instruments *of* self-control as they are instrumental *to* the security that allows us to make long-term plans. In this way, they are necessary to the process of forming our selves and of becoming tolerably decent people. In the absence of secure property rights, we would be forced to devote an enormous proportion of our time to consuming or protecting the things we have. Planning horizons would shrink, and so would our plans. And since others could take advantage of our own failure to consume or protect, we would be unlikely to see moral objections to taking advantage of them. In short, rather than allowing virtuous people to channel their virtues into real things, property is better viewed as a prerequisite to the attainment of the standard virtues (e.g., honesty, fairness, industriousness).

While property rights and autonomy are related, the relationship is not self-evidently what neo-Kantian arguments claim. First, as noted above, property rights seem to be related only instrumentally to autonomy. They are not essential to autonomy but are helpful, and the degree to which they are helpful varies according to individual circumstances. Second, because the relationship is instrumental rather than deductive, the shape of property rights cannot be derived readily from the notion of autonomy. The argument from autonomy supports secure property rights, but the concept of autonomy does not give determinate shape to the extent of the rights, the limits to rights to use or dispose of property, and the conditions under which the rights should change. The answers to those questions inevitably depend on analyses that are redolent of the utilitarian calculus described earlier. Proponents of natural-law approaches to property rights and of Kantian arguments make claims that can help us understand the connection between property rights and some important intuitions about what matters to individuals. But these arguments do not provide sufficient traction to explain the shape of property rules or to guide us in the work of determining the details of a property rights system.

Modern Arguments

Older arguments for property rights tended to focus on the relation of the property to an investment in finding or improving the property or to the way a secure right in property might affect an individual's sense of self or life choices. Modern arguments about property rights have tended to focus more on certain follow-on interactions that flow from the rights granted (though to a significant extent, the older arguments implicate the modern issues). Perhaps the most fertile source of new arguments traces to the modern utilitarian theorists' recognition of the competitive impact of property rights, in so far as they are inputs to production of other goods and services.[33] Since property rights effectively grant a monopoly to the holder, they create barriers to competition.[34] To take the simplest case, a property right in a desirable location for business excludes competitors from that same location. To the extent that this exclusive effect gives the holder some degree of monopoly power, he can charge a higher price to consumers than in a world where the location advantage was shared equally.

The effects of property rights are divided into dynamic and static effects. Dynamic effects include the incentive effects that we have considered earlier. For example, granting a property right in land enhances the owner's incentive to invest in that land to maximize the return from it. If an orchard owner feels secure that his apple trees will not be picked clean by strangers, he will take care to prune and fertilize the trees in order to maximize the yield.

The static effects of property rights include the monopolizing or exclusionary effect.[35] To get a sense of the static effect, imagine a case in which there are no dynamic effects. Return to the apple orchard example and suppose the apples are all ready to be picked, so that nothing that happens will affect the amount of effort put into growing them. And, suppose further, that the way the apples are picked and distributed will have no effect on future incentives to grow apples. Suppose the orchard owner has an advantage in location that puts him closer to his market than his rivals. As a result, the cost of supplying apples to the local market is $2.00 per bushel. For rivals, the cost of supplying apples is $3.00 per bushel. As a result, the orchard owner charges $2.90 per bushel and enjoys a local monopoly. Now, suppose the law required the owner to grant access to competitors at a rate that compensates him for the cost per bushel. Rivals then gain access to his apples, and they, along with the apple owner, compete in setting price. The apples now reach the market at a lower price, say $2.10 per bushel.

As this example shows, there is a static cost of exclusion. When the orchard owner could exclude the rivals, he charged $2.90. When he had to compete with rivals, the price fell to $2.10. Since $2.10 is (by hypothesis) sufficient reward to bring apples to the market, the additional $0.80 per bushel can be viewed as a surcharge that results from exclusion.

Although the amount of this surcharge from exclusion often is the focus of popular commentary on how well or poorly markets function, it is not the measure of the static cost of exclusion. The surcharge is simply a transfer from apple consumers to the orchard owner. It makes some members of society (orchard owners) better off and others (the people paying the extra eighty cents per bushel) worse off. But it is not a cost to the society overall. The money transferred from consumer to producer stays in the society and is used to buy other things that the consumers of apples make.

The static cost of exclusion—what constitutes a real loss to society—results from the reduction in consumption that occurs because exclusion allows the orchard owner to charge a high price. The static cost of exclusion is the sum of net benefits to society forfeited in a given time period as a result of exclusion. Thus, suppose ten additional consumers would have purchased apple bushels at a price of $2.10 per bushel, because each one values a bushel of apples at $2.40. For each transaction with each additional consumer, the net benefit to society is the difference between their valuation of a bushel of apples, $2.40, and the cost of providing it, $2.00. Those consumers do not purchase the apples at $2.10 and lose the additional value they would have gained purchasing the apples at that price. Apple producers lose the additional $0.10 they would have gained on each purchase. The static cost to society is $0.40 for each of ten consumers, or $4.00.

The apple orchard example illustrates the general trade-off between the static and dynamic costs of exclusion. The static cost of exclusion is minimized by allowing unrestricted competition among those who want the apples in the orchard. But this increases the dynamic cost, because the orchard owner's incentives to plant apples will be dulled if he does not receive the full reward, which is guaranteed by protecting his exclusive control. After all, the larger the expected yield at the moment the apples are picked, the more the owner should be willing to invest in the growth and maintenance of the apples.

The trade-off between dynamic and static effects is a general characteristic of property rights. The relation between these costs, however, varies in different circumstances. In the case of the apple orchard, the dynamic costs of forgoing property rights will be large and the static costs of granting them will be small. The reason is that there are many people who can grow apples that are perfect (or nearly perfect) substitutes for those of the orchard owner. Would-be consumers of the orchard's apples will be almost as happy to have apples from another orchard. If new growers find that they can make a profit, they will continue to plant trees, cultivate them, and bring apples to market until the price they can get for apples just equals what it costs to produce the apples. Because of competition, the static costs of giving orchard owners exclusive control of the apples in their orchards will be trivially small. At the same time, the costs of letting anyone who wants to come pick apples—costs of discouragement of cultivation needed for better apple production in the short run and perhaps for any apple production in the longer run—are large.

There are other cases, however, in which static costs of exclusion are likely to be large. Take, for example, any local monopoly, such as local telephone service (before the widespread dissemination of wireless technology) or local postal service. The local telephone monopoly could charge a monopoly price—that is, a price well above the amount necessary to cover its costs, which is the competitive price. It could do so because it had a property right in the exclusive supply of services to its market. Because the monopoly price exceeds the competitive price by a substantial amount, the static costs of exclusion—the forgone social benefit from providing the competitive level of supply of phone service—are likely to be substantial. In addition, because the monopoly price exceeds the competitive price, it could be reduced slightly without strongly affecting the monopolist's incentive to meet customer demands.[36] Given this, the trade-off between dynamic and static costs of property rights (here understood as the right of monopoly) is much weaker than in the apple supply example given above.

Summary and Conclusion

A persuasive argument for property rights—whether in information, land, or apples pulled from the forest—should be analytically coherent and also should fit the empirical evidence. Some theories—such as Locke's labor-mixing defense of property rights—seem analytically sensible only in a subset of cases. Some theories predict outcomes—the failure of markets to provide goods with public-good (nonrivalrous) aspects, for example, or the ability of authoritarian command-and-control systems to direct resources to their best uses—that turn out on inspection to be wrong or radically overstated. Some theories—such as neo-Kantian theories based on arguments from autonomy—make claims about property rights that cannot be connected in a meaningful way to empirical evidence.

Although it is subject to criticism on some grounds, a utilitarian, or cost-benefit, analysis provides both a coherent analytical framework and a basis for assessing empirical claims respecting specific property rights and existing property regimes. Intuitively, most people thinking seriously about legal rules gravitate to some form of cost-benefit analysis. The measurement of costs and benefits and the comparison of values across individuals present significant theoretical conundrums. But most of the practical questions respecting the arrangement of property rights can be answered by rudimentary cost-benefit analysis regardless of the questions generated by matters of theoretical dispute.

3

Intellectual Property

Invention and Expression

While *property* is a word familiar to everyone, the term *intellectual property* is not. Yet, everyone is aware of the types of activity that give rise to intellectual property and, at least at a general level, aware as well of the importance of those activities.

Look first at the activities at issue. Inventors pour time, energy, and large sums of money into efforts to make things work better, faster, and more effectively, to find new solutions to old problems. Writers, producers, singers, actors, and others devote their talents to creating books and films and music for us to enjoy. Firms develop products and services of a certain quality and use brand names to make it easy for us to know what to expect when we purchase a Steinway piano, eat at a McDonald's restaurant, get a coffee from Starbucks, or stay in a Sheraton hotel. We order Coca-Cola to drink in different places, expecting a pretty consistent product. And, thanks in part to the fact that Coca-Cola has been able to control the formula used to produce drinks sold under its label, that consistency is what we are likely to get.

The categories of activity discussed in the preceding paragraph are those that give rise to applications for patents, copyrights, trademarks, and trade secrets. These are the four major types of intellectual property rights granted by law. The typical reader will know the basic case for each of these types of property right—even if unfamiliar with the law that governs each one—and also will understand instinctively the importance of protecting inventive and creative activity.

Recall, for example, the discussion of modern medicine in Chapter 1. Medicine today relies heavily on drugs and biologic agents to combat diseases, to identify risks to our health, and to control the side effects of treatments. Modern medicine also relies on x-rays, sonograms, echo-cardiograms, computer assisted tomography (CAT scans), magnetic resonance imaging, and nuclear imaging to locate and identify fractures, cancers, heart malfunctions, and blocked arteries; to pinpoint tissue damage; and to discover internal injuries to nerves, muscles, and organs.

New drugs, biologics, and diagnostic tools have changed our life prospects. Consider a few examples. In 1922, 150 out of every 100,000 Americans contracted whooping cough, and in 1923 approximately 9,000 Americans died of the disease.[1] Following the introduction of a vaccine in the 1940s, that rate dropped steadily. By 1980, the infection rate from whooping cough was 1 per 100,000 of population.[2] With declining vaccinations (the result of complacency about a disease that had largely disappeared and concerns about side effects of the vaccine), the rate rose to 3 per 100,000 by the year 2000 with 12 deaths (in the entire population)—a substantial increase from twenty years before, but still a far cry from pre-vaccine levels.[3]

Tuberculosis was the third leading killer of adult Americans in 1900. By 2002 it was not even in the top sixty causes tracked by the Centers for Disease Control.[4] In 1953, 84,304 Americans were diagnosed with tuberculosis and 19,707 Americans died of the disease.[5] Things began to change that year with the launch of a national campaign to detect and treat tuberculosis,[6] and by 2002 there were only 15,056 diagnosed cases and 784 deaths in a nation of over 300 million people. Over that span, the infection rate dropped to one-tenth its 1953 level and the death rate (0.3 per 100,000) to less than one-fortieth its 1953 level.

As recently as 1940, a diagnosis of cutaneous malignant melanoma (skin cancer) was effectively a statement that the patient would die within a short time. The cancer rarely was identified at an early enough stage to be treated effectively, and the treatment regimes available consisted of poisoning the patient in hopes of killing the cancer cells before so severely damaging the rest of the patient's body that the treatment itself would prove fatal. By 2004, the combination of early detection and improved treatments gave patients diagnosed with cutaneous malignant melanoma cancer a survival rate of over 90 percent.[7]

Stories like these form part of the backdrop for patent rights. Of course, many factors can influence changes in morbidity and mortality rates for

diseases such as those described above. Public health authorities' commit-
ment to combating a particular disease can raise public awareness and
prompt a variety of private responses helpful in detecting and treating the
disease. And some diseases have been fought successfully without the help
of patented drugs, biologic agents, or equipment. That is not, however, the
complete story of modern disease control. One key element in each of the
stories recounted above is a patented product or treatment regime that
proved effective in disease control. The modern story of public health is
incomplete without inclusion of an increasingly important feature: that the
prospect of patenting discoveries and inventions has induced investments in
research and development of technologies for fighting disease.

Medicine is merely one field where the potential for an intellectual property right—a legal guarantee that the person who succeeds will have the
right to profit from that success by setting the terms on which others can use
the new invention or reproduce a creative work—fuels investment (in this
case, money necessary to explore preventatives, cures, treatments, and
detection technologies). Similar investments have propelled the discoveries
that have made our use of information and our means of communication
faster, cheaper, and easier over the past few decades. Part of the story is well
known. In the two decades following the production of Intel's 8086 chip, the
first generation of the basic architecture for personal computers, the cost of
a million computing instructions per second fell from about one thousand
dollars to under one dollar.[8]

A longer view of the history of computing progress is offered by Ray
Kurzweil:

> Computing devices have been consistently multiplying in power (per
> unit of time) from the mechanical calculating devices used in the 1890
> U.S. Census, to Turing's relay-based "Robinson" machine that cracked
> the Nazi enigma code, to the CBS vacuum tube computer that predicted
> the election of Eisenhower, to the transistor-based machines used in
> the first space launches, to the integrated-circuit-based personal computer
> which I used to dictate (and automatically transcribe) this essay. . . .
> Computer speed (per unit cost) doubled every three years between 1910
> and 1950, doubled every two years between 1950 and 1966, and is now
> doubling every year.[9]

As Kurzweil points out, Moore's Law, predicting the doubling of computing speeds every eighteen months from the introduction of the integrated circuit, captures only part of the landscape.

While other fields do not quite match the pace of change in computing or in medicine, there has been dramatic progress elsewhere as well. Communications, transportation, and entertainment were revolutionized in the twentieth century. The century began with mail carried by ship, train, and horse as the main form of long-distance communication; telegraphy as the primary vehicle for more immediate communication; and news delivered via paper and ink technology that, despite some advances in printing, was not a far cry from a hundred years before. Telephony, an invention of the late nineteenth century, was still a rarity for ordinary folks, even in the United States. Transportation remained slow and travel outside the main cities an adventure. Entertainment was either a live performance or some sort of self-entertainment such as playing an instrument or reading a book. There was a small market for musical recordings (phonograph cylinders, piano rolls), but the rise of a true mass market for that was still in the future.

The next 110 years saw the expansion of telephone networks and undersea cable lines; and the advent of microwave transmissions, satellite transmissions, cellular telephones, and Internet communications. Transportation evolved from horse, ship, and train to the nearly ubiquitous automobile, high-speed trains, and airplanes. The phonograph cylinder lost its place to the record, which was succeeded by cassette recordings, compact discs, and digitized music. Entertainment expanded to movies (invented in the nineteenth century and continuously improved in terms of technical effects), radio broadcasting, television, cable, satellite-direct entertainment, video recorders, and Internet entertainment. The result is a vast increase in the variety and amount of information accessible and the speed of transport, accompanied by a sharp decline in cost.

In each of these fields, investment in research and development has been driven in large part by the ability to secure profits through a legally protected patent, copyright, trademark, or trade secret. That is not the only reason for endeavoring to create new products, write novels, or build up a brand name, and not every investment in such ventures will be well made. Indeed, most investments will be lost, and even successful enterprises will often not be commercially successful. But the promise of commercial success, tied to the

legal right to control the innovation or expressive creation, is often a principal motivating force or a necessary condition for the activity essential to
innovation and creation.

Most importantly, intellectual property has served in modern economies
as a bridge between capital and the special type of labor that comes in the
form of innovation. Innovative concepts embodied in new products, through
design or through manufacturing process, often require financial backing in
order to make it to the market with reliable supply and quality. The capital-
ists who finance these innovations will not do so without the promise of a
reward.[10] Intellectual property forms a necessary ingredient in this supply
network: without the promise of reward, capital will not support innovation;
without capital, innovation will often be fitful and inadequate.[11]

Think of a rough analogy: oil exploration. Exploration is driven by the
expectation that a prospector can profit from pumping the oil from a well
that hits. There would be little incentive to invest capital and effort in trying
to identify likely locations for oil, to calculate how deep to drill and through
what geological impediments, if the fruits of successful exploration could
not be captured—if other people could take the oil as it came out of the well
without paying the prospector. Of course, there are some people who enjoy
the game of trying to find oil.[12] They like the excitement of trying to detect
something hard to find just as much as individuals who enjoy gambling
wholly apart from the money they win. But just as gamblers who consistently lose eventually come upon hard times, these people would not last
long in the oil prospecting business if there were no financial rewards from
their work. They would eventually tire of working without reward and the
pool of funds to support their efforts would evaporate. The more unlikely oil
is to find, the more costly to extract, the less will be discovered without the
security and incentive provided by a property right in the discovery. So, too,
with intellectual property.

Rights in Information and Ideas

Given the contribution innovation has made to our well-being, why treat
intellectual property as something different from ordinary property? Why
give intellectual property rights for limited periods of time, in contrast to
the general pattern of granting permanent rights to other property? Why

provide less scope for owners to control intellectual property than other property?

The standard answer is that intellectual property, embodied in things like songs and books, lacks the sort of exclusivity associated with other property. For most tangible property, one person's enjoyment of the property necessarily conflicts with or diminishes another person's enjoyment. With the subjects of intellectual property, however, it is easy for many people to enjoy the same thing at the same time. I can play a song on my radio loud enough for many people to enjoy it, provided they aren't annoyed by my choice of music. My hearing the song doesn't diminish the enjoyment someone else gets from it, and my playing the song doesn't use it up or make it less valuable for someone else who wants to play it another time in another place. Similarly, I can read a book or a newspaper and then leave it on a park bench for others to enjoy. Although at some point the physical object (newspaper or book) will become sufficiently worn to make reading challenging, my reading does not reduce the pleasure that someone else can gain from reading the copy later. Because my enjoyment does not reduce what is left for others, economists describe these items as nonrivalrous.

The core feature that explains why songs and books can be enjoyed by one person without diminishing what is left for others is that both are simply types of information. The song is information conveyed by audible music. The book is information conveyed by printed words. Neither is necessarily just bland information, as each includes emotive elements attached to the form of expression, as opposed to the underlying information expressed. But the emotive elements in writings and songs are essentially ideas, too.

Whether one refers to what is expressed as information or ideas, the key aspect of books and songs is an intangible quality not used up by one person's consumption. Indeed, in many cases sharing the good increases its value. Television executives have referred to this phenomenon as the "water cooler effect"—the value imparted by having seen something everyone else will be talking about around the office water cooler. Other commentators today speak of "network effects" as encompassing the benefits one person gets from having others share a particular experience or use similar goods. We return to this concept later and discuss some settings that generate strong network effects and other settings in which, contrary to these examples, information loses value as the circle of possessors expands.

Static and Dynamic Costs Again

The question, then, is what we should make of the fact that information and ideas, the essence of intellectual property, are largely nonrivalrous. As we noted in the previous chapter, modern utilitarian analysis compares the static and dynamic costs of property rights. Static costs are those observed at any given moment—costs that can be captured in one snapshot. Dynamic costs occur over time, or sequentially. We could not get a picture of dynamic costs in one snapshot; we would have to have a video camera rolling to see them. And like the idea of compound interest, dynamic costs are capable of a geometric progression.

Static Costs

The obvious static cost associated with a property right in a nonrivalrous good flows from its effect in reducing the use of that good. A property right confers the legal authority to limit use of property. As a general rule, property owners will want to restrict use of a good in order to exploit it fully or to realize its value (and for rivalrous goods some restriction is necessary, as such goods cannot be consumed simultaneously by several people).

Typically the limitation on use has two effects. The first effect of restricting access is that the right to use the property is allocated to the person willing to bid highest for it. This outcome, as explained in Chapter 2, tends to align use of the good with its highest economic value. The orchard owner who sells his orchard's apples wants to sell them to the people who will pay most for the apples. In the vast majority of contexts, this increases a society's welfare and wealth. As we noted in Chapter 2, property rights facilitate the *efficient allocation* of resources through trade.

The second effect flows not from the fact of restriction but from the degree of restriction. Giving a property right in a good may, depending on its scarcity, have a monopolizing effect, which in turn may give the owner considerable power over the price of the good. To the extent that the property at issue is, like apples, a standard good—one produced and sold in a competitive market—the owner will try to produce as much as possible of a good with the resources he has, endeavoring not to invest more in the process than he will get in return. The owner, however, is not able to exercise much influence over price. The apples he can produce will be such a small fraction of total apple production that a change in the amount he produces will have only a trivial impact on the price he will get for his apples.

If, however, the property at issue is one that is not a standard good, one for which there are limited alternatives available, the owner may be able to influence the price by supplying less of the good. And, indeed, the owner will have an incentive to restrict output to the point where the maximum profit is obtained, a point well shy of the socially desired output. The social ideal, from the standpoint of efficient allocation of society's resources, is to have goods sold to the point where the marginal cost of producing the last unit just equals the price obtained. In other words, any potential buyers willing to pay the cost of producing a good should be able to buy it rather than having to switch to some product the buyer values less. As we noted in Chapter 2, the static cost of monopoly—the cost of restricting output below the competitive market equilibrium level—is the loss of value to would-be buyers who value the good at more than its cost, though less than its monopoly price.[13]

For any good that is nonrivalrous, such as information, the social cost of limiting access seems on its face to be magnified.[14] It appears that there is only the social cost associated with limitation (that is, the monopolization effect) and not the benefit of efficient allocation as in the case of rivalrous goods. This is so for several reasons.

First, a property right in a nonrivalrous good will be valuable to the holder only if the good is scarce. Having a property right to a piece of information that everyone already has (e.g., "the sun rises every morning") will typically be worthless, since no one will be interested in paying for it. And it is unlikely that anyone would see a demand to be paid for using the information as reasonable; the instinctive reaction is that the user owes nothing to anyone else for acting on information so widely known. For this reason, property rights will typically be sought and granted only for nonrivalrous goods that are scarce, and this immediately implies some degree of monopoly power.[15] The owner of a plan for an effective cure for cancer has something of great value to others and will be able to charge a monopoly price to the first person who seeks access to his information.[16]

Second, if there is *no* cost associated with use of a good because there is no interference with other people's use of it, *any* restriction on access excludes someone who would pay more than the cost of his using the good. Of course, there is usually a cost to producing more of the nonrivalrous good, and for that reason it should be supplied only to consumers who are willing to pay a price that covers that cost. But once the good has been produced, restrictions on access would seem to undercut allocative efficiency by preventing the good from being transferred to people who receive a benefit that far exceeds the cost of the transfer. Ordinarily, in the case of rivalrous goods many, if not most, of the potential buyers who are unwilling to pay a monopoly price for a product also would be unwilling to pay a competitive price. From the standpoint of efficient allocation—of directing society's resources to those who value them most highly—those potential buyers are irrelevant in any calculation of monopoly's costs. For nonrivalrous goods, however, the loss in value to *every* buyer excluded by a higher price is, in theory, part of the social cost. That makes any grant of a right to limit access to nonrivalrous goods especially costly.[17]

Information and ideas have two other characteristics that, in a static analysis, make any limitation on access costly. One, which has been implicit in the discussion so far, is that as with other nonrivalrous goods (e.g., national defense) it is generally difficult to limit access to information and ideas—that is, they have the quality of non-exclusivity. Once information is disclosed to anyone, it takes effort to control access to that information. Information is, at least relative to other goods, easily shared and not easily corralled. That is the basis for the assertion that three people can keep a secret, if two of them are dead.[18]

The quality of non-exclusivity is slightly different from the absence of rivalry. Non-exclusivity deals with the cost of limiting access to a good; non-rivalry addresses conflicting interests in use of the good. I may have difficulty keeping you off my field, even though your use of one part of it doesn't conflict with my use of another part. Alternatively, your use of the field may reduce the value of my use, even though there is physically room for both of us and I would have to take costly measures to keep you out. For information and ideas, the characteristic of non-exclusivity means that the cost of transferring the information (not necessarily the item in which it is embodied, such as a book, but the pure information alone) is almost always less than the benefit that it would give to those who are excluded from it.

The other characteristic of information that affects the cost of limiting access to it is that its social value often exceeds its private value. In the language of economics, information and ideas frequently have "positive externalities," benefits to other people not captured by the person who produces or articulates the information or idea.

Some commentators have suggested that speech—the expression of information and ideas—always has higher social value than private value.[19] This goes a bit too far. Some expression has negative value for society, even though the speaker may derive benefit from the speech. Suppose a person with a stake in a particular product falsely claims that a competitor's product has potentially harmful defects, and the false statements persuade some people to switch from the competing product, to their detriment. The product they abandon is in fact safer than the product they purchase in its place. Society loses, but the speaker gains.

Other commentary claims that society actually gains from false statements, that the very act of confronting and combating falsehoods is socially useful.[20] Scientific knowledge, for example, has advanced at times thanks to scientists' investment in contesting a false thesis.[21] But false information can be socially harmful, misdirecting attention and leading to wasted energy and effort, all to no social gain. Equally off target is the claim that "the only cure for bad speech is more speech."[22] Imagine a false claim that a product produces serious, harmful health effects. Repeated denials may succeed only in impressing readers who missed the initial claim with the fact that there is a question about the product's safety. By the time the message about the product's actual safety penetrates the public consciousness, the firm that made the challenged product may be out of business.[23]

Information is not always socially useful, nor is its social utility always in excess of its private value. But information often has widespread value that is not easily captured by, or in some sense brought home to, the person who generates it.

Consider the discovery of how to navigate using the sun and stars. Celestial navigation made it possible to travel over vast distances at sea and to correct course at night. Diffusion of information on navigation brought European explorers to the Americas. The initial ideas about how to find one's way using the heavens had enormous spillover effects, and the benefits of the voyages made possible by improved navigation were spread broadly across peoples, places, and times far removed from the initial articulation of the enabling ideas.

Similar externalities are associated with creative expression as with scientific information. Novels and music can yield what might be termed cultural externalities, though whether the externalities are positive or negative can be debated. J. R. R. Tolkien's *Lord of the Rings* series and J. K. Rowling's *Harry Potter* books have created a whole set of terms and ideas exchanged among school children, creating new common currencies in each generation for the things they imagine. Rock music of the 1960s and 1970s also introduced its own set of symbols, idioms, and ideas, creating a bond within a coming-of-age generation and a cultural gap between successive generations.

The prospects for beneficial spillovers or externalities make it potentially more costly to impose restrictions on information, a conclusion that underlies much free speech jurisprudence in the United States and elsewhere.[24] The static picture, thus, is one of higher costs associated with assignment of property rights to information and ideas than generally will be associated with property rights in tangible goods.

Dynamic Effects

Higher static costs of property rights for information and ideas are only part of the story. In evaluating the proper shape and scope of property rights, we also must consider their dynamic effects.

Dynamic effects of property rights for information and ideas—the effects that take place over time—by and large can be expected to move in the opposite direction from static effects. That is, although static costs generally increase as property in information expands, dynamic costs tend to fall as property in information expands. The basic observation about dynamic effects, as we described earlier, is that property rights induce investment in finding or creating property. Thus, we could say that property rights produce dynamic benefits (encouraging innovation over time) or that they reduce dynamic costs (the reluctance to innovate because information is non-excludable).

Wendy Gordon argues that financial incentives associated with property rights can *reduce* investment in innovation.[25] This is likely to occur, in her view, when a creative expression induces a sense of obligation in the observer to "pay forward" the perceived debt owed to an original creator. When access to such expressions is monetized, as required by copyright law, observers of creative material may no longer feel such a sense of moral obligation.

We readily admit that perverse incentives can be created by property rights in information under special conditions. The case of copyright is one of the more controversial. But it is important to distinguish special cases from the general run of experience.

Many of the industries that are supported by intellectual property rights—pharmaceuticals, medical devices, and even the music industry—are full of individual innovators who appear to go to work happily without the slightest interest in financial reward. But take away the financial rewards secured by property rights in each of these industries and the result will inevitably be a reduction in the number of innovators employed. The fixed cost of innovation is the cost of employing talented individuals who are capable of generating useful ideas when given the resources and autonomy to do their work. The financial rewards secured through intellectual property rights enable innovative industries to pay for this fixed cost.[26]

Just as the nonrivalrous nature of intellectual property changes the static cost of restrictions on information and expression, it also alters the dynamic effect of rights to intellectual property. The changes run in opposite directions. While static (social) costs for rights to nonrivalrous goods (e.g., information) are higher than for tangible goods (e.g., apples), the dynamic effects of property rights will tend to produce greater social returns for rights in intellectual property than for rights in tangible property. The reason has to do with the ease of expropriation. With tangible property, it is harder for anyone to expropriate the property than it is with information and ideas. The non-exclusivity characteristic of intellectual property makes it easier to expropriate that property, reducing incentives to invest in its creation. Once an idea is known, it is easily copied. For that reason, a smaller portion of the fruits of investment in generating ideas and information are apt to be captured by the investor than is the case for the general run of other property. Higher social returns relative to private returns, which translate into higher static costs from restrictions on use of ideas and information, likewise translate into higher dynamic returns from the creation of rights in them.

This point merits underlining. On the one hand, society gains disproportionately from the innovation, from the vast number of potential uses of a drug such as penicillin or from the array of potential deployments of new computing technology or the cultural enrichment of a film or novel that looks critically at an aspect of the human condition. The very breadth of the gain and range of different uses generates large social benefits, and the benefits often build on one another. The nonrivalrous character of information encourages new and different exploitations of a beneficial idea. On the other hand, as noted earlier, there is a special difficulty in containing the benefits once the idea or expression is known. Together, these factors make the divergence between the social return and the private return from information greater than with other goods or services, and the dynamic benefits of property rights that induce investment in generating the information higher as well.

The commonly referenced dynamic effect of property rights, including intellectual property rights, is the increased incentive to invest in finding or creating property. In the case of intellectual property, that means investment in innovation and creation, in discovering information and ideas and in creating new expressions of them.

These are not the only dynamic effects of property rights. The rights also increase incentives to maintain property, to protect it against undue depreciation, to guard against "overgrazing," and to develop ideas that have greater utility to the public. Some scholars find these to be the most important aspect of intellectual property rights regimes.[27] Other scholars see little role for—and little benefit from—such "ex post" investments in intellectual property (those that take place after the initial inventive work).[28] The relative importance of "ex post" or "ex ante" incentive effects is ultimately an empirical question. As a matter of theory, however, the potential importance of both types of effect should be recognized.

As we explain later in more particularized discussions of the law, there is reason to expect that intellectual property rights give socially valuable incentives to preserve and enhance the value of property. Giving ownership rights to real property owners provides a basis for investing in crop rotation to maintain the land's fertility; for shifting cattle from one pasture to another to prevent overgrazing; and for seeking new, higher value uses for the land. Treating the land as a commons dissipates such incentives, just as treating the ocean as a commons leads to overfishing. Some of the rules of intellectual property law appear to provide similar incentives.

Balancing Costs and Benefits

The serious questions in evaluating intellectual property rights—in trying to assess the right scope and shape of such rights—are ones of magnitude. How do the static costs of such rights compare to the dynamic benefits? How much discouragement of socially valuable uses accompanies the grant of a particular property right? How much will the grant increase innovation? How much will it facilitate management of a valuable resource to discourage detrimental uses and to encourage valuable ones? All of these, at bottom, are empirical issues. As we emphasized in Chapter 2, property rights should be evaluated on the basis of their social costs and benefits, which will vary with changing economic and social circumstances. Empirical evidence, thus, should be critical to grounding considerations for design of property rights, including intellectual property rights.[29]

Unfortunately, little empirical evidence exists to shed light on the issues central to the design of intellectual property rights. In part, this deficit is an inevitable corollary of the fact that the costs and benefits of property rights in information are so hard to identify and to measure. How, for example, could one quantify the cultural effects from additional dissemination of books or music? From uses of information and ideas that *might* have occurred with lower impediments to access them? How can one determine how much additional innovation would occur with stronger property rights—or how much sooner it would occur—and what contribution those innovations would make to society?

As with much social science research, empirical investigation necessarily provides evidence that is only inferentially relevant to the issues at the heart of designing intellectual property rights. While we are unlikely to have empirical evidence showing exactly what contribution a particular feature of U.S. patent law or copyright law makes to the rate and value of innovation, we can see (table 1 below) that countries with stronger intellectual property rights tend to grow economically more than those with weak intellectual property rights.

Table 1 presents the results of an ordinary least squares regression of gross domestic product (GDP) per capita growth over 2002 and 2003 (average for the two years) on a measure of the strength of intellectual property protection, GDP in the year 2000, and (omitted from the table) the square of GDP in 2000. The measure of the strength of intellectual property protection is based on a survey conducted in eighty countries over the period 2002–2003 by the World Economic Forum.[30] Respondents rated their nation's intellectual property protection on a scale from 1 (weak or nonexistent) to 7 (equal to the world's most stringent). The average rating was equal to 4. Measures

Table 1. Ordinary least squares estimate of the relationship between economic growth 2002–2003 and the strength of intellectual property protection

Intellectual property protection Index 2002–2003	.95 (1.95)
GDP per capita in 2000	−.0003 (−2.31)
Number of Observations (Countries) = 78 R-squared = .08	

The regression also included the square of GDP per capita. The coefficient on that term was $-.6 \times 10^{-10}$ with a t-statistic of 1.61. The squared term takes into account the nonlinear relationship between GDP growth and base-year GDP.

of statistical significance called "t-statistics" are shown in the parentheses, and they indicate that the results of the table are statistically valid.

Table 1 suggests that if you compare countries of the same economic size, a one-unit increase in the perceived strength of intellectual property protection is associated with a .95 increase in the rate of economic growth. The average rate of growth in this sample of countries was 2 percent over this period.

Of course, the results in table 1 should be taken as preliminary evidence at best of the societal value of protecting intellectual property, because there are many other factors that influence economic growth that are not included.[31] The survey measure of the strength of intellectual property protection may appear to have a big impact on growth only because it is correlated with one or more of these omitted factors. In addition, it could be that economic growth leads countries to strengthen their protection of intellectual property rather than the other way around.

This information leaves us far from answering our cost-benefit question. Finding out that countries with strong intellectual property also grow faster does not tell us whether the laws cause faster growth, much less whether on balance they are socially desirable. Still, such evidence provides a clue about the laws' effect.

In the rest of this book, we are attentive to empirical evidence respecting intellectual property rights, but we recognize its limitations. Clues about the effects of intellectual property rights derived from empirical evidence typically can be assessed only in the context of broader considerations of the nature of intellectual property laws. For that reason, while looking to empirical evidence where helpful, we focus substantially on the most plausible predictions respecting the operation of the law. If the structure of the law suggests that it is likely to reduce dynamic costs (provides incentives to create) while at the same time limiting static (market shrinkage) and external costs, that provides a basis for inferring that the law is serving a desirable function.

Of course, intellectual property law consists of statutory and common law components, with common law taking up the largest part. The relative importance of common law is to be expected, since most of intellectual property law has been shaped through hundreds of court decisions analyzing specific dynamic-versus-static cost trade-offs. While no system of law making is perfect, the common law process is well suited for examining the incremental trade-offs—and the often-subtle changes in them over time—that shape intellectual property doctrine.[32] The statutory law process, on the other hand, has advantages with respect to non-incremental, foundational changes in the law—in other words, changes in the initial conditions from which the common law evolves. Statutes have set the initial conditions for some of our intellectual property systems (patent, copyright), while courts for the most part have determined their paths from those conditions by weighing incremental costs and benefits with respect to refinements on the scope of protection.

In looking at the effects of the law, it is essential to consider how the law in practice will drive these different costs. Some of the factors affecting the way the law will work in practice—such as administrative costs and error costs—are discussed in Chapters 4, 5, and 6. In these chapters, however, we concentrate our discussion on the primary shape and effects of the law covering the major headings for intellectual property rights.

Conclusion

The basic case for intellectual property rights is the same as the case for other property rights—the rights will make society better off by increasing incentives to find or create property, to preserve and promote property, and to allocate its uses wisely. The case for intellectual property rights, like other property rights, also recognizes that there are costs associated with exclusion. These costs include the static costs of excluding potential users of the property who would pay more than the marginal cost their use entails but less than the price an owner would charge. Intellectual property rights, like other property rights, are justified where—and only where—the costs of exclusion and related costs are outweighed by the benefits attending additional creation or discovery and the benefits of better management, promotion, and allocation of the property.

Intellectual property rights as a class are more controversial than ordinary property rights because they involve property in information (ideas and expression). Because information, unlike the tangible things falling under property law, is nonrivalrous and non-exclusive in character, the case for property rights is more difficult than that for land and tangible goods.

Whether property in information is a good idea is ultimately an empirical question—a question of the balance between costs and benefits. Even the most searching social science research, however, is unlikely to provide the empirical information needed to answer that question.

Often, when lawyers and policy makers are faced with questions of the balance between costs and benefits, the most useful thing they can do is to take a look at the law and see if it conforms with a reasonable expectation about how that balance should be struck to society's advantage. The inquiry may appear to be more suggestive than scientific, but it is often the most effective means for evaluating trade-offs in the law.

In the immediately succeeding chapters, Chapters 4 through 6, we examine the basic shape of patent, copyright, trademark, and trade secret law. Our examination of the fundamental features of these bodies of law leads to the conclusion that the law does a reasonably good job of trying to minimize the costs of providing property rights to information while promoting the beneficial incentive effects of such rights. We do not conclude that the law is perfect in this respect, but perfection is not the standard by which the law should be evaluated.

4

Patent Law

Patent Law: Property in Ideas?

The common description of the main headings of intellectual property law runs something like this: patent law protects novel ideas; copyright law protects creative expression; trademark law protects identification; and trade secret law protects contractual agreements against disclosing information. Each of these shorthand descriptions is basically accurate, but each also misleads in some degree.

We start with patent law. Patent laws trace back at least to the 1400s.[1] Although other grants of royal or communal privilege to produce certain items had been granted earlier, the "letter patent" had a distinct history. It was not a grant of monopoly privileges to favored individuals or groups seeking to exclude competitors from the market, akin to the guild system. Personal or political favoritism at times have played a role in patent-award decisions (as in England in the early 1600s),[2] but that was not the motive force behind patent law.

Instead, from the outset, the law was intended to reward the invention of something new, and the grants were expressly justified—in contrast to other monopoly rights—as encouraging the production of new products and the generation of new ideas. It is not surprising, then, that the first essentially complete patent system in Europe emerged at the same time as the flowering of new technologies in the Renaissance Era. The Venetian law on patents, adopted in the late fifteenth century, sets a pattern unlike guild protections and very much like modern patent systems. It does not single out a person or group for monopoly privilege, but rather provides for the award of a property right, for a limited period, to "every person who shall build any new and ingenious device . . . not previously made in this Commonwealth."[3] The law does not reserve the right to the government to set different terms for different inventions, or to tailor rules to suit the vagaries of political patronage. It confers on magistrates instead of other governing officers the authority to adjudicate and punish infringement.[4] The spread of patent law from its origins in Venice tracks both the diffusion of technology and the interest of governments in promoting new technology and in attracting those with skills for innovation.

Because the crux of the patent, thus, is to promote the discovery or creation of something new and to give exclusive rights to the person making the discovery or creation, it is common to think of a patent as granting property in ideas. To a significant degree, this is a fair characterization of patent law. More than any other body of intellectual property law, patent law does indeed protect the idea at the core of the property right. As we discuss, that is a key difference between the scope of patent protection and the scope of protection for copyright, for example.

Yet, patent law does not give protection to ideas as such. Instead, patent law—in its current forms around the world, as it has since its original incarnation in fifteenth-century Venice—protects *ideas reduced to application*. This is an important difference, and it is a clue that the law is framed with an eye to securing for society the dynamic benefits from innovation while at the same time avoiding unnecessary dynamic and static costs. The law's selection of subject matters that can be patented fits together with other components of patent law to produce a system that seems generally in keeping with our assessment of the costs and benefits of property rights in invention. In this chapter, we focus primarily on the incentive effects associated with selection of patentable subject matter, noting some other central features of the patent system within this framework.

Patentable Subject Matter

In the United States, a patent provides the holder the right to exclude others from making, using, selling, offering to sell, or importing the patented invention for a period of twenty years from the filing date. In order to be awarded a patent the idea must, as a rule, meet the statutory criteria of utility, novelty, and nonobviousness.[5] As explained below, the law has developed around these terms in a way that strikes a balance between the costs and benefits of property rights in ideas that at least is a plausible fit with what best serves society's interests. Instead of focusing on the statute's terms at the outset, we begin our examination of patent law by looking at examples of the types of ideas that can and cannot be patented and exploring the basis for the distinctions among them.

We can divide the set of potentially patentable ideas into four categories: mathematical formulae and results; physical formulae and results; ideas that describe processes, or "cookbooks"; and ideas that describe products (including machines). Mathematical formulae and results would include such things as Fermat's Last Theorem. Physical formulae include statements such as $E = mc^2$ or that force is equal to mass times acceleration. Cookbooks are step-by-step algorithms for making things. Machines are things that do work for us.

Mathematical Formulae

It is well known that mathematical results, such as the solution to Fermat's Last Theorem, cannot be patented. One common explanation for this exclusion is that mathematical results are in essence tautologies. The first person to show that $x^2-y^2 = (x-y)(x+y)$ may have provided something useful to many people, but this is simply showing that there is more than one way of stating a mathematical expression. The finding was truly "out there already," in the sense that the statement x^2-y^2 already has in it everything you need to know to find the factorization $(x-y)(x+y)$.

The "out there already" explanation, however, is insufficient as a general method of determining when a property right should not be granted. The fact that something is out there to be found doesn't mean there is no value in giving people incentives to go find it sooner rather than later. We encourage the discovery of things that are already in existence by awarding property rights to finders. That is established law for property rights on land and at sea. What, then, makes it different for ideas, or at least for *these* ideas? Why shouldn't the first to discover a mathematical formula gain exclusive rights to it?

Discovery Incentives
The answer lies in the balance between dynamic and static costs. On the one hand, some dynamic-incentive effects favor grants of property rights in ideas. The obvious benefit is encouragement of discovery.

Fame and advancement within the scientific community will motivate investment in mathematical discovery. Further, such discovery brings economic returns to those within the academic world, even without any direct financial stake in the discovery. These rewards will be sufficient incentives for much mathematical inquiry.

Yet, the incentive to discover mathematical formulae almost surely would be greater still if the discoverer could collect money from anyone else using his formula. Conferring exclusive rights over mathematical results would attract increased investment in mathematical discovery, and the social benefit from the additional discoveries might be substantial.

This dynamic gain is the motive for establishing property rights and should apply to patents for mathematical formulae in essentially the same manner as for other property. Unlike most other property, however, two offsetting costs probably dominate the benefits for this category of discovery.

Reduced Innovation: Dynamic and Static Costs
The first of these costs follows from the expectation that, without an offsetting adjustment, conferring property rights in mathematical results would dull incentives for some types of mathematical discovery, even as it increased incentives for others. If mathematical researchers had to send paychecks out every time their work built on prior mathematical results, whether or not the researchers had discovered their results independently, that could pose a serious impediment to mathematical and scientific inquiry.

In rejecting contentions that related types of innovations were patentable, the U.S. Supreme Court declared in one opinion that "a scientific truth, or the mathematical expression of it, is not a patentable invention,"[6] and added in another that "mental processes, and abstract intellectual concepts are not patentable, as they are the basic tools of scientific and technological work."[7] The justices in that case and on other occasions have expressed concern that allowing a patent for a mathematical formula would be tantamount to patenting an idea, which could block further research.

Of course, having to pay for inputs to research, including prior mathematical discoveries, is not in itself enough to defeat a claim to treat those inputs as someone's property. Scientists and mathematicians use computers, paper, office space, and other inputs that are costly. Anything that raises the cost of intellectual inquiry will deter some inquiry that otherwise would be undertaken. Yet, no one would claim that this consequence is sufficient to require owners of office space desired by mathematics professors to turn it over to them free of charge, or computer makers to donate work stations to the mathematicians.[8]

The costs to follow-on discovery from rights in earlier mathematical innovations, however, are not the same as those associated with ordinary physical inputs. Ordinary physical inputs, such as office space and computers, are rivalrous goods, typically sold in competitive markets. A rivalrous good cannot be used freely without interfering with its use by another, so the market's pricing of the good provides a mechanism for choosing the most socially valued among potential competing uses. This is not so for nonrivalrous goods, which can be used by different individuals for different purposes without diminishing the good's value.

For the special class of nonrivalrous goods represented by mathematical formulae, the social value may be large while the private value to an individual researcher may be quite small in expectation. Put differently, there is likely to be a wide divergence between the private and social value of the formula. Given this divergence, researchers will tend to be too reluctant, from society's perspective, to pay for use of the formula. The divergence between private and social value is likely to be greater for mathematical formulae than is the case with most ideas. Given the utility of mathematical results as building blocks to scientific research of any sort, their social value will tend to be greater than that of the typical idea. In addition, the nature of mathematical inquiry is such that a formula's utility often will be difficult to predict in advance of completion of the research relying on it. As a result, relatively few follow-on discoverers would be in a position to know that it was worth their while to pay the price charged by the patent holder. This is distinguishable from the mundane physical input—such as a pencil—where the private and social value of the input are pretty much the same in the average case and the typical researcher will have no trouble deciding whether its private value is greater than its cost.

In addition, the administrative costs of recognizing property rights in mathematical results are likely to be large in comparison to physical inputs. While sometimes a research design may be consciously built to follow on a specific formula, the ideas embedded in mathematical formulae cannot be excluded from a researcher's thoughts, providing an additional issue of defining when the use of such an idea in further research constitutes an infringement. Put differently, it is difficult to cabin ideas, especially the more abstract ones that have connections to many different strands of thought, and the integration of them into research concepts is not always observable or controllable in the same fashion as a decision to purchase a piece of equipment to use in research efforts.[9]

All of this suggests that providing rights to mathematical formulae would entail dynamic costs that exceed their innovation-promoting benefit. The costs will be substantial where rights to fundamental mathematical insights are at issue, not only because of the broad spectrum of potential uses but also because of the attenuated connection between the social benefit from many uses and the subjective value to the user.[10]

A second cost, closely related to the dynamic cost just described, is the static monopolization cost of a property right in mathematical formulae. Mathematical expressions form a language of science and of rigorous inquiry generally. They are used so frequently and in so many different settings that patentability would create a tax not only on research but on an array of activity that employ mathematical insights. The result would be an "inverse multiplier effect" that would shrink the market for rigorous intellectual inquiry built on mathematical foundations.

The static monopolization cost is perhaps better understood if we think of research fields as vertically related, with some fields supplying intellectual inputs to others. Mathematical research forms a primary market that supplies inputs to vertically downstream fields of scientific research. A monopolist who jacks up the price for mathematical results shrinks the primary market and has a ripple effect that shrinks all of the vertically downstream markets.

As discussed in the dynamic effects of pricing mathematical formulae, the balance between benefits to individual users and administrative costs (of identifying uses, pricing them, and collecting fees) may discourage use of the formula in large numbers of instances in which its use would yield social benefits. Even among those who are chary of withdrawing goods from the market processes that promote efficient discovery, management, and allocation, the static costs of giving patents for mathematical results would have to be viewed as enormous.

Although assertions about the magnitude of the costs we are discussing must be made warily, the balance of static and dynamic costs appears to tilt against granting patent protection for mathematical results. Granting property in mathematical results would run up static and dynamic costs strongly. The benefits from innovation incentives to first movers are likely to be swamped by the costs of innovation disincentives to later movers and by the static, market-shrinkage effects on scientific research.

Physical Formulae

As we move across subject matters from the most abstract to the most practical, the subject matter next closest to the world of practical things consists of physical formulae. The difference between mathematical formulae and physical formulae is that mathematical formulae and results are often tautologies while physical formulae are tested and testable against real-world processes and objects. For example, the physical formula $E = mc^2$ is not a tautology like $x^2 - y^2 = (x+y)(x-y)$; it is a proposition about the real world that can, at least in theory, be proven false by empirical testing. In this sense, a physical formula is a step closer to practical things than a mathematical formula.

The fact that a physical formula is not simply stating propositions that, however complex, must be true may seem to give it a greater claim to being made property. Yet, that difference is not of much significance. The physical formula, though testable, can be just as abstract as a mathematical formula and can be just as fundamental of a building block for later research. Where mathematical results form basic predicates for other mathematical expressions and for any exercise involving calculations based on them (such as engineering), physical results provide basic building blocks for understanding and reconstructing physical phenomena. Both types of formulae are available to be discovered in the same way. Both types of formulae are the products of research that builds on prior discoveries as well as on thought experiments and other theoretical inquiries. And creation of exclusive property rights can give rise to substantial static and dynamic costs for both types of formulae.

Consider the most famous equation implied by Einstein's special theory of relativity, $E = mc^2$. The theory explains that physical objects (mass) and energy are interchangeable, that every object contains within it energy that is stored, waiting to be released. The formula gives the exchange rate, so to speak, for mass and energy. It explains the creation of atomic energy (both the energy that is used to power everyday electrical gadgets and the fearsome energy of atomic bombs);[11] the way stars shine;[12] and phenomena that are critical to the design of television sets and global positioning satellites.[13] While the special relativity formula is distinct from most physical formulae in the scope and importance of its applications, it is prototypical of physical formulae in its connections to both earlier and later work.[14]

Given the basic building-block nature of physical formulae, such as the mass-energy-equivalence one, allowing researchers to patent them would create problems similar to those encountered in permitting researchers to patent mathematical statements. The factors that we examined in relation to the patentability of mathematical formulae—widespread potential application, the expected value to individual researchers (both in the primary and in vertically downstream research fields), and the administrative costs— seem similar for physical formulae. With patents, follow-on researchers would be deterred from carrying out their work. Demanding payment for the use of physical results would create large static monopolization costs. While there could be positive dynamic-incentive effects to innovation in physical formulae, as with mathematical formulae, the magnitude of the effect likely would be less than the costs associated with it.

The line between a formula such as Einstein's theory of special relativity and a directly useful product, such as a nuclear-fueled power plant, remains attenuated as with mathematical formulae. Indeed, that is the reason that it took forty years to go from publication of the formula (1905) to the capacity to release energy from uranium in sufficient quantity to detonate a bomb (1945). That time period is especially instructive when you recall that the search for ways to release energy had engaged teams of accomplished scientists for much of the period.[15] This suggests that physical formulae, like mathematical formulae, are unlikely to generate immediate market rewards, but that restricting their use could retard a substantial amount of research by scientists who will build on them. The same reasons that militate against granting patents for mathematical formulae suggest that granting patents for physical formulae would impose costs in excess of the benefits of increased innovation incentives.

Processes

Descriptions of processes for making things—what we have referred to as "cookbooks"—comprise the next category of potentially patentable subjects. Unlike the categories discussed above, processes are included in the set of things for which patents are granted. The U.S. patent law, for example, provides for patentability of "any new and useful process, machine, manufacture, or composition of matter, or any new and useful improvement thereof."[16]

Identifying what is a process that might be patented—and what separates it from a mathematical or physical formula, on one hand, or a product, on the other—presents a challenge. Potentially patentable items in this category range from descriptions of physical results to a step-by-step plan for making a product that seems almost indistinguishable from a description of the product itself.

Let us start at the abstract end of this spectrum. One could argue that $E = mc^2$ is not a physical formula, but a recipe for changing matter into energy. Obviously, if processes are to be patentable and physical formulae are not, patent law needs to distinguish between them. Patent law must require a certain degree of particularity. Otherwise, patents will be granted for physical formulae, masquerading as processes.

The same problem is observed with mathematical formulae. U.S. courts have woven an unsteady line of cases trying to make this distinction. In *Gottschalk v. Benson,*[17] the U.S. Supreme Court rejected a software patent on the ground that the patent effectively sought protection for a mathematical algorithm that allowed the conversion of binary-coded decimal numerals into pure binary numerals. Although it was described as a process, the court found that the procedure described in the patent application was a mathematical formula:

> The mathematical formula involved here has no substantial practical application except in connection with a digital computer, which means that . . . the patent would wholly preempt the mathematical formula and in practical effect would be a patent on the algorithm itself.[18]

Nine years after *Benson,* in *Diamond v. Diehr,*[19] the U.S. Supreme Court approved a process patent claim relying on a computer program, at the heart of which was a mathematical formula.[20] The formula and program provided a new, previously unknown, method of guiding the precise curing of synthetic rubber products. The court approved the patent on the ground that the algorithm at issue was embedded in a program directed at a particular use and product and thus, unlike the claim in *Benson,* was not tantamount to patenting an idea.

Courts and scholars have not had great success in attempting to find a line between *Benson* and *Diehr* that offers real guidance in determining what claims will be deemed efforts to patent ideas (pure mathematical formulae) and what claims will be deemed descriptions of patentable processes. The law seems to be developing, instead, discrete categories of claims—such as those for software patents—that are given separate treatment, through domestic law or through international agreement. Increasingly, in this arena, legislators and judges seek to provide categorical answers in place of the qualitative tests developed in case-by-case adjudication.

At the other end of the spectrum from abstract formulae are the directions to create an item in a specific way. These are the processes that patent law in fact protects. Here the law needs to distinguish what is protected as a particular *manner* of producing something from the physical *product* that is produced. A general description of a process—how to prepare hollandaise sauce—could cover all possible ways to produce hollandaise or hollandaise-like sauces, rather than one particular way of producing the sauce. A patent for a sufficiently general process description is functionally equivalent to a patent on the product (or class of products) itself—like a patent covering all cars, or all airplanes.

The distinction between a patent on a process and one on a product is important. If there are twenty ways to produce hollandaise, a patent on one of them may be valuable; it may be a better way to produce the sauce—one that costs less, takes less time, produces a better tasting sauce, or is less likely to yield a sauce that is too thin or too thick or that separates. But the patent on that process does not provide the patent holder with control over the alternative processes. The availability of those alternatives means that people other than the patent holder and his licensees can produce sauces that are likely to be substitutes for the sauce produced by the patented process. That limits the returns earned on the process and limits as well the static costs associated with higher prices for hollandaise and reductions in the amount of hollandaise produced (the twin hallmarks of monopoly).

The key aspect of process patents, then, is the scope of the claim allowed. The broader the scope and the more general the described process, the higher will be the static costs associated with it. At the same time, too narrow a scope will reduce the dynamic benefits of process patents. Patent law, for the most part, attempts to find the ideal point between these extremes, the point that should balance dynamic and static costs. How does it do this?

As patent applicants can be depended on to endeavor to broaden the scope of claims so far as the law permits, the law does not need guideposts to determine when a patent claim is not broad enough. The method by which patent attempts to find the right balance between static and dynamic costs is through *limiting doctrines,* rules that deny patentability to certain claims.

The most important limiting doctrine governing process patents is the requirement that the process lead to a particular, useful result. Patents are not awarded for laws of nature or physical principles,[21] mathematical formulae *(Benson),* or chemical formulae.[22] This rule implies that if $E = mc^2$ were offered as a process to be patented, it would be rejected because the formula does not give us a particular tangible result. Indeed, the distance between knowing the relation between matter and energy and knowing how to release the energy trapped in particular forms of matter is vast. We noted earlier that forty years, and quite a lot of effort, passed between the publication of the formula and first atomic bomb. The first nuclear power plant to generate electricity for commercial use appeared (in Russia) almost fifty years after the publication of the formula. On the other hand, as *Diamond v. Diehr* illustrates, a process that relies on a mathematical or physical formula in order to produce a particular product is patentable.

The reason for denying process patents to mathematical, physical, and other formulae and algorithms are the same as those covered earlier in this chapter—the deterrent to follow-on discovery and the static (monopolization) costs of protecting building-block ideas. The process in *Diehr* is distinguishable from the typical algorithm precisely because a process that results in a particular, useful result is unlikely to give rise to static and dynamic costs of the magnitude that would be observed in the case of stand-alone formulae and algorithms. Awarding a patent to a process that leads to a particular product would not deter follow-on discoverers who found that the mathematical formula at the heart of the patented process could be used to generate different products. And a patent covering a process for a particular product would be far more limited in scope and thus generate much smaller static monopolization costs than one covering a general algorithm that might apply to many production processes. This example suggests that patent law supports dynamic incentives while minimizing static (monopoly) and dynamic costs (deterring follow-on discovery).

The other key limiting doctrine in the area of process patents helps courts choose patentable subjects among those processes leading to arguably useful results. Cases such as *Benson* and *O'Reilly v. Morse* have stood for the proposition that process patents cannot be awarded to processes that are so abstract that they cover both known and unknown applications of the process.[23] As a practical matter, this is how courts can push the scope of patents toward the ideal level, given that applicants themselves will always seek the broadest possible application consistent with the legal rules on patentability. Put another way, since patent applicants are a force always pushing the law to expand the scope of protection, the best response the law could take to this force is to push back by developing legal principles for resisting overly broad claims for rights to patent processes.

Benson serves as an example of a case in which the sought-after process patent was denied because the process covered both known and unknown applications. The software program in *Benson,* converting binary-coded decimal numerals into pure binary numerals, could not by itself be limited to a specific product. Given this, the static costs and dynamic costs of a patent right could be quite large, depending on the range of possible applications. This does not imply that a new algorithm incorporated into a process used by a special type of computer could not be patented, because in that case there would be a particular application.

As we move from abstract formula to a process that yields a particular, useful result, we see that there is a further stage of refinement in which we select among several different methods of carrying out a particular process. The law would cut static costs even further if it limited the patent to a particular method, though this would involve some reduction of the dynamic incentive. As a general matter it is difficult to say how the law should make this trade-off between static and dynamic costs. Edmund Kitch, however, has explained that the law generally favors a broad right to the process.[24] One of his illustrations is a nineteenth-century case in which the Supreme Court upheld a patent on "a process of separating fats into glycerine and stearic, margaric, and oleic acids through the use of heat, pressure, and water at any temperature and in any apparatus that would work . . . even though the inventor himself had used only a few of the possible combinations that would work."[25]

The reason, according to Kitch, that the law awards a property right to the process, rather than a particular method of carrying it out, is in order to provide the best incentives for development of the patent's value. In a regime in which the patent right is limited to a particular method, the development of the patent would become, in effect, a common resource that would be inefficiently exploited. Consider, for example, the incentives of researchers.[26] The first discoverer would have a strong incentive to file, even though he may have hit upon the least efficient of several possible methods. At that point, his incentive to continue to develop the patent would be weakened by the fact that the information revealed could be used by competitors to find a more efficient method. Although this "efficient prospecting" function of patent law is distinguishable from the traditional innovation incentive, it is close enough for us to group it within the set of dynamic effects (see our discussion in Chapter 3).

The prospecting function coupled with the traditional dynamic-incentive effect suggests a good justification for the law's willingness to grant a property right in a process rather than a particular method of carrying out a process. Mark Grady and Jay Alexander have proposed a more general theory in which the breadth of the patent would depend on the extent to which the patent application signals the possibility for improvement.[27] Broad protection would be observed for those patents with a strong signal of potential further development, and narrow protection would be observed where the signal was weak. While this might be consistent with the degree of protection given in practice by courts, it is difficult to craft a reasonably clear and easily administered rule that has this distinction embedded in it.

As we noted before, courts and commentators have not been successful in articulating a clear line of reasoning to distinguish cases in which process patents are awarded and where they are not.[28] Notions such as that the invention was "out there already" or that it was not a "real invention" have been used to explain the cases. The cases are better explained by looking at the likely static and dynamic costs connected to a particular patent grant. These costs are related to the building-block nature of the invention to others in the inventor's field and the value of the invention to vertically downstream fields. An examination of these costs helps determine whether the patent is too abstract or general to be justifiable. Despite questions about the exact places and ways to draw the lines—such as whether a process patent can issue where a critical step is mental rather than physical or mechanical[29] or whether patents can issue for methods of doing business[30]—patent doctrine appears to be broadly consistent with the goal of minimizing static and dynamic costs.

Product Patents

The last category of potentially patentable things in our list consists of products—things that are made or discovered. This is the primary category for patents. The major advances in technology over the past two centuries have been associated largely with new products, such as the airplane, automobile, electric light, radio, telephone, television, transistor, and the various chemical compounds that comprise pharmaceuticals from aspirin to Zithromax®.

The cost-benefit balance for a patent on a tangible product is not the same as for the categories discussed above, but the law still must attend to the potential dynamic and static costs of particular rules. U.S. patent law is atypical in a couple of respects that we address later in this book, but the basic considerations for patentability of products under U.S. law are similar to those of other patent systems. There are other types of product patent under U.S. law (such as the plant patent or the design patent), but the archetypal product patent is the "utility" patent. That is the form we discuss here.

Recall that to obtain a patent, the product must meet three basic criteria: it must be useful, novel, and nonobvious.[31] Together, these criteria circumscribe patentability of products in a manner that is generally consistent with a balance of dynamic and static costs.

Utility

With the groundwork laid so far, it is easy to explain the function of the utility requirement. The utility criterion reduces both the static and dynamic cost of patents in two ways: by limiting the protection given to ideas and by enhancing the informational benefits of the patent system.

First, the utility requirement for product patents reduces static and dynamic costs by limiting the scope of property in ideas. A patent for a product that has no utility is effectively the same as a patent for an idea. Suppose, for example, a chemist invents a "wonder drug" that cannot be shown at present to cure anything, but in theory has the potential, perhaps in combination with other products, to cure hundreds of diseases. An application for such an open-ended patent would be denied under the utility requirement.[32] This makes sense for reasons that we have already set out. Where there is no specific present utility to a product, the cost of taxing future discovery and of monopolizing potential markets would seem to outweigh the benefit.

Another illustration of the utility requirement's denying protection to ideas is the distinction made, in product patents, between information and functional structure. A new type of accounting system or a new type of insurance form is useful largely for the information conveyed. A battery-powered car, however, is useful because of its function, which is embedded in its structure. The former is not patentable while the latter is.

The law's distinction between information and functional structure, though perhaps weakened by the recent development of business method patents, reflects the same balance between static and dynamic costs analyzed in the cases of mathematical algorithms and production processes. A product whose main function is to convey information, such as a new type of accounting system, poses the same problems for patent law as those observed in the case of mathematical algorithms generally. A patent on the information conveyed raises the cost of using information and chokes off future innovation. Given the cheapness of transferring and acquiring information, the costs of such a policy probably would be large relative to the benefits.

The second general way in which the utility requirement cuts static and dynamic costs is by enhancing the informational benefits of the patent system. It does this by ensuring that patents are not awarded for fraudulent products and processes; for example, products that falsely claim to have a specific utility. Recall that the inner workings of patented products, unlike those protected by trade secrets, are available to other researchers to study. That information would be of far less use to follow-on researchers if a significant share of it included bogus claims of utility.[33]

Novelty

The second requirement for a patent is that it be novel. Novelty is an easy requirement to justify. If the invention is not new, then the reward inherent in the patent is for diligence in pursuing an administrative prize rather than for innovation. The dynamic benefit of a patent system is the inducement to innovate. Plainly, if an invention is already known, used, described publicly, or patented (in the country of application or elsewhere), the patent is not a necessary incentive to this invention. Moreover, awarding patents for inventions already known or in use would have the perverse effect of encouraging latecomers to seek property rights in the innovations of others. In these cases, there is no dynamic benefit, and all that society gets from the patent is the static monopolization cost.

Granting patent rights also seems unnecessary if the applicant, knowing that patents issue only for new inventions, is willing nonetheless to describe the innovation in public documents without having applied for a patent— perhaps because the inventor gets immediate rewards in public notoriety or in academic standing sufficient to motivate disclosure. The same analysis would seem to hold if a patent applicant decides that the commercial rewards of being first to market a new item are so large that rushing to market is more important than rushing to patent. If the patent is not needed as an inducement, the benefit of patent protection cannot be invoked as a justification for incurring the costs. In addition, there is a reliance issue in this case. If an innovator rushes his invention to market without a patent, competing firms, realizing that the innovation is not patented, will replicate it. It would be chaotic as well as costly to allow the initial innovator to obtain the patent later and use it to oust the competitors from the market.

These examples suggest that the novelty requirement in patent law serves more than one function. At the most general level, the novelty requirement denies protection when the static monopolization costs seem large relative to the dynamic (innovation-inducing) benefits. However, the novelty requirement also serves the more specific function of preventing certain types of opportunistic expropriation. One type is when a noninventor expropriates the market value of an inventor's work by filing for a patent for an existing unpatented invention. If such patents could be acquired, opportunists would trawl for unpatented inventions, seeking to gain property rights over them. The other type of opportunistic expropriation is when an inventor first discloses his invention and then waits for someone else to find a valuable market for it, and then files for a patent.

In a world in which it is clear that the patent is not necessary to bring forth a particular invention (because the invention was already there before the patent), awarding a patent for that invention introduces static costs without any dynamic benefits. But in the real world it will not always be clear whether the patent award was necessary, and so the rules regarding novelty have implications for dynamic costs and benefits.

Dynamic-cost issues arise, for example, when the novelty requirement itself is a source of dispute. In the main, the disputes are over the determination whether an invention was in fact known before the patent filing. The novelty requirement is defeated not only if the invention was made by someone else, but also if something so close to it was in use or described publicly that the invention was "anticipated" by what was known to or discussed by others. So, for example, a patent on a particular, corrosion-resistant titanium alloy could not validly issue because an article published earlier had described titanium-molybdenum-nickel alloys in chart form that essentially describe the claimed invention.[34] It did not matter that the article did not have the same express description as the patent or that the article did not discuss the corrosion-resistant properties of the alloys suggested by its graphs. It was enough that the article showed a prior recognition of the existence of this alloy.

Courts and administrative authorities differ on the extent to which prior description needs to enable a skilled technician to actually produce or use the claimed invention—as opposed to simply describing it or something that might fairly be thought to encompass it—in order to defeat patent novelty.[35] That debate turns on the question of how much the dynamic benefit of patenting is diminished without the added financial encouragement of a patent for this last increment of invention. The answer to that depends on the frequency with which inventions are almost, but not fully, described in the literature; the time taken to proceed from what exists to completion; and the additional value of the completed invention relative to the added costs associated with the patents. Since there is no general answer to this question, the case-by-case approach observed in most patent regimes is what would be observed in any system that weighed the costs and benefits of patents. Our general point is that the unavoidable line drawing observed in this area suggests that the novelty requirement has significant implications for dynamic-incentive effects.

The other point at which dynamic considerations arise in connection to the novelty requirement is the filing date. Above, we noted that novelty is judged as of the time of filing: Was the claimed invention new as of that time or was it known, used, described, or patented earlier? In most patent systems, that is a fair approximation of the test.

The U.S. patent system has until recently differed from those in the rest of the world, in that the time for assessing the novelty of an invention is the date of invention, not the date of filing. However, the law in the United States is in transition, at the time of this writing, to a first-to-file rule, adopted in the America Invents Act signed into law in September 2011.

Under first-to-file, if James files a patent application on May 10 and Julie files an application for a nearly identical invention on May 22, the question is what was publicly described, used, and so forth, prior to May 10. Julie may assert that she perfected her invention in January and that James only perfected his invention in March, but the priority of rights to the invention is set by the date of filing. The relevant question on novelty is whether James's invention was novel when his application was filed.

Under first-to-invent, different issues arise. In a conflict between James's patent rights and Julie's patent rights, an arbiter would have to assess the factual basis of Julie's contention that she was the first to invent. The novelty of the invention is assessed at the time of the invention. But the fact that the date of invention, not filing, is critical means that the first-to-invent system needs rules to deal with acts that occur between invention and filing and to address problems that may be caused by excessive delay in filing.

Obviously, when filing is the key to priority rights, inventors have plenty of incentive to file without delay. Apart from its effect on the applicant's own rights, delay in filing carries with it costs in reduced disclosure to other researchers, including encouraging wasteful research expenditures. For instance, if a telephone has already been invented, failure to alert researchers misleads some into spending resources seeking solutions to a problem that has been solved. Resources spent on a race that is over are, in large part, all cost and no benefit.

Yet, when invention itself determines priority, a number of considerations might counsel delay in filing—such as uncertainty over the value of the patent, or the strategic value of waiting, like the dog in the manger, for a rival to prove the invention's commercial value. The individual inventor's incentive to file may diverge from the social incentive to file. If the system is designed to minimize social costs, additional rules are needed to address this problem.

The U.S. system, though in transition, has dealt with this problem by creating statutory bars to patents. So, for example, although published after invention (and, thus, not a barrier to a finding of novelty under U.S. law), an article describing the invention published more than a year before an application is filed will prevent issuance of a patent.[36] Similarly, if the invention is in "public use" or "on sale" for more than a year before the application is filed, the inventor loses his claim to a patent.[37] The statutory bars serve a gap-filling role that attempts to preserve the balance of costs and benefits associated with the novelty requirement in the United States and elsewhere.[38]

Nonobviousness

The last of the three basic requirements for patents is the requirement of nonobviousness. This requirement is close to, but different from, the novelty requirement. The novelty question is whether the invention was actually known or used or publicly described before a critical date (either invention, in the United States, or filing the patent application, almost everywhere else). Nonobviousness looks not to the fact of prior invention, description, or use, but to the distance between the invention and whatever came before.

In spite of this difference, it should be clear that the novelty and nonobviousness requirements serve the same function: denying patent protection where the dynamic benefits are small in relation to the static costs. Both requirements introduce a cost-benefit test into patent doctrine. While the utility requirement and the "limiting doctrines" governing scope (examined earlier in this chapter) function to limit or constrain gross imbalances between static and dynamic costs, the nonobviousness requirement (as well as the novelty requirement in uncertain cases) takes a more fine-tuned approach to trading off costs. It is concerned with the ratio of static costs and dynamic benefits even in settings in which the risk of unrestrained growth in either static or dynamic costs is minimal.[39]

Assuming that an invention is novel, the next question is whether it is sufficiently different from what was known before to merit protection against unauthorized use. If a reasonably skilled technician, familiar with the state of learning (referred to in patent law as the "prior art"), could have seen that the invention was possible, it will be deemed obvious and, thus, unpatentable.[40] In such circumstances, the cost of patent protection exceeds the likely benefit of encouraging innovation. When the distance between what was already known to those familiar with the prior art is slight, the invention can be expected to be introduced by someone within a reasonably short time. Although the patent applicant is the first person to actually complete the invention, in this case he has made only a slight advance in the timing of invention. Dynamic gains, hence, will be slight; static costs will be substantial.

The trade-off between static costs and dynamic benefits reflected in the nonobviousness rule implies additional limiting doctrines in patent law. A reordering of the components of some product, a change in proportions, and the omission or multiplication of existing elements are generally insufficient to meet the nonobviousness test.[41] Similarly, the substitution of different materials in an existing product or device fails the nonobviousness test.[42]

The usefulness of such a test is also implied by the potential dynamic costs that could be generated if no such test were in place. In *Hotchkiss v. Greenwood*,[43] the Supreme Court suggested that the nonobviousness requirement aims to ensure that patents have a sufficiently high quality. Otherwise, low-quality patents could effectively crowd out high-quality patents. For example, a patent awarded to a device that involves a mere reordering of elements of an existing device could effectively block a follow-on inventor from obtaining a patent for a significantly innovative variation.

It should be clear that the nonobviousness requirement is overinclusive. Some of the most significant innovations will appear to be obvious in retrospect. In the sciences, some of the best ideas appear to be obvious, or simple, in relation to their rivals. The Copernican system (sun-centered) is mathematically and visually simpler than the system of Ptolemaic epicycles. Anyone familiar with academic hierarchy knows the pressure on researchers to stay within accepted frameworks—pressure that leads them to keep plowing deeper within existing models before considering simpler and potentially more fruitful alternatives. Because of the incentives created by hierarchy, simple solutions are sometimes overlooked or discouraged. But the business world is less hierarchical, and simple solutions that are potentially profitable are more likely to be tried. As a result, the dynamic (incentive) cost of excluding obvious inventions from consideration for patents is probably not great.

Moreover, courts are fully aware of the overinclusiveness of the nonobviousness requirement. As a result, some pieces of circumstantial evidence, sometimes called "secondary considerations,"[44] have been invoked to justify the award of a patent in spite of retrospective obviousness. The most important such consideration is commercial success.[45] Some courts have held that if a product is commercially successful, then it must not have been obvious; otherwise, someone would have done it long before the patentee.[46]

The case of obvious inventions—and the costs associated with patents for these inventions—should be distinguished from the case of patent races. Sometimes several individuals or teams are seeking solutions to the same problem. This is not strictly a modern-day occurrence. Competing efforts were under way to solve the problem of communication at a distance, which gave rise to the telephone, with litigation for an extended period over patent rights.[47] Similarly, there were several different teams endeavoring to perfect means for manned flight at the time of the Wright Brothers success at Kill Devil Hills.[48] And while Thomas Edison is popularly credited with inventing the electric light bulb, in fact many other inventors were experimenting with ways to produce light with electricity, in order to replace gas lamps, and some had debuted working versions. Edison, however, came up with a better filament to conduct the electricity and then a much improved version of the filament that burned longer and more safely than other bulbs.[49]

In patent races, as in the case of obvious inventions, there is enough in the prior art to point toward something that more than one individual sees as a fruitful avenue for research. The issues with obvious inventions and patent races, however, differ. The law resists granting rights to obvious inventions because the innovation incentive from protecting the added contribution of the inventor is not worth the cost of protection. In patent races, there is a different issue. Even though the technological or practical problem to be addressed is obvious to others, the solution to the problem is not. Inducing investment in solving the problem by granting property rights is socially beneficial; and, by and large, the more obvious the problem being solved, the greater the social benefit from its solution.

Patent races are a concern to commentators because they can consume resources far in excess of what might seem an ideal investment in innovation. The dynamics of investment in pursuing patents can induce the contestants making serial choices about research to overinvest because of the winner-take-all quality of private returns from the race. Commentators have proffered several possible changes in the law to address concerns with patent races.[50] These changes, unfortunately, seem either practically unworkable or likely to generate even costlier problems for the patent system than the one they are intended to solve.[51]

Some Miscellaneous Exclusions

We have so far focused on the distinction between processes and products, and within the broad class of processes on the distinction between abstract ideas and useful applications. Products would seem to have a stronger claim to patentability because they are obviously not abstractions. Still, there are whole categories of things, including products, that are, or at one time have been, deemed unpatentable. These categorical exclusions (and the limits around them) can be explained by looking at the trade-off between costs and benefits associated with patents for these items.

Consider naturally existing animals, plants, and the substances derived from them without modification. These have been deemed unpatentable, under the exclusion for naturally occurring substances.[52] Why not allow a patent for the discovery of a new wild animal, such as Bigfoot or the Loch Ness Monster? The potential dynamic benefits of such a discovery would be difficult to identify. Unobserved animals, deep in unexplored forests or seas, have no known utility to people. To the extent that any utility might arise, it would be the result of finding substances from such an animal that benefit humans. But a patent awarded to discovery of the animal would dull incentives to any later researcher who would wish to study the animal to find useful substances. So there would clearly be a dynamic cost from awarding such a patent. There would also be the static cost of creating a monopoly in the market for the animal. With no identifiable dynamic benefits and rather clear costs, there is no case on utilitarian grounds for awarding patents for the discovery of new animals. The broad exclusion of patents for new animals is consistent with this argument.[53]

We can distinguish the case of a newly created or improved life form from finding a new animal deep in the forest. In *Diamond v. Chakrabarty*,[54] the Supreme Court upheld the patentability of a newly created life form, specifically bacteria genetically altered to consume petroleum waste. The new life form in *Diamond* obviously had a definite, useful, and beneficial application. A machine created to serve precisely the same function would have been patentable. The mere fact that it was a life form was not a sufficient reason to deny patentability.

We can also distinguish substances that are created from new life forms. If an explorer were to capture some new wild animal, he could not get a patent on the animal. However, if he extracted a chemical from the venom of the animal that had useful applications, he could patent the chemical, since it was not found in its final state in nature.[55]

At one time business methods were held unpatentable.[56] The law has changed,[57] though business method patents remain a matter of controversy.[58] As a general matter, the case for patenting business methods appears weak on cost-benefit grounds. New business methods will always be encouraged by market competition. A firm that introduces a new business method that either provides more value to consumers or reduces costs will outpace its rivals in the market. The advantage gained from adopting a successful new method gives the first mover a lead over industry rivals that can be self-perpetuating for some period of time, especially in businesses with strong network effects or brand identity. Business improvements by firms such as Wal-Mart, Starbucks, and Amazon, for example, appear to have given those companies advantages that lasted well beyond the time it took for widespread dissemination of the ideas behind those changes.

This is not something that calls for regulation, nor something that requires a special property right to induce investment in innovation. The normal process of dynamic competition, or Schumpeterian creative destruction, involves the continual introduction of new methods that lead at times to temporary monopolies but are eventually copied by competitors. Patents might provide an additional incentive to develop new methods, but they will also obstruct the process of dissemination and emulation that is core to dynamic competition. Given the ubiquity and frequency of the adoption of new business methods, it is by no means clear that society's welfare can be improved by allowing them to be patented.

Indeed, there is an inherent inconsistency in the notion of business method patents. Methods of conducting business are key instruments of competition, just as price setting. We tend to lose sight of this only when we focus on the short-term static competition involving aspects of price or quantity. Allowing business methods to be patented permits these instruments of competition to be turned into instruments of monopolization.

The Supreme Court addressed business method patents squarely in *Bilski v. Kappos*,[59] an opinion that endeavors to put the business method genie back in the bottle without creating a rule specifically addressed to that class of patents. The Court rejected the notion that the law can be read to incorporate a test for patentability that excludes or specially disfavors business method patents. On the other hand, the specific patent application at issue, one for a method of hedging risk, was rejected because it sought protection for an abstract idea.

The Court based its decision on the criteria for patentability on a straightforward reading of the Patent Act's terms: simply put, the term *process* includes business methods. Assuming that the process described meets other criteria under the law, the fact that the process describes a method for doing business does not remove it from patent eligibility. That well may be a sound approach for judges to take to legal interpretation. It is striking nonetheless that the Court paid so little attention to the incentive issues that led the Federal Circuit, in its earlier decision in the same case, to read those same terms as encompassing a patentability test that limits process-patent eligibility (the category in which business method patents arise) to processes associated with a machine or apparatus or the transformation of an item—a test that would have excluded most business methods from patentability.

The abstraction principle embraced by the Supreme Court may turn out to be a sufficient doctrinal tool for controlling the dangers posed by business method patents. That remains to be seen. A more difficult question is what consequences will flow from the *Bilski* decision's clear signal that the Court now looks primarily to the statutory language rather than looking through the language to the static and dynamic cost trade-off issues that the language is intended to capture—considerations that have shaped patent doctrine over the years of its existence. American courts historically have taken account of incentive effects and other related costs of patent rules in interpreting the broad language of the statute and in creating common law doctrines that limit the scope of patent protection. Indeed, the abstraction principle on which the Court rests its decision on patentability is an example of the type of common law rule that the court abjures in its general analysis of the statute. That in itself raises a question whether the difference is more a matter of the style in which the opinion is written or a more fundamental distinction in the mode of interpretation.

Beyond Patentability: Claim Construction and Infringement

The issue of patentability is only part of the law of patents. Much of the law deals with questions that focus directly on the scope of the right that a patent affords. The law of infringement addresses the extent to which a patent owner can exclude others from using the innovation covered by a patent. Two concepts lie at the heart of that inquiry: the scope of the patent and the nature of conduct that infringes on its exclusive rights.

The first step in enforcing patent rights necessarily is definition of the scope of the patent's coverage. As simple and straightforward as that concept seems, it provides no end of difficulty. After all, each patent at its core protects a novel idea that builds on and extends prior ideas. The exact contours of each specific novel idea—the peculiar innovation represented by a patent—requires definition in a way that allows others to know what is protected.

How patent law performs this function has implications for the social costs and benefits of the patent system. Beyond delimiting the general category of ideas that deserves protection, patent law must provide a mechanism for deciding what is protected by each patent in a way that minimizes potential confusion by would-be users (or avoiders) of that innovation. If the scope of patent protection is too narrow, investment in innovation is discouraged. If the scope of protection is too broad, the static costs of patents will overwhelm the innovation benefits. Indeed, failure to create clarity in the mode of patent interpretation generates both dynamic and static costs.

Over time, patent law has evolved special terms and claiming conventions that are designed to produce greater clarity in identifying what is asserted as the patented product or process, to separate the major (independent) claims from the minor (dependent) claims.[60] Apart from the specific rules that govern the language used and meaning given, the courts also have held that, despite the inclusion of contested factual issues within the arguments over claim meaning, construction of claim meaning is a matter of law (i.e., for judges to decide)—not something to be left to juries—a decision confirmed by the Supreme Court in *Markman v. Westview Instruments, Inc.*[61]

Since *Markman,* judges hold separate hearings to consider and dispose of contentions over the meanings of claims. Unfortunately, as former law school dean and Federal Circuit Judge Jay Plager (among others) has observed, federal district judges conducting the *Markman* hearings and issuing decisions on claim construction generally lack technical training or extensive experience with patents, leading to a less than ideally predictable set of decisions.[62] Concentrating more of the patent caseload in a court with greater expertise might help, but the ultimate issues may be too fact dependent and technical to be made much more predictable than current rules allow.

The uncertainty over application of rules for claim construction to specific patents in part reflects the natural difficulty over application of general legal formulae to specific settings defined by technical criteria. Much as commentators might wish that judges could improve at this task, it seems unlikely that there is any easy means to that end. In some measure, uncertainty also reflects efforts to inject flexibility into the law to accommodate the trade-off between costs associated with insufficiently specific claiming language, on the one hand, and those attributable to excessively detailed and specific claiming language, on the other. Similar trade-offs are seen in many areas of both law and life where too much information can reduce clarity, just as too little information can.

To address this problem, the law requires patent applicants to be sufficiently clear and precise in their claims to *enable* readers to make or use the particular innovation claimed.[63] But the law also incorporates two mechanisms for safeguarding against too narrow a scope for patent protection.

One mechanism is the statutory provision permitting claims in the form of "means plus function"—that is, claims that say something uses certain types of means or steps to perform a particular operation to yield a specific result and assert a right to exclusive control over all (closely) similar means used for the same function to produce the same result.[64] Claims in this form are interpreted in light of the sorts of structures included in the patent application's specifications and cover equivalent structures, allowing the innovator to reach a larger set of potential infringements than claims more narrowly tied to a specific structure.[65]

The other mechanism is a judicial creation, the "doctrine of equivalents." Like the means-plus-function approach, the doctrine of equivalents expands patent protection to limit opportunities for duplicating the innovation through approaches that are nearly, but not completely, identical. The doctrine of equivalents includes within the scope of patent protection all devices or processes that, in the long-used formula articulated by the Supreme Court, "perform substantially the same function in substantially the same way to obtain the same result."[66] Although recent decisions have narrowed the doctrine a bit,[67] the doctrine remains another way for courts to balance the risk of too narrow protection of innovation against the risk of too broad and uncertain coverage.

Conclusion

Looking at the most basic patent doctrines, we find that the law functions to reduce the sum of dynamic (incentive-based) and static (market-shrinkage) costs associated with patent rights. It does this largely by developing legal doctrines (limiting doctrines) that deny patentability. Those doctrines focus on the distinction between abstraction and particularity, and between information-conveyance and functional structure. Patent applicants naturally seek the broadest patent possible, which necessitates doctrines that can reduce the scope of patents and deny patents where the expected costs of protection exceed the expected social gains. At the same time, the doctrines cannot be entirely one-sided, as potential infringers have incentives to narrow the scope of patent protection. Doctrines looking to matters such as novelty and nonobviousness seek to find the optimal balance between innovation benefits and static costs.

The goal of this chapter is not to provide a comprehensive description of patent law, much less a full justification for every part of it. But our review of the basic patent doctrines suggests that patent law, like the law of property,[68] serves society's interest. Even though protection of intellectual contributions—of new ideas or discoveries reduced to a practical form—raises problems that are not observed in the case of property rights for tangible items, the system of protective rules that we observe seems to strike an optimal balance between social costs and benefits.

As we said before, whether the patent system is socially optimal is an empirical question that cannot be resolved once and for all by an analysis of legal doctrine.[69] But legal doctrine provides one empirical check for a theoretical argument. If courts appear to be setting up rules that avoid unnecessary or undesirable social costs, then we have to take that as a sign that the law is performing a socially beneficial function.

5

Trade Secrets

Keeping Secrets

Some of the best-known names among consumer products are based on intellectual property protected by trade secrecy. In some cases, the secret has been kept for a long time. Coca-Cola has been produced under a secret formula for more than 125 years.[1] Kentucky Fried Chicken's "11 herbs and spices" recipe has been protected by secrecy for more than 70 years.[2] Although both have imitators, no other firm has come up with a product that is exactly like Coke or KFC.

The longevity of these secrets is impressive—and unusual. Benjamin Franklin's famous aphorism about keeping secrets—that a secret can be kept by three people only if two of them are dead—has the weight of experience on its side. The betting odds favor Franklin rather than the stories of well-kept secrets. Think about the practical side of Coca-Cola's long-run success based on its secret formula. Over the century and a quarter of Coca-Cola's existence, who knows how many employees have had access to the secret formula? Any one of them could have mistakenly or intentionally revealed the process to someone outside the firm who might have then passed it on, allowing a competitor to legally produce a perfect substitute. Trade secrecy law has played a pivotal role in preventing this outcome.

At the outset of the previous chapter we referred to trade secret law as protecting contractual agreements not to disclose information. This is incomplete, as trade secret law also provides protection against disclosures that result from breaches of common law rights. The basis for enforcing trade secret rights might be a trespass—for example, a burglar who breaks into your plant and steals a highly profitable secret recipe used to produce oatmeal cookies (the example also works for chocolate chip cookies, brownies, and things that aren't goodies of the edible sort). But for most purposes, locating trade secret law within the realm of contract is appropriate; that is the legal and practical framework at the root of most aspects of trade secrets. Trade secret law, in this sense, can be viewed as an adjunct to contract law,[3] based in consensual arrangements that give access to protected information on specific terms, with tort and unfair competition law serving to back up those arrangements.[4]

The orientation of trade secret law, thus, is distinct from patent, even though the subject matter—information about useful inventive ideas—is largely the same. In patent, the law promotes a trade-off of disclosure of the idea in exchange for a time-limited right to prevent others from using that idea or very closely related ideas (even if independently arrived at). Trade secret law only protects against unauthorized disclosure of the idea by certain people who are bound not to reveal the secret or who came into possession of the information unlawfully.

The overlap between the subjects of patent protection and trade secret protection, coupled with the different orientations in their design, raises several questions: What is the scope of trade secret protection in relation to patent protection and what explains the difference? Is it necessary or useful to protect trade secrets when firms have the option of seeking patents? Should trade secret protection be viewed as a substitute for patent protection or a complement to it?

The static and dynamic cost trade-off framework developed in our earlier chapters also applies to trade secret law. As we explain in this chapter, the law appears to strike a (roughly) optimal balance between the static costs from market shrinkage due to monopoly pricing and the dynamic costs from weakening innovation incentives.[5] As with any area of law, of course, the conclusion that an overarching framework is socially beneficial does not mean that every single trade secret decision issued by a court will be justifiable. In addition, the balance of static and dynamic costs will change as technological conditions change, so that a particular rule that might have made sense in 1850 will not necessarily be sensible today. Still, the general rules of trade secret law appear to recognize property in information only where the innovation benefits are greater than the monopolization costs. That's a good thing—and not just for Coke and KFC.

Scope of Trade Secret Protection

We use the term *trade secret law* to refer to common law developed around the protection of trade secrets. Its basic parameters are set by the common law rules of contract and tort law. In this sense, trade secret law is not a distinct area of the common law. The distinctions that exist between treatment of trade secrets and other valuable goods are at the margins and involve relatively narrow deviations from standard tort and contract doctrines.[6] What gives trade secret law its distinctive standing is the focus of the law—the information protected by it—more than the legal doctrines that govern.

The contract law piece of trade secret protection is a matter of common sense. Go back to our oatmeal cookie example. If you have a secret recipe for mass-producing exceptionally tasty oatmeal cookies and want to hire someone to work in your cookie plant, your lawyer will advise you to insist that the new employee sign a contract limiting his freedom to reveal your secret recipe to others, especially rival cookie makers. The contract would serve several purposes: to signal to the employee the importance you place on maintaining secrecy (which reduces the likelihood of an accidental disclosure), to set up a penalty that would be imposed on the employee if he should reveal the secret to a rival (which reduces the risk of a purposeful disclosure as well), and to set up grounds for imposing a penalty on a rival who appropriates the secret and uses it under certain conditions (which limits incentives to induce wrongful disclosures and, by extension, backs up the employee disincentive to intentional disclosure).

If you did not listen to your lawyer, you would be taking a greater risk that the employee would accidentally or intentionally reveal the secret to a rival or to someone who passes it on to a rival, eliminating the primary competitive advantage you have enjoyed in the market for oatmeal cookies. Without the protection of a contract that limits the employee's freedom to reveal what he learns working for you, the employee might be paid by a rival simply to reveal the secret or might be hired by the rival and go off to the next job with your secret recipe in his hands. The contract would be one way to reduce the risk of these bad outcomes. That is one reason lawyers are paid to draft contracts—they can help protect you, and if you're prone to thinking about the risks to your business, the contracts can lower your blood pressure while reducing your risk.

Even though this legal advice can help reduce risks of having your trade secrets sent out into the world, a contractual provision may not be sufficient to prevent an employee from disclosing your secret to a rival. Suppose despite a nondisclosure clause in the employment contract, six months after being hired the employee leaves with the recipe in his hands and, more importantly, a thorough working knowledge of how you have produced your special oatmeal cookies. He may not have to disclose the recipe directly for the information to leak out. Moreover, it may be nearly impossible to prove that he has disclosed the recipe. Perhaps he has made suggestions to the rival on how to improve the production process, without ever revealing the recipe. Proving disclosure in court might turn out to be a difficult task. Given this, you may prefer to have something stronger in the contract, such as a ban on working for a rival within a certain period of time. But such restrictions on employment are subject, at a minimum, to a rule-of-reason test in every state (asking whether the length and scope of the limitation are reasonable) and are more broadly prohibited in some states, such as California.[7]

The rule-of-reason test governing noncompetition agreements was the common law's early attempt to balance static and dynamic costs—where static costs are the market-shrinkage costs generated by monopolistic pricing, and dynamic costs are the welfare losses that result from a reduction in investment incentives (see our discussion of these issues in Chapters 3 and 4).[8] A precursor of the common law rule-of-reason test was set out in *Mitchel v. Reynolds,* a case involving a noncompetition agreement between a baker named Reynolds and another baker named Mitchel.[9] Mitchel leased the bakery that initially belonged to Reynolds for seven years. The lease contract included a clause that prohibited Reynolds from returning to the same area to open up another bakery during the seven-year lease term. Reynolds returned, set up a competing bakery, and Mitchel sued. The court held that the contract was enforceable because it was reasonable. It was reasonable because the static costs were limited: the prohibition on competition applied to a specific area and for a limited time—constituting a particular rather than a general limitation, in the language of Lord Macclesfield. It was also reasonable because the prohibition was voluntary, meaning that it was a mutually beneficial and even, perhaps, necessary condition for the business transfer to occur. If Reynolds had not promised to stay out, it is doubtful that Mitchel would have leased his shop, risking failure if Reynolds returned to serve his old customers. After all, a major part of the value that Mitchel was buying was the customer base built up by Reynolds.

The case is a heavily cited precedent because its logic transcends the specific case of a noncompetition clause or even the conditions supporting the transfer of a lease (and, by extension, the transfer of a business) from one artisan to another. If those who want to acquire a business cannot be promised a valuable asset (a going concern with goodwill that will not be competed away immediately by the very people who created it), acquirers will not offer a positive price for the business. If potential acquirers will not offer a positive price for a business, that would reduce incentives for business owners to develop a valuable brand. While the brand may yield returns in the short term, part of the value of investing in a business comes from being able to sell your stake to someone else. To use a familiar analogy, imagine what you might do if you were told that you can live in your house as long as you want and make it as nice as you'd like, but you can't sell it. Being able to sell greatly increases incentives to invest in things that increase value. The decision in *Mitchel* reflected recognition that the noncompetition agreement supported incentives to invest in brand capital. The reduction in brand value that would have resulted from refusing to enforce such an agreement would constitute a dynamic cost to society.

It follows that if an employer uses a noncompetition agreement to prevent the disclosure of trade secrets, that agreement will be subjected, under the rule-of-reason test, to a balancing framework that is based on the same principles examined in our chapter on patents. In deciding whether to enforce a noncompetition agreement, courts attempt to find the best balance between static and dynamic costs.[10]

If the employer does not have a noncompetition clause in the contract or a specific prohibition on the communication of certain information about his processes, he may still attempt to prevent a rival firm or ex-employee from using trade secrets that fall into their hands. The question confronted by a court in this scenario is whether it is a secret deserving of protection (assuming the employer has taken reasonable steps to protect it).[11] Employees often acquire at work a lot of information that would be valuable to rival employers. Indeed, almost any on-the-job training that enhances an employee's productivity is valuable to rival employers. To use Gary Becker's terminology, "general human capital"—based on training that enhances an employee's productivity at tasks that are also performed in other firms—is valuable to rival firms; "firm specific human capital"—based on training that does not enhance an employee's productivity to rival firms—is not valuable to rivals.[12]

If courts hold that *all* human capital (even the most general human capital) acquired on the job is protected under trade secrecy law, then no employee would be able to switch jobs. The static costs of such a rule would be enormous because it would force employees to stick with their initial employer, like the system in professional baseball before the adoption of free agency but on a global scale. On the other hand, if every bit of information transferred to the employee that had value to rival firms were considered part of that employee's general human capital (and, therefore, beyond the scope of what employers can limit), then there would be no effective protection of trade secrets. Dynamic costs would be high in this scenario, because it would drastically reduce incentives for firms to develop some special processes that might confer both benefits to consumers and competitive advantage in the market; without an ability to protect those innovations, the advantage could be quickly negated in most instances—at least so far as the advantage depends on knowledge that one employee could take away.

The courts, therefore, have had to draw a line around the definition of a trade secret. The line probably has failed to provide perfect protection of trade secrets, but the line is clearly necessary. For example, Ed Kitch discusses the case of *Wexler v. Greenberg*,[13] where the defendant, a chemist, developed several useful chemicals for his employer largely by reverse engineering (and then slightly modifying) the products developed by rival firms. When the defendant left his employer to work for a competitor, which then began to manufacture similar products, the former employer sued. The court refused to find that the products were protected by trade secret law. The products were not developed by the employer using information guarded as secret and then shared in confidence with the employee. The court regarded the information as more in the nature of general knowledge of the industry—something beyond the scope of an employer to control.

Although contracts protecting commercially valuable private information are common and the absence of a clear contract limiting disclosure or other use of the information at issue in *Wexler* weighed in the court's decision, a contract prohibiting disclosure or limiting work options is not necessary to protect trade secrets. The law defines a trade secret as information that provides a competitive advantage and that the possessor has made reasonable efforts to protect from disclosure. There is nothing in the law that says that the possessor has to have a contract limiting disclosure with his employees for trade secret law to provide some degree of protection.

The noncontract-based features of trade secret protection rely on principles of tort and property law. Even if you have not signed a contract with employees prohibiting disclosure, the law provides some protection, provided that the information falls within the legal definition of a trade secret: it has competitive value, and the possessor has made reasonable efforts to maintain secrecy. As put by one early U.S. trade secret decision:

> In the case at bar there is a contract about the employment in which Cornelison agrees not to disclose trade secrets, but the law about such secrets is too plain to require extended comment. If one person has a trade secret which is valuable to him, and another person enters into confidential employment with him in and about the business which demands the use of that secret, and by such employment learns the secret, he cannot utilize this secret knowledge to the disadvantage of his employer. If he does so, he robs his employer. That is the contract relationship between them, and it makes no difference whether it is expressed in writing or not. If not expressed, it will be implied.[14]

The tort and property law principles that protect trade secrets authorize the law's intervention when a secret is taken through force or fraud. However, the definitions of force and fraud are a bit more elastic than in the tort setting. Consider a taking by force. If the rival procures the secret by holding a gun to your employee or breaking into your plant in the middle of the night, he has violated trade secret law. Of course, he has also violated the criminal and tort laws of every state. No one should be surprised to find that the civil law will impose a penalty when a trade secret is procured by force, as in the examples just considered. The penalties consist of a claim for damages on the part of the possessor and an injunction against the use of the secret by the taker (the rival).

Under the Economic Espionage Act of 1996, trade secret theft is also a federal crime.[15] The statute was applied to an effort to sell Coca-Cola's secrets in U.S. v. Williams,[16] a rather typical if disheartening example of trade secret opportunism. Joya Williams, an executive assistant at Coca-Cola, told her co-defendant Ibrahim Dimson that she had confidential Coca-Cola marketing documents and a product sample, and that people sold this sort of information "all the time in corporate America".[17] Dimson wrote a letter to Pepsi offering to sell the information, which Pepsi promptly faxed to Coca-Cola. Coca-Cola called in the FBI, which began an investigation culminating in the conviction of Williams and Dimson under the Economic Espionage Act.[18] Perhaps the least expected part of the incident is that Pepsi alerted its rival—showing that the firms are both sensitive to protecting their secrets and not eager to encourage an "arms race" in subverting that pillar of each firm's business.

A more interesting case is *E. I. DuPont de Nemours & Co. v. Christopher*.[19] The defendant, a rival of DuPont, hired a pilot to fly over a new plant being constructed by DuPont in order to take pictures of the layout and better understand DuPont's manufacturing process. The court found that the defendant had violated DuPont's trade secrets. This is clearly not a case of force, in the popular sense of the term, or of fraud. However, it is arguably a case of constructive force as traditionally understood in the common law. The early common law on flyovers treated them as trespasses and, therefore, constructive force, based on the theory that a landowner possesses rights to the space congruent with the boundaries running both beneath and above his land.[20] That early law made sense back in the ancient period when a fly-over, if successful, involved a low-orbit brush with trees at best. The early prohibition has been weakened in the modern law by the necessity of allowing commercial aviation. Flyovers beyond five hundred feet by licensed aircraft have generally been exempted from trespass law prohibitions.[21] The decision in *Christopher* can be seen as a return to the earliest tort law rules governing flyovers, but limited to the particular instance of a flyover for the purpose of gathering trade secrets. Nothing in the changed law accommodating commercial and general aviation was at issue in the case, and the sense of the older rule applied.

Christopher is an illustration of how traditional tort rules operate to provide modern trade secret protections. The rules defining legal breaches are those of tort law, updated, or, in the case of *Christopher*, retrieved from the past in order to provide a more effective web of protection for trade secrets.

As we noted earlier, trade secret law also requires reasonable care on the part of the possessor to maintain secrecy. The definition of reasonable care is unclear a priori.[22] One could argue that DuPont had not taken reasonable care to maintain its secrecy because it had not constructed an opaque awning over its construction site. However, to make this argument is to answer it at the same time. It would have been quite costly for DuPont to hide its construction site from planes flying overhead. Moreover the likelihood of someone discovering the plant-layout secrets on a random passenger flight would have been close to nil. Given this, it would not have been reasonable for DuPont to construct an opaque awning over its construction site. Doing so would have required a great expenditure to avoid a cost that was negligible in expectation.

The reasonable care required by trade secret law is consistent with the reasonable care suggested by the principles underlying trespass law. The reasonable care required or suggested by trespass is simply a refusal to invite outsiders onto your property and, in order to avoid disclosure, the necessity of covering parts of the property that you do not want those outsiders to see from outside of the boundary. Trespass law does not require warnings to outsiders to stay off the property; the trespasser violates the law by an unauthorized entry onto the land. DuPont would have failed to exercise reasonable care if it permitted trespassers to walk onto its property on a regular basis to observe the layout of the new plant as it was being constructed. If DuPont's rival had been invited to go on a tour of the plant and during the tour discovered all of the secrets about the plant layout, DuPont would have lost its trade secret protection.

Moving away from the trespass context, reasonable care imposes a greater burden on the possessor of a trade secret. The possessor is required to take the care that would be reasonable provided that others with whom he interacts comply with the established tort and criminal laws.[23] Suppose officials from DuPont had gone to a trade conference with details of their plant in a file contained in a briefcase. If one of the officials showed those details to participants at the conference, then he would have breached his duty to take reasonable care to protect the secrecy of the information. If the official instead had left the plans sitting out in the open on a table as participants passed, that would also be a breach of the duty of self-protection. On the other hand, if the plans were locked up in the briefcase and a conference participant picked the briefcase lock to gain access to the plans, then the DuPont official would have complied with his duty of self-protection and the lock-picking conference participant would have violated the law.

Not only is trade secret law's duty of self-protection somewhat greater outside of the trespass setting, it is also greater than the corresponding duty imposed by the criminal law. If a conference participant read and copied DuPont's plans, that would be equivalent, in terms of the information transferred, to stealing the documents outright. If the participant had stolen the documents, he would be guilty of theft (and liable for trespass to chattels) and liable under trade secret law as well. However, if the participant merely reads and copies the information that is left open to public view, there is no violation at all. In other words, theft of the information, the matter that is the most valuable, is perfectly legal in this example. Because the possessor left the information open to public view, he has forfeited his right to bring an action under trade secret law after the information is stolen. But if he had left something valuable on his desk and walked away temporarily, he would by no means have forfeited his right to bring an action for conversion if a conference participant had taken the item.

The reasonable care requirement of trade secret law is a clear indication that the scope of protection that it provides to information is much narrower than that offered by patent law. Patent law does not impose a reasonable care requirement on the part of the patent holder to prevent infringement. Patent law does not require the patent holder to expend effort to inform potential infringers of the existence of the patent; on the contrary it is the duty of the infringer to find out about the existence of the patent.

Information versus Things, and the Duty of Reasonable Care

There is no requirement in the law of trespass governing real or personal property that the owner take reasonable and proper steps to protect the property against trespass. A landowner is not required to maintain a fence in order to have a valid trespass claim against someone who enters his land without an invitation.

Why is there a reasonable care requirement in the trade secrecy context, but not in the context of other types of property? This is a puzzle that has not been explained in the literature on trade secrets.[24]

We think the core reason is that the common law treats information differently from tangible objects. If you throw a rock at someone, you will be found guilty of battery even if you did not intend to hit him (say, only to scare him away). If you harm someone's reputation by making accusations against him in the newspaper, you may be found guilty of defamation, but there have always been privileges and defenses available.

Hurling rocks and hurling harmful accusations are two ways to hurt someone. The law is much more generous to you if you use accusations. The reason is that it involves information, the economics of which we examined in the Chapter 3. Because information has positive externalities, the law is reluctant to punish people for the simple act of conveying information.[25] In comparison to ordinary negligence or trespass law, the law provides a subsidy to conveyors of information.

This applies to the disclosure of trade secrets. The law imposes a requirement on the holder of a trade secret to take reasonable steps to guard it because it is reluctant to punish someone who happens upon the secret and discloses it without knowing that the holder intends to keep it secret. For the same reason the law requires the innovator to have evidence that the discloser knew or had reason to know of the wrongful character of his disclosure.[26]

Protection Strategies Given Incomplete Legal Protection

As we suggested at the start, the contract and tort law rules protecting trade secrecy have played a role in protecting some of the most valuable secrets in the market. But legal protection is far from complete. The courts have had to limit tort and contract-based protection to prevent the employer from gaining a monopoly in skills that are valuable industrywide, and to permit the free movement of employees. In light of this, trade secrecy is often one of many strategies a firm will adopt in order to protect commercially valuable information.

One obvious extra-legal strategy an innovator can adopt to protect secrets is to hire only family members. Family members may not make the most productive employees. The range of skills available in the rest of the world (and even in the immediate community) commonly exceeds by a fair margin the skill sets possessed by family members alone. And family members at times bring to work at a family business their peculiar needs to act out emotional issues connected with having more successful relatives. However, the cost to a family member from revealing a trade secret generally will be greater than the cost to a nonrelated employee. The family member's own wealth is often linked to that of the founding innovator and typically cannot be enhanced by selling confidential business information for less than its full value to a rival firm. Moreover, the informal sanction of ostracism is a substantial penalty to the family member. The prevalence and success of family-owned businesses may be due in part to this feature.[27]

Another extra-legal method is to divide the information up among employees so that no one has the complete secret.[28] For example,

> To protect the secrecy of the composition of KFC Seasoning, KFC has designed a blending system for making the seasoning. With permission from KFC, one part of KFC Seasoning recipe is blended by Sexton and another part is blended by Stange. Neither company has knowledge of the complete formulation of KFC Seasoning nor of the other's specific activities in the production of the other's part of the product. Both companies have entered into secrecy agreements with KFC, binding them to maintain the confidentiality of that portion of the KFC Seasoning formula to which each is privy. KFC's relationship with both Sexton and Stange has existed for more than 25 years. No other companies are licensed to blend KFC Seasoning . . . After KFC Seasoning is blended by Sexton and Stange, it is then mixed together and sold directly by Stange to all KFC retail operators and to distributors acting on behalf of KFC retail operators.[29]

Thus, in addition to the protection provided by trade secrecy law, KFC has adopted a policy of divulging only components of its secret recipe to the firms that supply its franchisees. This is an inefficient way to do business, but the alternative is to accept a greater risk of disclosure.

Patent or Secret?

Private Choice Issues When Secrecy and Patenting Are Viewed as Substitutes
Given the greater scope of patent protection—which is available against any imitator, even unknowing imitators, rather than being limited to those who wrongly disclose the secret information—one might ask why anyone would choose to rely on trade secrets. There are several reasons.

Filing for a patent is costly, while the costs of keeping something secret can be kept manageably low in some cases. On an economic basis, an innovator might decide that the private incremental value of patent protection relative to trade secrecy is not worth the additional cost.[30] For example, the innovator might think that it is unlikely anyone will ever figure out or reverse engineer his secret. In that case, he might gain just as much effective protection from trade secrecy as from patent law at a much lower cost. Further, if he believes that the innovation is durable—again, Coca-Cola is a prime example, as demand for the drink has not declined substantially over time due to changing tastes or the availability of other substitutes—trade secrecy may be preferable because it can last well beyond the patent term. Or the innovator may fear that the disclosure required by patent law will guarantee that someone will find a noninfringing method of producing a substitute innovation within a few years, and that he can at least get a longer lead time over rivals under trade secrecy.[31] We could go on with permutations of these examples.

It is often assumed that trade secret protection is a path that provides weaker protection, as a substitute to a patent, but for a lower expense. That is sometimes true, but both parts of this assumption depend on the particular conditions. As our examples above suggest, trade secrecy can give stronger protection in both forestalling creation of inexact substitutes using information disclosed in a patent filing (not all of which would necessarily be deemed infringements of a patent) and preventing the proliferation of exact substitutes for a longer period than patent protection affords.

Our examples also suggest that enhancing trade secret protection through contractual restrictions can be expensive. It involves writing and possibly enforcing contracts with a potentially large number of employees, or finding other ways to keep those employees from revealing the secrets to rivals, including tilting selection toward employees more likely to share the employer's values rather than employees with better skills. For a sufficiently large enterprise, trade secret protection may not be cheaper than seeking patent protection.

Another factor bearing on the choice is the fact that if you rely on secrecy to protect your innovation rather than filing for a patent, you run two risks with respect to the innovation property right. First, a rival may come along and patent the innovation, and then you may lose your right to use it.[32] The patent law will refuse the patent to the second innovator only if the innovation is revealed in a way that constitutes public information.[33] Second, you will lose the right to obtain a patent after you use the innovation for one year without filing.[34] Even if no one else can patent the innovation, you no longer can patent it—and if the secret information becomes known, you no longer have any protection.

Social Choice Issues

The fact that an innovator might prefer trade secrecy over patent raises a troubling issue. Perhaps the costs that we argued in the previous chapter that patent law doctrine appears to control—static (market shrinkage) and dynamic (innovation discouraging)—could grow to a much larger extent under trade secrecy.

Patent law limits the static cost of protection by favoring limited and specific claims and disfavoring general and abstract claims. The first question to consider is whether an innovator could avoid this constraint through trade secrecy. This is unlikely.

For abstract results, such as mathematical and scientific formulae, most innovators do not have a financial stake in secrecy. Their reputations as scientists are directly related to the widespread dissemination of their work. A patent system, if it awarded patents to abstract results, might encourage such innovators to patent in order to earn fees from follow-on researchers, but trade secrecy would offer them nothing.

There are some obvious exceptions to this argument. A scientific researcher within a corporation might develop a formula that permits the corporation to develop a superior production process and thereby enhance its profits. If the formula has a general application to a large set of production processes it might be used to monopolize several markets. Still, this exception is unlikely to result in great static costs, for several reasons.

First, if the innovation has many applications, its use will spur simultaneous efforts to discover it independently. Once discovered independently, its value *as a secret* disappears. This is distinguishable from the patent case, where a formula that could easily be discovered independently could serve as the basis for a stream of monopoly rents for the life of the patent (twenty years). Thus, independent efforts to discover the formula will increase directly with its value, and if the formula is one that could be discovered independently within the life of a patent, then trade secrecy will generally impose a lower static cost because the secret will be discovered before patent protection would have ended.

Second, if the formula is one that is unlikely to be discovered through independent research during a span as long as a patent term, its static cost is still likely to be less than that of a patent when viewed over the long run. The reason is as follows. Suppose the formula is one that is both highly valuable and highly unlikely to be discovered independently during the term of a patent. Then the trade secret has a monopolizing effect that is either the same as or greater than the patent. But there is still a crucial difference. The trade secret's invulnerability to independent discovery indicates that it is a truly unusual discovery. It has a monopolizing effect only because it enables its holder to satisfy the market at a lower cost (or higher quality) than rivals because of its superior production process—in other words, the secret provides a substantial efficiency advantage.

This is also true of a patent that generates a monopoly, but patents exclude rivals who could have just as easily duplicated the innovation independently, including rivals who might have been only a few hours behind the successful patent applicant in perfecting the innovation. Trade secrets exclude only those rivals who could not have just as easily duplicated the innovation independently.[35] The monopolies that result from trade secrets are more likely to be efficient, in the sense of reducing long-term supply costs,[36] from the innovation's development to the fruit that it bears, than the monopolies achieved through patent. This suggests, in turn, that the static costs of the most valuable trade secrets are offset to some extent by efficiency gains.

Third, if the formula has a general scope of application, then it will be valuable to many firms, in many different industries. The formula will have a market value that can be ascertained easily by looking at the additional profits generated by its use. Over time, the formula will be sold or licensed to other firms; even if licenses are accompanied by contract provisions binding licensees to maintain secrecy, as dissemination occurs in this fashion, there is a substantial likelihood that the formula will no longer remain a secret. In short, the ordinary pressures of the market are likely to ensure that a formula of general application that is potentially valuable in many production processes will not remain a secret for a long time.[37]

The result could be different where the formula poses a potential national security risk. The U.S. government monitors patent applications and stays on the lookout for innovations that could have important military uses. These innovations, when discovered by officials in the government's Disruptive Technology Office, are cloaked in even greater secrecy until a decision is made by the government to permit the information to be released. In other words, the federal government applies something akin to an eminent domain rule, without compensation, to innovations that have potentially important military applications. After pouring years of hard work into a new process or product, the innovator may find his work product in essence taken by the government. The innovation's details may remain secret, but that secrecy is of little value to the innovator.

The upshot is that trade secrecy is unlikely to serve as an alternative to patent as a method of monopolizing a large segment of the economy, and where it has substantial bite, the static costs of trade secrecy are likely to be offset by efficiency gains. An innovation that is denied a patent because of its abstraction, generality, or broad scope of application is unlikely to return as a trade secret capable of imposing the same static costs that would have been imposed under patent law.

Now consider the dynamic costs—the costs legal protection of information could have in the form of diminished follow-on innovation prospects. In the patent case, follow-on innovation is diminished because of the taxing effect of fees for licensing use of the information. In the trade secret case, follow-on innovation is diminished because the information is never disclosed.

Still in this analysis, as in the static analysis, the number of attempts to independently discover the innovation will be directly related to its value. If independent discovery efforts fail to reveal the secret, then the innovation is (probably) really valuable to society. If it cannot be independently discovered, it must be a very significant innovation. As such, it probably offers extraordinary gains in efficiency as well as the potential for monopolistic pricing.

In addition, this analysis overstates the reduction in follow-on innovation that results from the bottling up of information in the form of trade secrets. The fact that an innovative process is protected as a trade secret does not mean that no potential follow-on innovator ever gets hold of the secret. It only implies that the potential follow-on innovators who get hold of the secret do so through the consent of the holder. Trade secrets are revealed and information gets out.[38] The recipients generally will be prohibited by contract from using the secret in competition with the holder, but it would be impossible to stop them from using the information gleaned from the secret to engage in related follow-on innovation.

Overall, under trade secrecy, dynamic costs (in terms of the discouragement of follow-on innovation) are more likely to result than under patent law, though the difference is not as great as it appears superficially. Moreover, the efficiency gains resulting from the secret innovation are likely to be correlated with those costs. As Friedman, Landes, and Posner have noted, trade secrecy allows the innovator to prove the patent office wrong, to society's benefit.

As we noted earlier, trade secrets can be difficult and costly to protect. If it were simply a matter of preventing trespassing spies, the costs would be quite manageable, as *Christopher* suggests. But the costs of preventing employees, or former employees, from revealing trade secrets can be large. The employer could write a contract specifying the precise secrets that are not to be revealed, but by revealing the secrets in the contract the employer would have damaged his own effort. Alternatively the employer could write a contract barring the disclosure of secrets, but then when a disclosure occurs the employee might defend himself on the issue of whether he had really disclosed a secret. A more powerful tool for the employer would be a noncompetition clause that bars the employee from working for a rival within a certain period of time.

Each of the contract clauses just discussed can be viewed as an instrument designed to prevent the disclosure of secrets by employees. The narrowest clause, specifying the secrets that cannot be disclosed, is potentially self-defeating and difficult to enforce. The broadest clause, the noncompetition provision, is much easier to enforce. The cost of writing and enforcing a narrow clause, would be passed on, at least in part, to employees in the form of lower wages, and perhaps to customers in the form of higher prices. An optimal contract between employee and employer would choose the clause that minimizes the joint costs of specification, compliance, and enforcement.

The state law on noncompetition agreements has important implications for the private and social cost of enforcing employment agreements protecting trade secrets. If the state law prohibits noncompetition agreements, as in California, then it will force employers to find a more expensive alternative to protect secrets. Those employers could try to enforce narrower agreements, which would be considerably more expensive. The costs of enforcement would operate in effect as a tax on wages, reducing take-home compensation and employment levels. Alternatively, the employers could hire family and friends, expecting the sanction of ostracism to serve as an adequate deterrent to theft of secrets. Or, the employer could screen hires more carefully to find employees that are more trustworthy. It may seem to be an entirely positive feature among employees that trustworthiness and bonding are being stressed by the employer, but there is a hidden cost in the rejection of potentially productive employees who fail to pass the bonding tests.

Another approach that employers could take in response to a prohibition on noncompetition clauses is to enter into an agreement not to poach employees from each other. Interestingly, such an agreement appears to have been in operation among high-technology firms in California, where the state prohibits noncompetition clauses.[39] The agreement suggests that the difference between the mobility of high-technology workers in California and Massachusetts, a subject of study and discussion,[40] may not be as great as it appears superficially. Unlike California, noncompetition clauses in employment contracts are enforceable in Massachusetts.[41] It has been suggested that this difference could explain a more dynamic and fluid market for ideas in California. But the employers may have blunted, and would certainly have incentives to blunt, this dynamism through tacit agreements not to poach employees from each other. Such an agreement is a per se violation of Section 1 of the Sherman Act. But if the agreement is tacit, the law makes it difficult to prosecute under Section 1.[42]

Lastly, if each of the foregoing options for circumventing a state prohibition on noncompetition clauses seems unappealing to the contracting parties, the employer can opt for the patenting strategy. Indeed, this is consistent with the evidence that patenting rates appear to be higher in areas where noncompetition clauses are not enforced.[43]

The employer and employee have incentives to design an optimal regime for protecting trade secrets. Laws that obstruct those efforts increase the private and social costs of trade secret protection. In the high-tech sector, such laws—e.g., California's prohibition of noncompetition agreements—seem difficult to justify on the ground that employees are unsophisticated; the technology firms pride themselves on their ability to attract the country's best test takers. If prohibited by law from adopting the most efficient contracts for protecting trade secrets, firms will adopt alternative methods that result in lower wages and levels of employment, as well as weaker innovation incentives resulting from the dilution of protection.

In the end, the overall social desirability of trade secrecy, relative to patent, is an empirical question. Previous economic analyses of trade secrecy, by William Landes and Richard Posner and by Robert Bone, have offered cautious assessments of the social value of trade secrecy. These authors, especially Bone, have stressed dynamic costs of secrecy (i.e., reduced follow-on innovation) and have suggested that trade secrecy offers some benefits to society as an alternative to patents but largely as a necessary gap-filler given the incompleteness of patent protection. Our assessment is a bit more optimistic. The dynamic costs of secrecy probably have been overstated. More importantly, the most successfully protected secrets are likely to be process innovations that have the most value in the market; in addition, the secrets that are most commercially valuable are those that offer the greatest efficiency advantages to the holders. Those efficiency gains are likely to be transferred by the competitive process to consumers in the long run.

Patent and Secret?

We have so far followed the common approach by assuming that the innovator will choose between patent and trade secrecy. But it is not entirely correct to view the two choices as substitutes. In some instances, they can serve as complements.[44]

Consider the incentives of a patent applicant who knows that he also has the option of secrecy. In most cases, a patentable invention, like any idea put into application, can be broken down into several phases. The simplest division is between a core prototype idea, upon which a later version will build, and the revised model. To simplify, suppose the patent applicant has a choice whether to file for a patent once he has the prototype or to wait and apply once he has completed the plans for his revised model. Suppose in addition that the revised model is a substantial improvement on the prototype.

There are trade-offs to be weighed in the choice between filing at prototype or revision stage. If you file at the prototype stage, you minimize the risk, by filing early, that a rival innovator will beat you to the patent. On the other hand, there is a risk in patenting at the prototype stage. Once the patent has been granted, the information from the prototype becomes public. A rival may be able to invent around and produce a version that is equivalent to your revised model. Alternatively, a rival may simply build on your prototype and make such a big improvement that he is able to produce a version equivalent or better than your revised version that is either patentable or is likely to be found noninfringing with respect to your patent. Given this risk, it may be preferable to wait and file at the revised version stage.

In this scenario, trade secrecy offers a complementary strategy rather than a substitute.[45] Suppose it is possible to get a patent for the basic, stripped-down version of the prototype, one that reveals as little information as possible about the revision while still maintaining patentability. One strategy would entail filing early on the prototype and relying on trade secrecy to protect the elements of the revised version. This strategy requires deliberately leaving out information that would signal the revised version to a rival but including enough information to patent the prototype version. To some extent, this is a strategy that is common. Filing for a patent takes time, and innovators often continue to improve the product or process after filing for the patent. But the strategy can be pushed a bit further by stripping the prototype to a workmanlike core and keeping the most significant innovations under the cloak of trade secrecy.

Another way of thinking about this strategy is that it relies on trade secrecy for those elements of the innovation that can be efficiently protected through secrecy. Thus, if there are some elements of the invention (in revised form) that are unlikely to be found through reverse engineering or through independent invention, those elements might be more effectively protected through trade secrecy. Through a combination of patent and trade secrecy, the inventor obtains a greater level of protection than provided by either system alone.

The upshot of this approach is that innovators are likely to file earlier for patents, but with applications that reveal less information. The social welfare implications of these changes are unclear. With earlier filings, information on innovation reaches rivals sooner and starts the process of inventing around and revising sooner. On the other hand, with less informative filings, the effort to invent around will begin from a lower base level of information.

In our chapter on patent law, we discussed the Kitch thesis that broad patents facilitate the continuing development of an invention.[46] If the patentee is awarded a narrow patent, according to Kitch, he will be reluctant to develop the innovation further, because the information revealed could help competitors. For this reason the law favors broad patents for processes, for example. However, if secrecy is viewed as a complement to patent, then the negative incentive effects of narrow patents are not necessarily going to arise. If the patentee is awarded a narrow patent, he can continue to develop the innovation further under the cloak of secrecy. Secrets are more costly to society than patents, at least in one dimension, because of the loss of information to the public, but they may also provide a stronger spur to innovation. The incentive-dilution problem identified by Kitch appears to be limited to the instances in which the firm cannot protect its information through secrecy.

Moreover, to the extent that firms use secrecy as a complement to patenting, there is a stronger case for recognizing narrow patents, contrary to Kitch. If firms rely on secrecy for the best post-patent innovations, broad patents would not lead to more information being revealed; they would only be used to block potential competitors. Hence, where secrecy is likely to be used as complementary protection, courts should favor narrow protection.

Of course, this last observation ignores the costs of varying rules with circumstances. Certainty respecting legal rules has real value, not least where property rights and financial investments are in play.

Conclusion

Trade secret law presents very few puzzles since it is really just a collection of offshoots from contract and tort law. The puzzles, to the extent there are any, involve the practice of using trade secrecy as a substitute for or complement to patent. When viewed as substitutes, there are many reasons someone might choose trade secrecy over patent, even though patent protection is broader in significant ways. When viewed as complements, trade secrecy may permit the innovator to obtain a stronger level of protection than that provided by patent law alone.

As we have stressed throughout, the desirability of trade secrecy protection relative to patent is an empirical question. On a priori grounds, we see little reason to believe that trade secrecy leads to greater social costs than does the patent system. True, trade secrecy denies society the information made public through the patent system, but that information may still be transferred by consent of the possessors. In addition, secrecy may also offer greater rewards to inventors, thus serving as a stronger spur to invention. Given that the resources devoted to independently discovering trade secrets will be directly proportional to the market value of the secret, we expect that the secrets that are best protected will also be the ones that provide the greatest benefits to consumers in the long run.

6

Copyright Law

Property in Expression

While patents and trade secrets focus on promoting the development of new ideas by creating rights to their use, copyright law focuses on a different aspect of the world of ideas and information: the particular qualities associated with the expression of ideas. Copyright protects expression by prohibiting the reproduction and distribution of a copyrighted work as well as the creation of derivative works based on a copyrighted work.

Even more than patent law, copyright law has come under fire as an interference with the creation and dissemination of new ideas. Professor Larry Lessig captures the spirit of the anticopyright arguments:

> In the name of protecting original copyright holders against the loss of income they never expected, we have established a regime where the future will be as the copyright industry permits. This puny part of the American economy has grabbed a veto on how creative distribution will occur.[1]

In Lessig's opinion, shared by others who take a pessimistic view of this body of law, copyright has become a looming impediment to creative work (as well as to important facets of our freedom), and the obstacle it presents to the creation and dissemination of new ideas is growing rapidly. That argument has been advanced in various forms, and with varying degrees of certitude, by respected scholars as well as by others who are invested in particular projects that serious attention to copyright inhibits.[2]

Yet most of the assault on copyright—carried primarily in works that are themselves copyrighted—overstates the law's flaws and undervalues its benefits.[3] Like patent law, copyright law is structured to avoid unnecessary or undesirable static costs, while remaining consistent with its goal of supporting incentives to create (reducing dynamic costs). To be clear, there is ample evidence that the actual intention of those who created the legal framework for copyright was not necessarily congruent with our conception of social good. While copyright law includes strands taken from the authors' rights approach of Continental European systems, the Anglo-American versions also have roots in efforts of publishers to establish monopoly rights over printing—rights that, in their initial form, were a debatable fit with broader social interests.[4] Our contention, however, is not that the actual intention of those who frame the law comports with social good—rather, it is that, because of the way competing interests have interacted over time with the institutions that produce our laws, the structure of the law is broadly consistent with social good.

In large measure it is because these two major intellectual property regimes share the goals of promoting the expansion of innovative work and minimizing the costs associated with it that the basic scheme for copyright differs substantially from that of patent law. In particular, four major differences should be noted.

The first important difference is that copyright is available only for non-utilitarian forms of expression, while patent is limited to ideas that are embedded in "useful" form. While there is some blurring at the boundaries between the two legal regimes, this distinction has implications for the way the protections of patent and copyright law function.

Second, there is no real bar to the grant of a copyright. Unlike patents, a copyright can be secured for any original, expressive work of art, literature, or music (along with a few additional categories, such as mask works, that are treated as analogs of the primary classes of expressive creation).

Third, the scope of protection under copyright is far narrower than under patent law. Patent law provides broad rights of exclusivity, including rights against conduct that works a modest and inadvertent infringement—even reaching products and processes arrived at entirely independent of any knowledge of the patent. For legal restrictions to apply, it is enough that the infringing activities or products duplicate what is covered by valid patent claims. Copyright's protection is merely against copying; although this slightly oversimplifies copyright's purpose, it nevertheless captures the claims at the heart of copyright's domain. In copyright law, even an identical product, independently arrived at, will not transgress.

Finally, copyright protection lasts far longer than patent protection. In the United States (and most other nations) a patent lasts for twenty years from the date on which a patent application is filed (formerly seventeen years from the date on which a patent was issued), but U.S. copyright lasts for the author's life plus an additional seventy years (a term that has been extended several times and, as a result of rule changes over the years, has produced a few fillips in computing the exact timing of copyright expiration).

These attributes of copyright can be, and are, discussed and debated as freestanding matters, but in truth all of these attributes are parts of the same effort to construct a property right that suits the category of activity protected. And while each aspect of copyright reasonably can be argued to be either too protective of the underlying activity or not protective enough, for most categories of expressive activity, copyright law seems to provide a reasonable set of rules.

Getting to Copyright

Copyright's Domain: Nonutilitarian Expression
The first difference between patent and copyright is the defining character of the two domains. Patent law promotes the discovery and public introduction of useful inventions by protecting the ideas at their core, subject to the requirement that the ideas be reduced to a practical form and actually introduced into the practical world. Copyright law, in contrast, promotes the contributions of literary, artistic, and musical creativity by protecting specific expressions of ideas in those arenas from direct copying or imitations so close as to be essentially the same as copies. (We come back later in this chapter to the questions of what the "essentially the same" category of copying covers now and what it should cover.)

The limitation on copyright's domain has two main elements: it comprehends only the aspect of creative work that is expressive, not its utilitarian applications; and it reaches only the qualities associated with expression, not the underlying ideas that are being expressed. These elements both define a category of innovation that is separate from the subject of patent law and restrict the ambit of what is protected within that category. Both elements are essential to the balance of social costs and benefits in copyright law.

Nonutilitarian Works

The first part of the restriction around copyright—its limitation to nonutilitarian aspects of creative work—essentially serves to channel legal protection to the right framework. Useful ideas that can be embodied in practical inventions get one type of protection that is deeper but of shorter duration, while creative expressions get protection that is longer but shallower.

If the social calculus of costs and benefits for protection of these classes of activity were the same, no such separation would be needed. But the different subject matters do have different costs and benefits associated with their creation and protection, and the different legal regimes generally provide a better fit for their distinct subject matters than either would if applied across the board.

On Protecting Literary and Artistic Expression—Not Ideas

The second part of the restriction of copyright's domain—its limitation to protection of specific features of expression, not of the ideas expressed—also makes sense from a broader societal standpoint. For things in patent law's domain, the difficult activity—what really calls for enormous investment of time, energy, creativity, and money in the typical case—is not coming up with a general idea, but coming up with a way to make it happen.

Take, for instance, the idea of manned flight. For thousands of years, humans imagined what it might be like to fly, even if, as with Icarus, that didn't always have a happy ending. But the idea of human flight foundered on the practical problem of designing a mechanism that would actually take people into the air, keep them up, move them forward, and let them land safely.

The special insight of Wilbur and Orville Wright was the *idea* of how to solve the problem: what combination of materials and design would support flight. It was a *practical* idea—not an abstraction, but still an idea—that was their special contribution. Put differently, the mechanical part of actually making a plane, the artisanship of construction, was not the aspect of invention that separated the Wright brothers from other aspirants trying to solve the problem of manned flight. The concept that would make the plane fly was the key. Patent law is intended to induce and reward just that sort of inventive idea. Practical conception, not production, is the object of patent law's affection.

In copyright's domain, a different object is rewarded: here, creative *expression* is what separates the gifted from the pedestrian far more than the ideas expressed.[5] The idea of reproducing human likenesses has been with mankind for millennia, but that doesn't solve the problem of actually making a painting that looks real—a two-dimensional image that seems three-dimensional, that looks back at the viewer, that creates a sense of intimacy or serenity or passion. The initial production of works of art requires the genius that is special; and bringing the fruits of that genius into being requires investment in working out the details of a piece, of mixing the right colors, making the right brush strokes, drawing the right lines. What distinguishes a Rembrandt or Vermeer, a Sargent or Manet, from the run-of-the-mill artist isn't the idea behind their paintings but the expression of it. Specific compositions may be especially creative, but the basic ideas for most great art works, even down to a fairly deep level of detail, can be found in numerous other efforts.

So, too, most acclaimed literary works are famed for the special turn of phrase and twist of plot, not for the idea that provides the framework for the book or play. Boy meets girl and falls in love; hero saves the day; successful and acclaimed man or woman falls from grace. Basic story ideas are almost all well-known and endlessly retold. The same is true of this plot: boy and girl from the wrong families or wrong sides of some other social divide fall in love, tragically as it turns out (though some modern versions stress the comic aspects of an unlikely love match). Even when we know where the plot lines lead, Shakespeare's *Romeo and Juliet* still can impress with its wondrously crafted phrases.

Society benefits by keeping its Shakespeares engaged in working out exactly the right way to express the thoughts and feelings that are already so often expressed by others in ways less enduring than "a rose by any other name would smell as sweet." It is the elegance and poignancy of expression that speaks to us across generations. Society is better off giving incentives to authors to get that right—not by encouraging a rush to be first to claim protection for a story of frustrated love between souls whose ardor leaps over familial enmity. It is better off having its da Vincis and Michelangelos and Rodins—and its Picassos and Modiglianis—do the work needed to find the right modes for presenting images that will inspire and delight instead of rewarding the first to convey the idea of a smiling woman, a handsome young warrior, a man deep in thought.

Copyright Law's Take on Expression-versus-Idea

Of course, as in the case of patents, rights seekers have incentives to obtain the broadest rights possible. Who wouldn't want protection for a general idea of the kind found in the Montagues versus Capulets (and Hatfields versus McCoys, Jets versus Sharks, Abie's Irish Rose, Bridget Loves Bernie, and endless other variations)? But granting property rights in ideas of that sort carries all of the potential costs we identified earlier in the context of mathematical algorithms and physical results.

The law recognizes this problem and denies copyright protection to information and ideas of a general nature, such as how to do something. In *Baker v. Selden,*[6] the Court denied protection to a general system of accounting described in Charles Selden's copyrighted book. Selden had developed a method of laying out bookkeeping forms to improve accounting. The defendant adopted a similar method, though with a change in the order of some entries. The Court denied the attempt (by Selden's widow) to enforce a copyright on the ground that this was really an attempt to gain protection over the basic plan or algorithm rather than its particular expression. In Justice Joseph Bradley's words, "no one has a right to print or publish [Selden's] book, or any material part thereof, as a book intended to convey instruction in the art, [but] any person may practice and use the art itself which he has described and illustrated therein."[7]

The instinct at work here can be analogized to the abstraction principle discussed in Chapter 4. We saw in Chapter 4 that patent law would deny protection where the right sought would protect an abstract idea or plan. Because the abstraction principle is a harsh rule in operation, it can be defended only as a rule of thumb that gives the right answer on average. There are many abstract ideas that take quite a bit of ingenuity to discover. In a perfect world, their discoverers would be given some protection for their ideas. But in an imperfect setting, general rules have to be applied that deny protection in cases where it would be socially desirable in order to avoid granting protection to a much larger number of cases in which it would not be socially desirable. Given the large static costs of protecting abstract ideas, patent law declines to award rights in them except so far as the ideas are embedded in a particular, useful application.

Copyright law provides the same answer, rejecting efforts to stretch the law's protection to cover general or abstract ideas. In fact, copyright arrives at that point more readily and emphatically, for good reason. The cost of protecting an abstract idea would be greater in copyright's domain than patent's because the term of protection is much longer for copyright. And because the special benefits of art and literature tend to come more from the manner of expression rather than the idea itself, because the ideas embodied in art and literature so often already are well-known, the costs of expanded protection for ideas are not offset by any increase in the pace at which new ideas are developed and introduced to the public.

The Case of Inseparable Idea and Expression?

Suppose the idea and the expression are merged, in the sense that there is only one way to do something and to express it? Consider, for example, an insurance form that pretty much has to proceed in a certain order for it to make sense. Protecting expression in such cases effectively protects the underlying idea. When that occurs, courts generally deny (or sharply limit) copyright protection.[8] That is one reading given to *Baker v. Selden,* although the more general distinction between idea and expression seems to us a better fit.

The merger of idea and expression might not be a problem for copyright if the idea is itself essentially artistic, such as the vast, elaborate imaginary playground that J. K. Rowling builds into her Harry Potter novels. Even if some of the ideas behind the settings, creatures, and games envisioned by Ms. Rowling are not susceptible of expression in many different ways, the notion of a merger of expression and idea doesn't occur for such cases. The ideas themselves are sufficiently distinctive and creative—so infused with the sort of originality that copyright is intended to protect—that it would seem odd to deny protection against infringement on that ground. But giving protection to a particular expression when it is so closely connected to an idea as to be virtually the only way to implement it is problematic where the idea is primarily one for doing things in the workaday world, as with Selden's accounting system.[9]

Notwithstanding the penchant of commentators for broadly invoking concepts such as the merger of idea and expression to explain judicial decisions, implementation of the law has been more sensitive to other distinctions, such as the type of idea expressed.[10] The static cost problem—the costs associated with protecting ideas that have traction in the ordinary world but are not reduced to practice or vetted in the same way as those behind patents—explains why protection should be denied in cases such as *Baker v. Selden*. While those costs are a legitimate concern in patent, they loom even larger if the idea is a similar practical one whose creator seeks a right to exclude others from using it for a longer term than patent provides and with less scrutiny.[11] The concern here, however, must be balanced against a contrary concern that courts implementing the copyright law not be so quick to see ideas merged with expression as to undercut the valid protection of literary and artistic expression under copyright.

Copyright's Domain: Originality's Open Door

The second distinctive feature of copyright law, which like the limitation to nonutilitarian expression helps define copyright's domain, concerns the prerequisites for obtaining copyright. It addresses the essentially empty set of requirements for obtaining copyright, a description that overstates the point, but not very much.

Under patent law, there is a process for examining the novelty of the idea embodied in patent claims, inquiring how easy it would have been for someone versed in the prior art to foresee this next step in the development of the technology at issue ("nonobviousness"), and assessing whether the distinctive contributions described by the patent's claims merit protection. To be sure, patent offices are notoriously overburdened and understaffed; this coupled with the problem of limited knowledge for the centralized decision-making that supports utilitarian claims for property rights in the first place plainly affects government officials' decisions on patent novelty. More than a few patents have been awarded for inventions that sound obvious or trivial, such as Amazon.com's infamous one-click buying patent.[12] However, despite the flaws, patent examination is a serious process, and contests over the novelty and nonobviousness of patents frequently lead to patent invalidation.[13]

Our point here is not to defend or condemn the present shape of patent awards. When dealing with a large potential universe of cases in which the initial judgment may be right or wrong, it often is more cost-effective to wait for someone to flag problematic cases than to invest more up front in better initial decision-making. That is why sometimes it is better to rely on "fire alarms" rather than invest in "police patrols" (to borrow terms from Mathew McCubbins and Thomas Schwartz).[14] It is at least plausible that the same analysis would support the decision not to invest greater resources in getting the first-level decision on patent novelty right.

The critical point for copyright, however, is that the contrasting levels at which patent and copyright law set the bar for an initial award of property rights is striking. If the bar in patent is perhaps too low, in copyright it is nearly resting on the floor. For some specific purposes, compliance with formalities of copyright registration with a central authority has been needed to gain (or continue) legal protection.[15] But for most purposes, copyright has only two conceptual requirements in U.S. law: "fixation" and "originality."[16] Fixation requires that the expression be set in some tangible medium—it excludes simple, unrecorded oral presentations of an idea, for example. Outside a few unusual cases, fixation has not been a significant issue in copyright law.[17]

Originality has been only slightly more of a speed bump for copyright. In the main, the requirement is not that a writing or picture be truly original in the sense of being significantly different from what came before. Rather, the constraint is primarily that the work is produced by someone as his or her own creation, as opposed to being a direct copy of someone else's work.[18] The prerequisite of creativity or originality is routinely distinguished from novelty. Judge Learned Hand famously explained that a second author who re-created independently an exact duplicate of a prior work would satisfy the requisites of copyright, despite the fact that his or her effort created nothing new or unknown.[19] In this sense, the originality requirement does little more than exclude from copyright eligibility works that would violate an existing copyright.[20]

Courts at times have invoked another aspect of originality, described usually as the requirement of "creativity," to set out a minimal quantum of intellectual effort as a prerequisite to copyrightability.[21] Although there is some variation across decisions, generally the level of creativity demanded is vanishingly small.[22] Almost any level of creative effort that produces an independent work of art or literature or music suffices for copyright. Simple geometric designs, for instance, have been held to satisfy the originality-creativity requirement.[23]

Why set the bar so low for originality? For those who take a moral rights view of copyright or who ground protection in the connection of the expression to the personality and autonomy of the author, there is no reason for limiting protection to works of significant creativity. So long as the work is not infringing on what is due other authors, the effort that went into the work's creation and its connection to the persona of the author is sufficient.[24] What explains the low bar, however, if the point of copyright is, as pragmatic and utilitarian supporters would have it, to encourage creating new works of art, literature, and music and making them available to the public?

One justification for this choice is that the alternative would require government officials—whether in the office of the Register of Copyrights, the courts, or elsewhere—to parse the degree of originality and creativity in different works. Unlike in patent law's domain, in fields like art and literature such judgments inevitably will overlap with matters of opinion that form the basis for political contests. Is *Apocalypse Now* original and creative, or does it lack originality, doing little more than placing Joseph Conrad's *Heart of Darkness* in the jungles of Vietnam? That question can be answered by reference to politically neutral criteria, but how confident will creators be in the neutrality with which the criteria are applied by officials whose prospects for advancement come from the government that is shaping policy for the war in Vietnam?

Officials need not consciously seek to suppress dissent or punish criticism of an incumbent administration's policies for biases on such questions to exert subtle influence on determinations of this sort—a recognition that underlies other limitations on the scope of government power.[25] Many decisions on originality won't implicate political judgments, of course.

Yet there are obvious risks of tilting public discourse on issues of political salience when assessing subjective qualities of literary, artistic, and even musical works.[26] These risks would magnify the costs of having government officials assess the originality of an applicant's work before granting copyright protection. The administrative costs of a system of prior approval based on assessment of originality suggest a sufficient reason to reject it.

Probably the key reason, however, for such a low barrier to the award of copyright protection can be found in an assessment of dynamic (innovation-related) and static (monopolization) costs. In the patent system, it would be inefficient to have a low bar for awarding a property right. It would encourage inventiveness, to be sure, but it would also encourage numerous efforts to gain monopoly control over markets. As we argued in Chapter 4, the static monopolization costs of indiscriminate patent awards would easily overwhelm the dynamic innovation benefits.

In contrast, the balance of static and dynamic costs is different in a system of indiscriminate copyright. While it is true that everyone gets a property right to their expression, that property right does little, in most cases, to exclude others from exploiting rights in their own independent expressions. Unlike the case of patent, which protects ideas, the static costs from protecting expression are relatively small.[27]

Because the static cost of granting indiscriminate rights is relatively low, copyright protection provides the most encouragement to whatever happens to sell in the market for expression. This inevitably leads to protection for expressions that are so trivial that it would seem unnecessary to protect them at all. Interestingly, the general inability of objective observers to determine the degree of originality in someone's expression provides a reason why the dynamic benefits of copyright protection are likely to be substantial. There are no well-identified standards that would allow an objective observer to determine originality and greatness in art; a Warhol can command much the same appeal in the art market as a Rembrandt. While originality and superiority in art are subjects that experts will assert they can judge by "objective" criteria, they are almost always determined more by the recognition and acceptance that the work receives in the market than any criteria an expert claims should govern. By granting an indiscriminate property right that generates a reward only when the work is successful in the market, copyright effectively targets its inducements to the precise qualities that make some works of expression stand out among others.[28]

Admittedly, the modern world of art and expression is so closely intertwined with promotion and preference-shaping that it would be ridiculous to assert that the line between high-quality and low-quality art is determined entirely by commercial success. However, there is a vast population of independent critics who are wise to the promotional efforts, and there has always been a healthy degree of skepticism applied to questionable claims of greatness in the world of modern art. The works of art and literature that stand the test of time usually do so because they have features, sometimes hard to pinpoint in the art world, that make them superior to the vast majority of similar works in their ability to convey an image or to evoke an emotion. These features are probably better rewarded by unfettered access to copyright than by a system that attempts to identify them as a precondition to gaining protection.

Copyright Scope

The length of copyright differs markedly from patent, as does the scope of rights conferred by copyright. These two distinctions between copyright and patent are closely related. On the one hand, the longer the term of protection, the higher some costs associated with grant of monopoly rights; on the other hand, the more narrowly those rights are defined, the smaller those costs. The costs of granting a property right, of course, are only one side of the coin; the other side is made up of the benefits of granting the right (or the costs of not granting it). As we explained in Chapter 2, societies recognize property rights precisely because the rights serve important interests. In all events, the trade-offs made in constructing the current system of copyright law involves relatively narrow and long protections. We begin with the scope of copyright.

Rights to Copy—More or Less

The limited protection given by copyright is, primarily, a right to control actual copying. Given the division between expression and idea, the essential goal of copyright has to be protection of the expression against unauthorized taking. A broader right than that would inevitably morph into a right to control the ideas embedded in the expression.

In practice, the scope of the right conferred expands or contracts along three pivot points: derivative works, fair use, and third-party liability. These are the headings under which the law asks what works are so similar to actual copies that they should come within the property right, what actual copying should be permitted even though it violates the prohibition against unauthorized reproduction, and who besides the person actually making a copy should be subject to the law's enforcement.

In all of these determinations, the law has been sensitive to two, some-times competing, considerations. One, which focuses on the relationship between creator and work, combines the effect on incentives to invest in creativity and attention to implications of a sense that creative work incor-porates aspects of social or personal identity other types of work may not. The other focuses on broader cultural implications of protection.

The incentive-effects piece of this is easiest to grasp. The investment required is less obvious in many types of creative work, but it is substantial nonetheless. Anyone who has painted a portrait or written a book or com-posed music can attest to that. While the flash of genius—the song that emerges whole from a sudden insight or the literary composition that virtu-ally writes itself—occurs, it looms larger in myth than in reality. Real expres-sive work entails hours of painstaking rewriting, of laborious attention to the details of a painting, of careful chiseling of stone.

Think, for instance, of moviemaking. No one doubts the investment that is poured into the cinematic magic, into finding just the right shot in just the right locale, or any of the myriad other details that create the motion pic-tures that entertain and inspire. People working in other fields may scoff at the notion that this is real work, but like anything else that takes a special eye, these crafts at their best take not merely genius but effort and persis-tence as well.[29]

It is harder for people raised in the Anglo-American legal tradition to appreciate the argument that expressive work merits special protection because it captures aspects of social or personal identity that other work might not. This is the avowed predicate for most of the world's authors' rights regimes. Many European copyright systems rest on that understanding of the reason for protecting expressive work.[30]

We don't deny that this connection might be important to shaping the law,[31] but it is less obvious that it has a useful life separate from the incentive-effects argument. With a few notable exceptions,[32] the shape of copyright laws designed to protect moral claims of authors and those tied to utilitarian social goals do not differ markedly.

The other consideration juxtaposed to the incentive effects on creation of

expressive works focuses on the effects they have on our collective experience, our culture. Works of expression that gain a large audience—not necessarily something that occurs within a few years or even decades following
their creation—can become engrained in popular culture, sometimes sur-
viving several generations or more.[33]

The connection of literature and the arts to culture is both amorphous
and profound. Works of art and literature can become important sources of
information on social conditions at the time the works were written or contain insightful descriptions of seemingly permanent features of our lives.
They also provide a shared vocabulary of terms and expressions and reference points that help frame thinking about enduring themes in the human
condition. In other words, they can provide a window to our past, a capsule
of our present, or a mirror to our own souls. The special nature of the works
can be framed in economic terms as cultural externalities or spillover effects,
as they provide benefits to society not captured entirely by those who possess them.[34] Whatever terms one uses to describe this phenomenon, analyzing the costs and benefits of copyright protection for these works involves
more than just a comparison of dynamic and static costs as ordinarily conceived. Some effort should be made to take cultural effects into account as
well. As we explain below, the law seems to be doing this.

Derivative Works—The Outer Edge of Copyright
Although copyright doctrine has numerous twists and folds, two particular
elements mark the law's efforts to allow expansion of protections and to create
exceptions to copyright's reach: protection against unauthorized creation of
derivative works and exception for infringements that fall within the category
described as "fair use." We briefly describe both elements of the law.

In addition to the right to prevent unauthorized copying or performance
of protected works, copyright carries with it the right to control the production of "derivative works" based on the original. So, for instance, someone
who holds the copyright to a novel has the exclusive right to make a movie
based on the novel or to approve a translation of the novel. This protection
lasts as long as the copyright term. Courts originally approached this exclusive right on a case-by-case basis, denying the right to exclude in some cases,
granting it in others.[35] Later, the copyright statute was amended to grant
stronger protection to rights-holders.[36]

The change in the law could be defended as an efficient response to changes in the technology and economics of core copyright businesses, those that rely principally on the production of copyrighted work. Over time, the returns to original works from initial sales of the work declined relative to the returns from other sales. Take the case of motion pictures, where revenues from initial domestic releases now make up less than 25 percent of total revenues for most major films, while foreign releases (often adapted for particular audiences through subtitling or dubbing) account for between 10 and 25 percent and returns from releases in other forms (such as DVD—sometimes in altered or expanded versions—and interactive games based on the film) comprise anywhere between 50 and 75 percent.[37] As the value of the other releases and related works built on the original film have risen, so have the consequences of ceding control over the spin-offs from the initial investment in production. Attention to the incentive effects for creating the initial expressive work counsels expansion of the rights associated with it. One can view this as another example of property rights expanding in response to technological change, as we discussed in Chapter 2. However, there is a risk that statutory enhancements of copyright security, in contrast to those that result from the common law process, will overshoot because of the one-sided pressure of lobby groups.

Implementation of the law on derivative works generally has been sensitive to the considerations identified here. The rule embodied in the cases is that works that do not "transform" a copyrighted work sufficiently to support a new copyright generally are viewed through the same lens as direct copying. The question of what to do with such works generally doesn't hold courts up for long.[38] The more serious question is whether a particular work that is built on an earlier copyrighted work draws so heavily on the earlier work's particular expression that it constitutes a derivative work, within the province of the right holder to control, rather than a new, independent work. Not surprisingly, that question has come up in relation to some of the best known and most popular literary and entertainment creations.

The television series *Seinfeld,* for example, gave rise to *The Seinfeld Aptitude Test,* a book of questions and answers about scenes, characters, and events from the series. The producer of the series sued the author and publisher of the book for copyright infringement. The defendants claimed that the book had taken factual material, rather than protected expression, from the series and that the book had transformed any protected expression by creating a question and answer format for assessing readers' knowledge of the series. Judge John Walker, writing for the U.S. Court of Appeals for the Second Circuit, rejected those arguments.[39] The "facts" taken from the series were all fiction, part and parcel of the expression that is protected by copyright, and the transformation was "slight to non-existent."[40] The court also rejected the argument that any infringement should be excused because Castle Rock, the copyright holder, had chosen not to produce derivative works based on the series, essentially ceding the field to others willing to create such works. The court rebuffed this, too, quoting the district court judge:

> It would . . . not serve the ends of the Copyright Act—i.e., to advance the arts—if artists were denied their monopoly over derivative versions of their creative works merely because they made the artistic decision not to saturate those markets with variations of their original.[41]

A similar result was reached in litigation over a work based on the Harry Potter books of author J. K. Rowling. Rowling, along with Warner Brothers Entertainment, which produces films based on the Harry Potter books, brought a copyright infringement action against RDR Publishers claiming that its planned publication of *The Harry Potter Lexicon* violated existing copyrights.[42] The *Lexicon* contained snippets of information about an extraordinary range of characters, creatures, objects, events, and places, arranged alphabetically. The information was almost entirely taken directly from Rowling's work but arranged to facilitate checking on things from the intricate, imaginary world of Potter without having to find where in the seven books or movies they appear. The trial judge had no trouble finding that the *Lexicon* was a derivative work that appropriated copyrighted expression without authorization. The book did not so much copy the Harry Potter novels as capitalize on their popularity by providing a guide to the perplexed—not in the sense of a critical commentary but in the sense of a selection and reordering of descriptions already contained in Ms. Rowling's novels.[43] In the court's view, this was something the copyright holders had the right to produce, not to produce, or authorize others to produce—a right that was theirs alone.

Notably, the *Lexicon*'s author, Stephen Vander Ark, for many years prior to his decision to publish it, maintained (as he still does) a heavily trafficked Web site devoted to Harry Potter trivia. Ms. Rowling had not objected to the electronic version, but took exception to the book form. While it is not clear whether the book would have been less complementary to the novels than the Web site or whether Ms. Rowling would have authorized someone else to produce such a work, the essence of the property right—of the right to control the use and reproduction of a copyrighted work and the creation of works based directly on it—is to place that decision in the right-holder's hands.

Following the district court decision, the defendants filed and then withdrew an appeal, and then announced a new, expanded, revised and re-titled version with considerable original commentary from Mr. Vander Ark explaining matters in his own words, as well as quoting from Ms. Rowling's work. In the end, the particular expression of Ms. Rowling was left within her control, while information that went beyond mere repackaging of her words was put into public hands—which would seem just the balance the law should strike.

Fair Use—Copyright's Safety Valve

Where derivative works doctrine reflects the effort to decide how broad a scope copyright will enjoy—how far rights will be recognized to control more than simple, direct reproduction of a copyrighted work—fair use doctrine asks when direct uses of copyrighted expression should be permitted, when what would otherwise be an actionable infringement of legal rights should be excused. The law on fair use, though now codified,[44] is traced back to Justice Story's searching analysis of the problem in *Folsom v. Marsh*.[45] Fair use doctrine is a safety valve against putting too much power in the right-holder's hands.

At the outset, the doctrine seems a bit out of place. The definition of property right generally implies the power to control use and to exclude unauthorized users. That is the essence of intellectual property rights as well as other property rights. The decision to place temporal limits on intellectual property rights marks them as different from some—though by no means all—other property rights. So does the decision to restrict the ambit of what can be controlled by the intellectual property right-holder—such as copyright's limitation to control over copying either directly or effectively in creating derivative works that closely track the expressive elements in the underlying copyrighted work. It is reasonable to question what role the doctrine of fair use then plays. If reasonable choices have been made in setting the time and scope of copyright, why provide within the law another mechanism for compromising the rights?

The accepted economic explanation, originally offered by Wendy Gordon, is that the fair use doctrine provides a way of reaching socially desirable outcomes when negotiation costs are too high—when those who benefit from a particular use of copyrighted work are too numerous, scattered, and marginally affected to negotiate a price for using the work.[46] This certainly is a plausible explanation for the doctrine, which emphasizes factors that could be assimilated into a test for market failure due to high transaction costs that prevent socially beneficial agreements.

The current test asks judges to look at four factors: (1) What is the nature and purpose of the use? Is it educational and non-commercial? Does it simply copy the work, or transform it substantially? (2) What is the nature of the work that is being copied? Is it a work that describes important factual information (that presumably might be of special public benefit if more broadly known) or one that is fictional and entertaining? (3) How much of the copyrighted work has been taken? Does it constitute a large proportion of the original work? (4) What effect will this use likely have on the market for and value of the work?

These factors could be organized to assess whether the transaction cost of getting permission to reproduce a work is high (given the number of potentially benefited individuals), while the dynamic cost on authors' incentives is insignificant relative to the external benefits of copying. That "market failure" approach can explain a number of fair use cases.[47]

Yet it is not clear that this is the complete explanation for the fair use defense. The defense is invoked often in disputes between two publishers or similar commercial enterprises. Not only would they seem well positioned to negotiate without extraordinary costs or at least to trade blanket licenses; they also would seem able to capture enough of the value potentially interested individuals place on the material at issue to negate any supposition of market failure.[48]

In cases like this, where transaction costs are low but rights-holders don't want to sell, the market failure argument resolves into a claim that has two component parts. The first is the supposition that there is a broader public that not only cannot readily participate directly in negotiation over the rights but also will not publicly value access to the copyrighted material in the particular form at issue highly enough to purchase it. The second part is an assumption that, despite the first supposition, members of the unrepresented public still either subjectively value the new access to infringing material in the aggregate enough to merit a (theoretical) purchase of use rights from the copyright holder or are going to be benefited in ways they can't appreciate *ex ante* but that confer aggregate value in excess of the costs the uncompensated use would have for the rights-holder.

These assumptions are not generally disprovable any more than they are provable. The spillover-effects assumption is associated with dissemination of speech that has political associations.[49] That is certainly logical, as the benefits from such speech may be difficult to appropriate. Yet there seems to be no shortage of paying enterprises engaged in such speech, from *The New York Times* and *The Wall Street Journal* to *The Drudge Report* and *Salon* to Rush Limbaugh and Rachel Maddow—the list could go on and on. Similarly, the assumption that the uncompensated use of someone else's expression will benefit a broad public sufficiently to justify the taking of the initial work is plausible enough in a range of settings, but it depends on a belief that the settings can be identified with some accuracy by government authorities whose judgment then will substitute for actual market transactions.[50]

A different approach to the fair use doctrine doesn't see it as an antidote to market failure in the ordinary sense. Instead, the doctrine is a backstop, or safety valve, for difficulties in the application of other doctrines—difficulties created in some cases as a result of an expansion of protection through statutory innovations. This alternative points the way toward considerations that should be accommodated in the other doctrines but might be less readily emphasized in those doctrines than in the form of a separate fair use defense.

Seen this way, the problem addressed by fair use doctrine is not one that occurs only in copyright law. With any set of complex considerations, the process of applying the rules (including legal rules) designed to harmonize those considerations often generates errors that cannot be efficiently reduced by restating the rules themselves. This happens when the existing rule does a good job of dealing with the most common cases and changing the rule to improve its application to a particular group of other cases—for instance, by creating a more complicated rule that incorporates considerations relevant to those less common cases—will increase errors and error costs overall. In such instances, the law sometimes provides a collateral avenue for reaching the right result in unusual cases.

Consider, for example, our prior discussion of cases in which a copyright holder seeks to prevent publication of a derivative work. The right-holders prevailed in the Seinfeld and Harry Potter cases, discussed above. Another derivative work case sought an injunction to publication of a novel based on Margaret Mitchell's classic *Gone with the Wind*. Alice Randall wrote a book called *The Wind Done Gone*, which looked at the life of a civil war family from the eyes of the slaves. The copyright holder of *GWTW* sought to block the sale of *TWDG* as a derivative work, succeeding in the district court but losing on appeal.[51] The characters in *TWDG* were clearly patterned on those in *GWTW*, though their names were changed, and much of the story line was taken from Ms. Mitchell's book. As the district court said, "[*TWDG*] uses fifteen fictional characters from [*GWTW*], incorporating their physical attributes, mannerisms, and the distinct features that Ms. Mitchell used to describe them, as well as their complex relationships with each other. More-over, the various [fictional] locales, . . . settings, characters, themes, and plot of [*TWDG*] closely mirror those contained in [*GWTW*]."[52] The new work, on this view, appeared to the district judge much like the sort of derivative works enjoined in the other cases.

The writing in *TWDG*, however, was original, even if it was a far cry from the quality of the older novel. Indeed, the negative reaction of critics was part of the basis for the claim that *TWDG* not only preempted a possible authorized sequel but diminished the market for other derivative works based on *GWTW*. Yet the action for copyright infringement, rather than for disparagement of a trademark,[53] did not turn on whether the later work was as good as the first but on how much it depended on the special aspects of the first's expression. Application of the law respecting derivative works would seem to preclude an injunction in that case. Not only was the writing entirely new, the perspective of *The Wind Done Gone*, especially so far as matters of race are concerned, was radically different from that of *GWTW*. Prevailing views of race relations changed dramatically between the time of the initial work, 1936, and Ms. Randall's work more than sixty years later. It seems evident that a work with such a different portrayal of race relations in the antebellum South would fall outside the initial copyright's reach.

That was not the basis on which the appellate court reversed the lower court. Instead, the appeals court grounded its decision in fair use doctrine. It found a substantial likelihood that Ms. Randall's publisher would prevail because her work was sufficiently transformative, important to the public, and distinct from the market for *GWTW* that its borrowing from that novel would constitute fair use. The court viewed skeptically the prospect of *GWTW*'s rights-holder proving that *TWDG* diminished the market for a sequel to that work. In our view, the same result could have been reached by construing *TWDG* not to be a derivative work within the purview of *GWTW*'s exclusive control rights. But the safety valve of fair use allowed the court to arrive at that outcome.

Similarly, in *Campbell v. Acuff-Rose Music, Inc.,* the Supreme Court invoked fair use, rather than a construction of derivative work, to permit use of prior copyrighted expression.[54] The Court's decision, allowing the band 2 Live Crew to invoke the fair use defense for its "Pretty Woman" takeoff on Roy Orbison's hit song "Oh, Pretty Woman," was widely seen as holding that parody is favored under the traditional fair use test.[55] It is fair enough to assert—without empirical support—that parody can have substantial social value. So, of course, can other forms of satire and social commentary. More-over, the line between parody and other writing is by no means self-evident. Ms. Randall's publisher characterized her work as parody, obviously in an effort to come within *Campbell*'s protection. But not all different perspectives or different styles constitute parody of the work that they begin from.

Perhaps, the justices meant to say that use of an earlier work's expression for a derivative work that pokes fun at the original is less likely to be authorized, no matter what its social value. The issue then would not be any traditional conception of transaction cost—the cost of negotiating over the rights—so much as evaluation of factors that correlate with the dynamic and static costs of the use.[56] The result again may be correct, but it rests on a highly impressionistic empirical judgment. The parties at issue in *Campbell* plainly could negotiate; they simply were not going to reach the outcome the justices thought most beneficial to society. Whatever the right outcome in *Campbell,* it seems to fit better with the "safety valve" view of fair use than with the "market failure" view.

This is a good point to return to the framework we have relied on in previous chapters, though with some slight modification here. Intellectual property for the most part strikes a sensible balance between static and dynamic costs. For copyright the standard analysis might be modified to account for occasions in which there are strong cultural spillover effects. Mathematics serves as a language of science; similarly fashion, art, music, and literature serve as languages of ideas and emotions. Cultural spillovers can provide a reason for tapering the property rights implied by copyright, at times. The safety valve function of fair use reflects an implicit recognition of this point. At the same time, these spillovers also can provide added reasons for valuing copyright's enhanced incentives to create the works that yield spillover benefits.

Third-Party Liability

The third pillar of the current U.S. law effectively framing the scope of copyright's protection concerns the degree to which third parties can be held liable for their role in facilitating or encouraging copyright violations. Although copyright cases often involve three major players—publishers or motion picture producers or recording companies—risks to the economic interests of copyright holders increasingly come from widespread, low-visibility copying by individuals. The rise of photocopiers, video recorders, digital technologies, and the Internet have made copying of literary works, motion pictures, music, and software—almost any copyrighted material—cheap and easy. Until relatively recently, it took painstaking and often highly skilled work to make a high-quality copy of most copyrighted material. Now that is within almost anyone's reach.

Copyright holders could simply acquiesce in widespread copying. More than a few commentators have urged them to do just that. It is possible that some businesses will find suitable alternative revenue streams to compensate for the losses attributable to ubiquitous low-grade piracy. But for many copyright holders, the losses seem large enough to diminish the likelihood of profiting from investments in producing copyrightable products. Why spend the millions or billions needed to create new software or to make the next blockbuster film if the expected revenue stream is going to be diverted into a million rivulets that cannot cost effectively be tapped by the creators? Those who want to let a thousand flowers bloom (free of copyright claims) tend not to be the same folks who invest in planting and tending the flowers.

The question for people making those investments, thus, has often been whether there is a way to corral the technologies that make copying cheap and easy or to treat revenues from their sales in part as substitutes for the revenues lost from the copyright violations they facilitate.

In most cases, the answer has been no. Manufacturers of photocopiers, for example, are not required to reimburse authors and publishers for the copying that their machines enable. This outcome is in line with the general rule that manufacturers of products are not liable for the use of their products to violate the law. In general, both efficiency and notions of personal autonomy militate against making product manufacturers responsible for what customers do with their products.

That is not a complete end to the matter, however, as courts and legislatures have carved out exceptions to the norm against liability. Those exceptions provided grist for arguments in favor of third-party liability for copyright violations. Three major federal court cases over the past twenty-five years have spelled out the terms on which third parties may be held liable under U.S. copyright law.

Sony v. Universal City Studios, Inc.,[57] *A&M Records, Inc. v. Napster, Inc.,*[58] and *MGM Studios, Inc. v. Grokster Ltd.,*[59] have established the basic proposition that firms marketing technologies with substantial legitimate uses will not be absolutely (strictly) liable for their use to infringe copyright. But when the overwhelming majority of the use is for copyright infringement, and especially when the technology is marketed to encourage as well as to facilitate infringement, courts will find the firms liable as contributory infringers. A similar approach has been adopted legislatively with respect to enterprises that operate Web sites, making the enterprise secondarily responsible for rights violations carried by its site when there is reason to expect that infringing material is being posted.[60]

In the case of technologies that facilitate copying, the law has an intuitive economic justification. Technologies that facilitate copying increase the flow of information in society, which is ordinarily desirable. However, the technologies also make it far easier to infringe copyrights. The law's goal is to put the burden of risk from misuse of the technologies on the party that most efficiently can bear the risk, a test consistent with the balance between the social costs and benefits of these technologies.

The general problem is the same as that historically associated with technologies that have introduced risks. For example, in an old English case, *Rickards v. Lothian,*[61] a tenant of a building sued the owner for installing a lavatory, because someone snuck into the lavatory at night and deliberately caused an overflow of water that damaged the tenant's property on the floor below. The question in *Rickards* was whether the landlord should be held strictly liable (given that he had nothing to do with the intruder) for introducing a risky technology (water supply) into the building. The court's refusal to hold the landlord strictly liable established a principle of tort law that limits strict liability to technologies that throw off risk far in excess of their spillover benefits.[62]

The question posed today is how to balance the benefits from file-sharing Web sites, and other technologies that facilitate copying, with the risks they create. In many cases, the Web sites and other technologies will have benefits that far exceed the risks, although some will fail that test. The law's present approach does not ask that question directly, but poses a related question when the Web site or technology encourages, profits from, or turns a blind eye to infringement. It effectively allows for liability if the Web site operators do not take reasonable steps to prevent and correct copying (or if the operators make their money from the violations, as Napster and Grokster did) but does not impose strict liability on them.[63]

If the law imposed strict third-party liability on all technologies that facilitate copying, it would effectively make the owners of those technologies bear all of the risks associated with their introduction even though they could not, at the same time, lay claim to all of the benefits introduced by the technologies. This would be, in effect, an inefficient form of taxation, forcing technology entrepreneurs to assume the risks to third parties while allowing the general public to reap the spillover benefits. The result would reduce society's wealth, as fewer technologies that could facilitate copying would be introduced in the future. At the other extreme, permitting those who produce and profit from new technologies to promote or facilitate copying with impunity when they easily (cost effectively) could take steps to discourage or terminate copying would shift the cost of new technologies to copyright owners (or, equivalently, allow technologists to expropriate the rewards from novel and creative expression). That could allow technologies to flourish even though their social costs substantially exceed their benefit. Obviously, a middle ground is needed that provides incentives to ensure that benefits and costs of new technologies are aligned with decisions respecting them.

The doctrines setting the scope of control over derivative works, permitting fair use, and placing reasonable bounds around third-party liability define a scope of copyright entitlements that seems roughly congruent with a cost-minimizing approach. It may not be absolutely right in every application or in view of all future technological innovations, but the overall structure and major attributes of copyright law seem to provide a reasonable and relatively constrained set of rights.

Copyright Term

In contrast to the scope of copyright's protections, which are much more limited than patent rights, the length of copyright substantially exceeds the term of protection provided for patent. Copyright term, now set at the life of the author plus seventy years for most purposes, has increased significantly over the last hundred years. Initially, national copyrights in the United States, like those in eighteenth-century England, were awarded for fourteen years, with a possible renewal for another fourteen years. This was extended in 1831 and has been revised upward periodically over the last two centuries. The 1909 U.S. Copyright Act set the first copyright term at twenty-eight years, with a possible twenty-eight-year renewal, although just a year earlier the major international accord on copyright had adopted a rule that copyright should last for the life of the author plus fifty years, a term embraced by U.S. law in the 1976 copyright act.[64] The 1976 law also provided for a life-plus-seventy-year term for one category of previously unpublished works. The life-plus-seventy term was made the norm with passage of the Sonny Bono Copyright Term Extension Act of 1998.[65] Although the last of these extensions was challenged as violating the Constitution's provision for "limited term" copyrights, the Supreme Court in *Eldred v. Ashcroft* pronounced the modified copyright term as long but not unlimited, and constitutional.[66]

The ideal term for copyright—the term that best accommodates interests in promoting useful expression, in encouraging broad public dissemination, and in avoiding the costs associated with limitations on using expression—is not something that legal or economic analysis will be able to pinpoint. For any category of expression, the right term will be more a matter of guesswork than analysis. Further, there is no reason to believe that a single answer will be best for different categories of expression (for novels, how-to books, documentaries, dramatic motion pictures, children's films, art, song compositions, software programs, and so on).

What is capable of analysis is the basis for belief that a longer term is justified in response to changes in the technology of copying and the economics of expression. As described above, copying has gone from a laborious, labor-intensive project requiring considerable skill—think of the monk spending years creating a duplicate copy of a manuscript in the Middle Ages—to something anyone can accomplish readily and inexpensively. At the same time, markets for expressive works have become more global, complex, and interconnected. Movies from Mumbai can have audiences now in Minneapolis, Miami, and Manhattan, just as Hollywood films can play in theatres and on DVDs and computers from California to Calcutta, Caracas, Canberra, and Cannes. The number and diversity of derivative works spun off from successful creative efforts have grown, and the economic returns from these other works have grown as well.

At the same time, the proportion of profitable expressive ventures seems to be declining, especially if pared back to profitability based on the initial expressive work. More and more, Hollywood studios' fortunes rise or fall with the results of a small number of releases. The size of the take from the biggest winners in any year will have an enormous impact on the business's overall profits. But despite the best efforts at prediction by the most knowledgeable industry insiders, it remains a matter of some mystery just *which* among the many offerings will carry a studio in any given year.[67] Who would have thought, for instance, that an animated movie about an overweight, out of shape, kung-fu-loving panda would generate nearly a billion dollars in revenue in two years between U.S. box office, foreign box office, DVD, and video game sales? We have seen no empirical evidence explaining why uncertainty might be rising, but the greater number of markets (and the lower familiarity of those markets to the people who traditionally have been responsible for deciding what to invest in each film) logically would correlate with higher uncertainty. The same appears to be true in other core copyright industries.

If all of the biggest hits run out of steam quickly, then copyright term is not going to affect the investment in producing new expressive works. The scope of copyright protection, rather than the length of protection, then would be key. But if many of the most successful works enjoy popularity that continues not only across geographical spaces and types of follow-on works but also across time, the length of copyright protection becomes another critical factor in inducing the desired investment in creation.

Obviously, the shorter the copyright term, the more likely it is that investment in new expressive work will be truncated. Equally clear, the magnitude of that effect will increase with the prospect for easy copying (especially easy, widespread, hard-to-detect copying). It will increase as well with uncertainty about which expressive works will be successes. And, lastly, it will also rise with the costs of producing the works. All of these forces—increased ease of copying, greater uncertainty about the returns to any particular expressive work, and greater initial production costs for many types of expressive work—seem to be at play in today's world. On all of these margins, then, changes threaten investment support for copyright, and that translates into a basis for longer copyright terms.

One factor that moderates the positive return from longer copyright terms is that investment decisions are time sensitive—those making the decisions rationally discount future earnings, so income that is farther away in time is worth less in present investment. The upshot is that after a relatively short period (well shy of the current life-plus-seventy-years term), potential revenues are too far in the future to have much effect on investment in creating new works. The analysis will change so far as relevant decisions are made on an ongoing basis about additional investments in maintaining the value of the expressive work.[68] These investments need to be taken into account in designing the optimal copyright (or other intellectual property) term.[69] But for the initial investment, it will not matter much how far out in the future the rights extend past the point where the discounted present value of that income approaches zero. At the same time, the social cost, in present value terms, falls at roughly the same rate. The question, thus, is whether continuing copyright protection into the future incurs static costs that exceed the dynamic cost of leaving expression exposed to being freely appropriated too soon.

Consider four alternative approaches to copyright term: a short fixed term, a permanent copyright, a short initial term with an option for renewal, or a longish fixed term. Again, admitting the absence of solid data to allow rigorous evaluation of these options, there still are a few observations that seem sensible guides to choosing the right framework.

The first possibility, a short fixed term, likely will create substantial dynamic costs, unduly discouraging investment in creating expressive work. The second option, a permanent right, mirrors what is done with respect to most property, and it has its advocates in the world of intellectual property as well. But information, which is intimately bound up with many of the subjects of copyright, can be distinguished from most other types of property. Even though copyright doesn't protect the broad ideas associated with expression, a permanent right raises especially difficult questions when we think of the cultural effects of copyright and the protection of derivative works. Permanent protection could raise the cost of obtaining socially valuable new expression or new uses of the copyrighted expression, given the costs of identifying holders of very old rights and assuring that there is no infringement on them. Additionally, so far as the rights are associated with particular sorts of restrictions on use, there is a "dead hand" problem of limiting unforeseen future benefits from specific uses.[70] So far as the expression has substantial positive spillover effects, it may be desirable to have some sort of tapering of protection, at least at the boundaries of copyright involving derivative works or transformations. To be sure, tapering has costs in terms of the forgone investments in maintaining the value of a copyright and promoting it, and in light of this a hybrid rule consisting of a permanent right at the core involving outright copying of original work and a tapered right at the boundary involving transformations may be optimal.

The renewable term option certainly is a possible solution to problems that might exist with either short or permanent copyright terms, but it is not clear that the costs associated with renewal filings and a concomitant need to provide mechanisms for ascertaining which copyrighted works have renewed their term are less than any gain from eliminating rights in the remaining works. Presumably, rights-holders for the most profitable works will renew, which means that those who are most likely to enforce their rights will enjoy a longer term. However the permanently renewable option raises the same "dead hand control" problem as does the option of a permanent right. Conceptually, a preferable approach would be a sliding scale scheme that recognized that permanency or permanent renewability has a stronger basis at the core involving explicit copying than at the edges involving borrowing of concepts and markers. The obvious cost of any approach that has a sliding-scale quality is the increased administrative cost and error cost associated with less bright line rules, although current law deals effectively with the judgment calls this scheme would entail through determinations on the scope of copyright protection.

The last option, a standardized, longer copyright term seems at least as likely to be the best alternative as the other choices. Most of the complaints about copyright's longevity are voiced on the basis of particular anecdotes or particular activities that require some accommodation with existing rights-holders. Yet, time after time, practical solutions to that sort of need have been worked out. We understand the objection that current copyright law does create special problems for some businesses, but we are unwilling to advocate a significant change in the law simply out of concern that such solutions may not be identified for some specific class of enterprises or activities.

Conclusion

Copyright law continues to evolve in response to shifting technological, economic, and political considerations, and some of the changes in the law have generated considerable controversy. In addition to debates over matters such as the fair use doctrine, the scope for protection of parody and similar works, the application of the law to impose liability on third parties, and the term for copyright—all of which remain in play to some degree—the application of the law to reproduction via the Internet has proven controversial (a matter discussed further in Chapter 8). None of the lines drawn by the current law is unimpeachable. All of the particular determinations on copyright length, scope, and reach rest on unprovable empirical assumptions. Yet all of the major elements of copyright law, if not clearly right, seem to be reasonable approximations of what would constitute a socially desirable balance.

7

Trademark Law

A trademark, such as the product name Coca-Cola, is really nothing more than a label. Given this, it would be natural to assume trademark law to be a relatively narrow and inconsequential field. After all, patent law and trade secrecy law deal with inventions, and copyright deals with such things as books and musical compositions. When thinking of the subject matters of patent, trade secrecy, and copyright, no one questions the degree of ingenuity or effort invested in the ideas and information protected by the law. But in the case of trademark law, the information protected seems comparatively trivial—how much effort goes into thinking up a name like Cracker Jack?

Unlike patent and copyright, trademark law is not designed to encourage the work that goes into inventing the information that the law protects. Why should the law spend enormous resources to protect silly names that people invent over lunch? The basis of trademark is somewhat different. Since its common law roots in the law of unfair competition, trademark law has aimed to prevent a species of fraud, or closely related, the palming off of one person's goods as those of another. This is a far more serious issue than safeguarding silly names.

Trademark law is surprisingly complicated and full of details. It is not our goal in this chapter to explore all of those details, for there are so many that only a well-paid trademark lawyer would have the motivation and patience to explain them. At bottom, the law confronts the same trade-offs between the costs of monopolizing markets (static costs) and the benefits of market-expanding innovation (dynamic benefits) examined in the previous chapters.[1] Trademark doctrine strikes a defensible balance between these costs and benefits.

In the course of applying our framework to trademark law, we hope to clarify the relationship between trademark and efficient markets, a topic that has led to a chorus of scholarly critiques of trademark.[2] Competition for marks is a lot like competition for location, since a good brand name can help attract consumers while a bad brand name will not help or may actually turn consumers away. As we explain below, there is no reason to believe that unregulated competition for brand differentiation and related brand names will lead to the best possible outcome. Trademark law, rather than assisting firms in their effort to establish an optimal set of property rights, actually seeks to correct some well-known types of market failure. This is the perspective from which trademark law should be viewed.

The Functions of Trademark

It is overly simplistic to refer to a trademark, as we did at the outset, as nothing more than a label. The trademark is a label identifying the source of the product, but it is more fundamentally a signal. As a signal, the trademark serves several functions.

The functions of the trademark signal can be grouped into two broad categories consistent with our general approach: (1) supporting market-expanding investments, and (2) gaining some degree of power over price in the market. The former function affects the category of dynamic costs (or benefits) that we have discussed in previous chapters, and the latter function affects primarily the category of static costs.

Recall that dynamic costs are observed over time. If we reduce the return on a particular investment today—say, in growing corn—the cost of that decision, in terms of a reduction in corn crops, will be observed in the future. Dynamic effects often involve the future capacity of a market, whereas static costs typically involve a diminution in the size of a market with a given capacity at a given moment. It is the difference between possibly having no market at all and having a market with a higher price and lower quantity than would otherwise be observed.

Dynamic Consequences

There are many ways to think of the dynamic effects of a trademark. We will offer a few here, but we do not mean to give the impression that this is an exhaustive survey.

One way to think of the dynamic effect is that the trademark supports or improves *quality-enhancing investments* in a product. The reason is that a trademark enables consumers more easily to distinguish your product from those of others. Given that consumers can more easily distinguish your product simply by looking for the trademark, you can feel relatively secure that investments you make into the quality or the promotion of your product will be captured in the form of enhanced sales or more valuable sales. In other words, the trademark ensures that the benefits of promotional and quality investments will be captured or *internalized* to the party making the investments.

To see why this is so, suppose trademarks were not allowed, or suppose all products within a given market had the same trademark and were physically indistinguishable. If you made an investment to enhance the quality of your product, no consumer would be able to distinguish your product from those of other sellers. If information got around reasonably well, consumers might eventually discover that the average quality of products in your market increased as a result of your investment. But they would not be able to tell that your product was any more valuable than those of a rival seller. Because they discovered that the products in your market had improved, they would buy more and be willing to pay more for them. As a result, all sellers in your market would benefit from your investment. If there were one hundred sellers in your market, you would enjoy one one-hundredth of the benefit from your investment in the quality of your product.

Now, one could argue that this outcome may not be so bad after all. Indeed, it has been argued that the law should *not* aim to internalize the benefits from investment per se, but instead ensure that enough of the benefit is internalized to lead you to invest whenever investment is good for society.[3] In this case, however, the two goals are the same. Suppose that for every one dollar you invest into quality enhancement, you gain one dollar in increased profits and ninety-nine rival sellers also gain one dollar in profits. Then you will invest up to one dollar in quality, but no more. The gain to society from your invest-ment is one hundred dollars. Although you would be willing to invest up to one dollar, it would be even better for society if you were willing to invest up to one hundred dollars. So it is clear that although the inability to internalize the full benefits of investment in quality may not put an end to your invest-ments, your incentive to invest will be excessively weak relative to the overall gains. Maybe that is not so bad after all, but it could be a lot better.

And, it could be a lot worse. After you have invested one dollar and realized that ninety-nine dollars of the benefit went to your rival sellers, you might have second thoughts about repeating that action. Indeed, you might realize that it is far better to let your ninety-nine rivals do the investment. That way, you avoid spending anything and you gain from their investments. Why not reap where you have not sown, if it is there for the taking? But if everyone thinks this way, investment in quality declines to the bare minimum.

The scenario in which everyone waits for his rival to do the investing is the result of *free riding*. When sellers are unable to distinguish their goods from others' goods, consumers view each good as a perfect substitute, giving each seller has an incentive to free ride off the quality investments of other sellers. Of course, if everyone free rides, then no one makes any substantial investments in quality,[4] and the quality of goods in the market spirals downward over time.

The trademark signal also has what can be described as a *bonding* or *hostage-creating* function.[5] Assume the signal functions to distinguish your products from others and you have invested substantially in quality. The signal allows you to reap the full benefits of your investment in quality. But it also has the effect of creating a bond or holding you hostage to that enhanced expectation of quality. If you fail to maintain the quality level, your trademark loses its value. The investment in quality in order to enhance the value of the trademark is like a bond that you forfeit the moment you cut back on investment.

Closely related to the bonding, or hostage-creating, function is the role of a trademark in sending a *credible signal of quality*.[6] Anyone can put a label on their product and promote it. Anyone can grab a megaphone and yell to the public, "Buy Brand X because it is good." But talk is cheap, and eventually everyone realizes that. It would be a different thing, however, if you invested a conspicuously large sum of money into the promotion of Brand X. Consumers would then reason that there is a high chance Brand X really is good, because otherwise only a fool would invest such a large sum in promoting it.

Lincoln famously said that you can fool some of the people all of the time, all of the people some of the time, but not all of the people all of the time.[7] It follows that a decision on the part of a rational actor to spend a conspicuously large sum on promotion of a trademark is either an effort to fool many for a short time, a few for a long time, or simply telling the truth. But as the sum invested into promotion increases and persists over time, it becomes less and less likely that the seller is trying to fool anyone. The investment would eventually be wasted if it is not backed up by quality. It would be reasonable for the consumer to infer that large and persistent investments into the promotion of a brand constitute a credible signal that the brand's quality is indeed high.

As this last description suggests, the trademark can become, over time, something greater than it was at the outset. At the initial date that a branded product enters the market, the trademark is simply a label identifying its source. But after large, persistent, and conspicuous investments in quality and promotion have been incurred, product perceptions become associated with the trademark and the trademark itself becomes a reliable signal of quality. Consumers began rationally to rely on the trademark's promise of quality.

It is common to see the trademark's function described primarily as a means of *reducing consumer search costs*.[8] This is an important function, and it overlaps with the functions described to this point, and others still to be described. It is obvious that a prominent and distinctive label identifying the source makes it easier for the consumer to distinguish the trademarked product from other such products. When consumer search costs are reduced, this has implications for the real cost of the product to the consumer (static costs and benefits) and for the size of the market itself (dynamic costs and benefits). Since we will discuss static costs in a separate section below, we will reflect briefly on the dynamic effect here.

The dynamic consequences of reducing consumer search costs have been explained already as part of our preceding discussion of the functions of trademark law. When search costs are reduced, consumers can more easily distinguish one product from another, which internalizes the benefits from investment in quality and promotion. With the benefits internalized, free riding is less likely to be observed. Of course, this is not just a matter of having shinier chrome on a branded bicycle. When sellers cannot internalize the benefits of quality investment and promotion, they may decide to cancel new products or to exit the market entirely. Thus, reducing search costs has a dynamic consequence over time, because it enhances incentives to introduce new products or to extend product lines under a specific brand.

Static Consequences

We have so far confined ourselves to a consideration of the dynamic consequences of the trademark signal, and now we will take up the static consequences. The search-cost-reducing function of the trademark, in addition to the dynamic consequences discussed above, has important static consequences. The cost of search is a real cost to the consumer of entering the market. The real price a consumer pays is the sum of the cost of finding the good, the cost of transacting for it, and the sticker price of the good (unless discounted from the sticker). Any device that reduces the search cost reduces the real price consumers must pay for goods. Thus, trademark reduces static costs by effectively reducing the real price consumers pay when they enter the market. This means that more goods are sold within markets of any given capacity.

In contrast to the static benefit (or cost reduction) just described, the trademark can also increase static costs, by enabling the seller to shield itself from some competition. In other words, trademarks can generate static costs by empowering the seller to hike its price above the level that would be observed in a competitive market.

To see how static costs are created by the trademark, we will first have to consider the domain of available trademark signals. Judge Friendly, in *Abercrombie & Fitch Co. v. Hunting World, Inc.*,[9] set out four types of possible trademark: (1) generic, (2) descriptive, (3) suggestive, and (4) arbitrary or fanciful. Generic terms refer to the class of items to which the seller's product belongs. For example, the words *orange* or *car* are generic descriptions of general categories of goods. Descriptive terms actually describe some important feature of the good—such as the term *versatile* for a certain type of luggage, or *sturdy* for a type of bicycle. Suggestive marks are in part descriptive but also serve a distinguishing function—"Mustang" (a car), "Grand Voyager" (a mini-van), and "Coppertone" (a suntan lotion) are examples. Lastly, arbitrary or fanciful marks do not have a descriptive function in any sense, and typically have no meaning at all other than in connection to the item that it brands—e.g., "Polaroid" or "Kodak."

Suppose a seller of oranges chooses the generic term *orange* as his trademark. If he could gain legal protection for the use of the term—that is, if he could use the law to prevent other sellers from using the term *orange*—he would have an advantage in the marketplace for oranges. Other sellers of oranges would have to find some other terms to describe their goods—e.g., *orange-colored citrus fruit*. With his rivals forced to use alternatives to the generic term, the seller who monopolizes the generic term would have an immediate appeal to consumers who had not studied the market carefully. Only consumers who had sufficient experience or who had studied the market would know that many of the *orange-colored citrus fruits* available in the market were perfect substitutes for the orange.

As a mark, the generic term is like a desirable location from which to sell your product. Acquiring control over the generic term is a lot like acquiring control over the central marketplace of a town. The most natural place where consumers would go to shop would be exclusively yours and rival sellers would have to find ways to entice consumers to visit their shops in all sorts of untraveled spots.

More generally, one can think of the incentive to acquire a mark as similar in many respects to the incentive to acquire a desirable location in a geographic market. Each seller has an incentive to gain control over the location that is attractive to the largest number of consumers.

Competition for location was first described by economist Harold Hotelling.[10] Competition for a desirable mark is, similarly, a type of *Hotelling competition*. Imagine a beach that is 600 feet long, sandwiched by rock barriers. Two ice cream sellers would like to locate their stands on the beach to sell ice cream to beachgoers. The most desirable allocation of the two ice cream stands would put one at 200 feet from the left barrier and the other at 200 feet from the right barrier. This would minimize the distance that the average consumer would have to travel to obtain ice cream. But the competitive process will not generate this result. If the first ice cream vendor chooses the location 200 feet from the left barrier, the second will choose the location 210 feet from the left barrier. That way, the second vendor will get the business of all of the beachgoers located 206 feet from the left barrier all the way to the right barrier. Of course, once this happens, the first vendor will move to the right of the second vendor, and both will keep moving right, leapfrogging each other, until they are smack in the middle of the beach—one vendor located 295 feet from the left barrier and the other vendor 295 feet from the right barrier.

Unregulated competition for marks would have the same characteristics as Hotelling competition for location. The only difference is that instead of

competing for the best physical location, sellers compete for the best location within the domain of potential brand names. Viewed from this perspective, the acquisition of exclusive control over a generic term is similar to
acquiring exclusive control over a very desirable physical location. Indeed,
given the burden foisted on competing sellers, acquisition of exclusive control over a generic term is a bit like the ice cream vendor obtaining control
over the entire beach, forcing his rivals to sell from beyond the barriers.

Acquiring exclusive control over the generic term would permit the seller
to charge a supracompetitive (i.e., tending toward monopolistic) price.
Because rival sellers would be forced to choose alternative names that are
different from the generic, the search costs to consumers who wish to purchase the item from rival sellers would increase.[11] For example, in the case of
the orange seller who acquires exclusive control over the term *orange,* consumers would have to search for other orange sellers among the many other
sellers of items labeled citrus fruits. If the search cost is one dollar per transaction, then the orange seller would be able to add a surcharge of up to one
dollar to his oranges while still retaining all of the consumers who enter the
market in search of oranges.

As this example illustrates, the acquisition by sellers of exclusive control
over generic terms imposes static costs on society. Such control permits the
seller to charge a monopolistic price,[12] which reduces the quantity sold on
the market.[13] Moreover, such control increases the search costs for consumers who wish to find alternative sources of supply. Thus, the one potential static benefit of branding—reducing search costs—is canceled, while the
cost of monopolizing markets is enhanced. And although our focus is on
static costs at this moment, we should add that dynamic costs—costs from
reduced investment incentives—are likely to result in this scenario too. Rival
sellers who are shunted to the boundary of the market by the first seller's
acquisition of the generic term will find their incentives to invest in quality
and promotion reduced. Because consumers face higher search costs in
finding them, rival sellers will receive a lower return on every dollar invested
in promotion and quality-enhancement.

Acquisition of exclusive control over descriptive terms can have the same
harmful effect on competition. Descriptive terms are often necessary to
identify a submarket within a broader market. Sellers of "versatile" luggage
or "sturdy" bicycle frames may cater to a specific subgroup of consumers
who are looking for a particular attribute in a product. Gaining exclusive

control over the most natural term describing a specific submarket may generate static costs similar to those observed in the case of control over a generic term. The size of the costs would be determined by the number of consumers in the submarket and the extent of search-cost barriers put in the way of rival sellers.

As we move toward suggestive, arbitrary, and fanciful terms, the search-cost barriers thrown in the way of rival sellers decline. "Coppertone" communicates quite well the function of the suntan lotion that bears the name, but there are other suggestive names that could be used by rivals that would not put them at a significant disadvantage in getting the attention of consumers. For the most part, suggestive names take up desirable space in the domain of brand names, but they also leave plenty of room for other sellers to locate near consumers—to continue with the beach analogy, the other ice cream sellers can find room on the beach to compete against the first ice cream seller. This is obviously so in the case of fanciful names.

Of course, even a suggestive or fanciful name can become so thoroughly identified with a general category of products that it essentially gives the seller who controls it exclusive control over the beach. In theory, the name Coppertone could become a general description of suntan lotion. If a sufficient number of consumers begin to equate the product's name with the generic category, rival sellers will be at a disadvantage if they are unable to use the name. Denying rival sellers access to the name would increase search costs in the market and permit the initial seller to add a monopolistic surcharge to its price. This is especially likely where a product creates a new market. New generic terms like *aspirin* and *cellophane* have come about from this process.

We have so far focused on the static costs generated by the first mover's acquisition of a brand name. The first seller, we noted, has an incentive to acquire the most desirable term in the domain of names—and a term may be desirable largely because it increases the search costs to consumers looking to purchase from rival sellers. We compared this to an ice cream seller taking the most desirable spot on the beach and relegating his competitors to sell from undesirable locations, or from beyond the beach boundary.

We have not considered the incentives of the second firm to enter the market. If the first firm has used a generic term in its brand name, the second mover will obviously wish to have access to the same generic term. The second seller of oranges would want to identify his products as oranges rather than as "orange-colored citrus fruits." This is desirable Hotelling competition. But as we noted before, it does not lead to the best possible allocation of brand names as signals to consumers. It could be that the second seller is actually selling a slightly different product—perhaps oranges with a slightly different flavor. It might be better for all consumers for the second seller to take a different name to communicate this feature to the subgroup of consumers who would be especially interested in his product. But the second mover's strongest incentive is to locate in a space in the brand name domain that gives him access to the largest pool of consumers. Thus, differentiation through the choice of brand names will not be driven by the competitive process into the precise arrangement that best serves the interests of consumers.

More troubling, suppose the first seller has adopted a fanciful name—one that does not by itself impose search barriers in the way of a second seller in the market. Suppose the first seller of oranges labels them "Orion" oranges. Suppose in addition that Orion oranges turn out to be especially popular with consumers. The second seller will then wish to label his oranges "Orion" oranges. Again, this is Hotelling competition; this is locating on the beach right next to the first ice cream seller. The name Orion has proven to be successful at attracting consumers. Why not locate in the same space of brand names and sell to consumers already there? Moreover, the competition benefits consumers to the extent that the original seller of Orion oranges will have to engage in price competition with the new seller.

If the Orion oranges sold by the first and second movers are the same, it is hard to see how consumers could be harmed, at least in the short run, by the second mover's decision to adopt the same name. The fact that consumers could not distinguish the two by name would not be costly, because the products are the same. And since the products are the same, consumers would be indifferent between the two sellers. However, if the products sold by the first and second movers differ in quality, then the second mover's adoption of the same name does generate new search costs for consumers. The second mover generally would not want to use the same name if it sells oranges that are more attractive to consumers than Orion oranges, but it would especially want to use the name if it sells oranges of lower quality. Consumers would have to study the market in order to distinguish the original Orion oranges from the new Orion oranges. Thus, the second mover's decision to adopt the same name as the first mover, where there are significant quality differences, generates static costs in the form of additional search by consumers. Moreover, the second mover's adoption of the same name as the first retards price competition rather than enhancing it. The new market price will be a blend of the prices for high- and low-quality oranges, which benefits the low-quality seller and penalizes the high-quality seller.[14]

The upshot is that the competitive process originally described by Hotelling provides an analytical framework for assessing static costs and benefits resulting from unregulated competition for brand names. First movers, if able to obtain protection for any brand name that they choose, will have incentives to stake out a position that raises search costs for consumers who wish to purchase alternatives. The easiest way to do this is to use a generic or descriptive label, or to use a name that is likely to become generic over time. Second movers will choose any name that has already shown its power in attracting consumers. If there are no quality differences between the two sellers, the choice of the second mover will impose no losses on society (in the short run), and indeed will benefit society by enhancing price competition. But in the presence of quality differences, the second mover's decision to locate closely to the first in brand name space raises search costs for consumers and diminishes price competition.

If we imagine each distinct brand as taking some space on the beachhead of consumer preferences, unregulated competition will not lead to the best (i.e., consumer-welfare maximizing) assortment of brands, nor to the best (i.e., search-cost minimizing) allocation of search costs for consumers. For any given allocation of brands, clustering and exclusion among marks will generate inefficiently high search costs for consumers. Trademark law could easily improve upon this outcome.

Regulation of Trademarks

The question we turn to now is whether the law responds to some of the problems described above. Although in general, trademarks reduce search costs, they can sometimes be used to increase search costs, and there can be negative as well as positive investment incentives. Does the law restrain some of the decisions that are likely to be costly to society?

The law of trademark has evolved from the common law on unfair competition. Although lawyers tend to think of trademark law as part of intellectual property law today, it is an outgrowth of tort law. Indeed, one of the early tort law casebooks, that of John Henry Wigmore, includes a section covering "tradal imitation," which presents excerpts from important early trademark cases.[15] Many modern trademark cases are based on a federal statute, the Lanham Act.[16] However, the Lanham Act merely permits plaintiffs to sue in federal court to enforce substantive rights that have been determined by the common law of unfair competition and trademark. In other words, the Lanham Act serves a primarily procedural purpose, easing enforcement by permitting registration of trademarks and the filing of lawsuits in federal courts. But the reasoning behind trademark doctrine has been developed over hundreds of years by courts examining tort actions among businesses.

First, consider the most obvious function of the trademark, which is to distinguish one seller's goods from those of other sellers. The common law has protected trade names at least since the seventeenth century. In an English case from 1618, *Southern v. How,*[17] the court upheld a tort action brought by one clothier against another who had copied his mark. Thus, the most basic function of trademark, to allow goods to be distinguished, which reduces search costs and expands markets, has been enforced by the law for quite a long time.

The central issue in the common law trademark infringement cases was whether the mark of the alleged infringer could be *confused* with that of the plaintiff (the original trademark).[18] When the second user adopts the same mark as the first user, confusion is obviously likely to occur. The confusion rule extends the law's protection of the original mark more broadly to instances in which the second mark is not precisely the same as the first one, but is close enough to cause confusion to the typical consumer.[19] The specific confusion scenario the law aims to prevent is that in which a typical consumer would be led to do business with the holder of the second mark under the belief that he is actually the holder of the first mark or part of the same business as the holder of the first mark. For example, in one of the early U.S. cases, *Mossler v. Jacobs,* the court enjoined the use of the name "Six Big Tailors" by the second user, where the first user had operated for many years under the name "Six Little Tailors."[20] The court noted that confusion was likely because many businesses were referred to by abbreviated titles, and that "Six Tailors" is all that many consumers might have in mind when they searched for the services of a tailor.[21]

Though a rather straightforward case, *Mossler* illustrates how courts have developed a common law of trademark confusion. Courts have noted how confusion results because of the search environment,[22] cognitive limitations,[23] and habits of mind such as the tendency to abbreviate. The reasoning of *Mossler* suggests that even if the second seller had used the label "Six Big Tailors of the Windy City" (the case was from Chicago), the outcome, a finding of infringement, would have been the same. The risk of confusing "Six Little Tailors" with "Six Big Tailors of the Windy City" would appear to be minimal. However, in the real environment in which consumer search takes place (e.g., with cars honking from behind the car of the searching consumer), the names are similar enough to result in the second mark user receiving traffic that was initially intended for the first user.

Just as substantial differentiation may be insufficient to avoid a finding of confusion, substantial similarity may not lead to a finding of confusion. In a market of sophisticated purchasers who search within an environment with no time constraints or distractions (no cars honking behind them), similar marks may not generate a serious risk of confusion among buyers.[24]

The confusion requirement itself is an illustration of the law seeking to reduce the sum of static and dynamic costs. The law does not give the trademark owner a property right in the mark. The law protects the mark only when confusion is likely. This is a desirable rule in light of search costs and investment incentives.

First, the confusion rule limits protection to instances in which there is a serious risk that the second mark user will free ride off of the goodwill investments of the first user. Such free riding can take place only where there is a significant risk of confusion between two goods in the same market. If confusion does occur and part of the customer base of the first mark user is siphoned off by the second user, the first user's incentives to invest in quality and promote his product will be weakened. Investment incentives are maintained by the confusion rule.

Second, the confusion rule denies protection when the first user has acquired a name that contains important terms identifying the market in which he sells and when consumers are sophisticated enough to distinguish first and second users who use the same terms. Recall that the first mover in the Hotelling competition model will appropriate the most desirable location in the market. In the set of brand names, the first mover will have incentives to acquire terms that define the very market in which he sells—generic terms or descriptive terms. But if the first mover gets exclusive control over such terms, he will effectively increase search costs for buyers seeking goods from his rivals—that is, he will relegate his competitors to the boundary of the market. If a second user adopts some of the same terms, without risking confusion to buyers, that will reduce search costs and enhance competition by permitting the second user to enter the same market. The law permits some degree of imitation in this scenario.

One classic illustration of this latter point is the case of a splinter group from a social (or religious) society. Obviously, this is outside of the business context, but societies provide services to their members just as businesses do. In *Supreme Lodge Knights of Pythias v. Improved Order Knights of Pythias*,[25] the plaintiff (a secret society) tried to enjoin the "Improved Order" from using the name "Knights of Pythias." The court noted that it was common for splinter groups to retain the name of the original parent organization, as is observed among churches, and that anyone who knew enough about the societies to seek to join either of them would know that they were different and would not be confused by the similarity of names. In a sense, the name Knights of Pythias defines a market for the society. If the original order could prevent the splinter group from using the same name, it would effectively push the splinter group to the boundary of the market and increase search costs for individuals who wanted to join the splinter group.

In addition to the confusion requirement, the common law developed specific rules that reflect the same effort to maintain investment incentives while minimizing the static costs of market exclusion. Perhaps the most important of these rules is the absence of protection for generic marks.[26] The scenario in which an orange seller acquires exclusive control of the term *orange* is not permitted under the law. This prevents a seller from strategically foisting large search costs on buyers who seek to purchase from rivals. The initial mark user can protect his investment incentives just as well by adopting a fanciful or arbitrary name, which will not put search-cost obstacles in the way of rival sellers.

The common law denied protection for descriptive terms as well,[27] though modern law developed under the Lanham Act provides protection for descriptive terms where they have acquired "secondary meaning."[28] A descriptive term that has acquired secondary meaning has become understood, within the minds of consumers, as a term identifying the particular seller rather than a term identifying a relevant market.[29] Since, as we noted earlier, descriptive terms can serve to identify or define a relevant market, this rule has the same justification and effect as the denial of protection for generic terms.

Under the common law and also under modern federal trademark law, a mark could not be protected unless it was in use.[30] This rule prevents a seller from acquiring all of the names that would be useful or desirable in identifying a seller within a certain market and leaving it to rivals to use their inventiveness to find palatable trade names. In the absence of this rule, sellers would have an incentive to "name-squat" in order to force rivals to choose names that put them at a disadvantage in competition for consumer attention.

Several scholars have suggested trademark law has moved in the direction of permitting mark owners to gain a property right in names. The key piece of evidence supporting this alleged "propertization"[31] of trademark law is the development of the dilution doctrine.[32] Under the dilution doctrine, the first mark user can prevent a second user from employing the mark even though the two are not in competition with each other and there is no risk that existing consumers will be confused by the second mark.

As in much of trademark law, there is a noticeable reluctance on the part of courts to establish the dilution doctrine as the equivalent of a property rule. Many courts have looked for evidence of possible confusion, which might occur because the first seller might be expected to expand into the market of the second seller,[33] or because the products of the first and second seller appear to be technologically related.[34] At least for cases following this approach, the dilution doctrine can be viewed as an expanded version of the confusion rule, where confusion takes into account the likelihood of entry and the widespread recognition of national brands. But dilution cases still extend the protection for mark owners beyond the narrow confines of confusion over the actual source of goods.

However, critiques of the increased propertization of trademark law are overdrawn. Even under the modern dilution regime, the crystallized rules denying protection to generic terms and minimizing protection for descriptive terms remain. The dilution doctrine reflects, to some degree, a modern reassessment of the balance between static and dynamic costs. The confusion test is a flexible balancing test, or standard, that is capable, like the negligence rule of torts, of reaching different conclusions as the inputs to the test change. And with the growth of national marketing campaigns for brands, the inputs to the balancing test have changed.

The case for dilution doctrine is a straightforward one. Suppose one firm sells cars and the other firm sells some unrelated product, such as candy. If the first seller adopts "Orion" as its mark, the dilution doctrine may prevent the second seller from adopting the same mark, even though the average consumer is not going to confuse a carmaker with a candy seller. In the presence of a national market of both brands, there will be spillover effects. If one firm creates a positive image for the brand, that will spill over to the other firm. Here, the free-riding problem arises. Since there are positive spillovers from brand promotion, both firms would have an incentive to let the other firm do the promotion. Hence, the dilution doctrine is useful as a method of preventing free riding on brand promotion. It follows that there are dynamic benefits, in the sense of promoting investment, that are generated by the dilution doctrine.

Another version of the same problem involves opportunistic behavior. A firm in an unrelated market may have an incentive to adopt the mark of the first seller in order to gain a positive initial reaction from consumers. This is no effort to fool consumers, but to bathe in the favorable light of an established brand. But if one thousand firms do the same, eventually the brand loses its value to the first seller. Consumers who have confronted the brand in use by many different firms of varying quality will have no reason to associate it with the first seller.[35] If this scenario seems objectionable once one thousand firms attach themselves parasitically to the established brand, why let one firm do it?

Yet another version of the problem involves disparagement of the mark. Uses that diminish the value of a trademark by suggesting associations at odds with the brand image—think, for example, of uses of the Mickey Mouse character to promote products that are polar opposites of the clean-cut, child-friendly image that helps support Disney's appeal to children and families—also free ride on the investment of the mark owner and first user. And, as in the dilution cases, the disparagement impairs the value of the mark.

Indeed, uses of the mark that directly conflict with the image of the first user may be appealing to second users precisely because they gain an immediate recognition and hold on the attention of consumers. But this immediate hold that results from presenting a dissonant image damages the first mark user by potentially giving the dissonant image greater salience to the consumer than the original image. Direct consumer confusion may not exist, but there is nonetheless an economic basis for protecting the mark.

What about the static costs of the dilution doctrine? They appear to be minimal. If the Orion car manufacturer and the Orion candy manufacturer are not in the same market, then allowing one firm to gain exclusive control over the trademark will not necessarily have any implications for competition. Ordinarily, permitting one firm to gain exclusive control over a mark has negative implications for competition when that control effectively shunts the other firm to the boundary of the market. But that is not a risk where the firms are not in the same market at all. Far from reflecting a new propertization of trademark, the dilution doctrine reflects a sensible striking of the balance between static and dynamic costs.

Our defense of modern dilution doctrine takes as its premise the view that common law courts have developed the doctrine in the process of balancing static and dynamic costs. When protecting exclusive control over a trademark has no implications for competition, the static costs of trademark protection are minimal. However, this does not imply that the dilution doctrine should always be given the most expansive interpretation possible. While clear rules should be the mainstay of legal rights, courts should have the flexibility to decide on a case-by-case basis the extent to which the dilution doctrine will protect brand names.

Our defense does not necessarily extend to the new propertization that has come about from legislative intervention, such as the Trademark Dilution Revision Act of 2006.[36] The statute overturned several common law rules limiting the protective effect of dilution doctrine.[37] Indeed, our defense of intellectual property law is grounded in the common law's flexibility to take trade-offs between static and dynamic costs into account in every single dispute. It is through such flexibility that an appropriately structured set of rules are derived. Recent legislative interventions have ousted the courts from their traditional function of developing trademark law and expanded protection in some instances beyond the level that would be consistent with a rational balancing of static and dynamic costs. This is one sense in which the propertization critique hits its target.

Another sense in which trademark law has reflected a property-law-like approach is a special context involving remedies. Under the common law, plaintiffs who had been injured or who were at risk of injury from trademark infringement could enjoin use of the mark by the second user. If they had suffered damages, they could also receive a damage award. There was also the possibility of a restitutionary award based on the unjust profits earned by the infringer.[38]

However, under the common law the restitutionary award was limited to those cases where the infringing party acted with intent to infringe.[39] In other words, the plaintiff could receive an *accounting,* or an award of the defendant's profits from infringement, only where the defendant knew of the prior use of the mark and attempted to use it for the evident purpose of exploiting the consumer goodwill developed by the first user. This feature of the law was very much like property law, which permits plaintiffs to receive a restitutionary award only where the trespasser has intentionally stripped assets from the property owner.[40]

Under the modern law based on the Lanham Act, the accounting award is available to the plaintiff even where the defendant has not acted with intent to undermine the mark.[41] In this sense, trademark has developed a very aggressive property-like approach by stripping gains from trademark infringers whether or not they acted with intent. This feature of the law is of questionable value, since it strips profits even from individuals who infringe innocently.[42] The one justification for this policy is that the Lanham Act includes a registration provision, which provides notice to all firms that wish to use a mark that has already been registered. One could argue that in the presence of a registry of marks, all cases of infringement are intentional or at least reckless.

Although we have said relatively little about the theory of remedies in our previous chapters, our remarks here apply with only minor variations to other topics of intellectual property. Compare trademarks to patents. In the trademark setting an injunction does not put the losing defendant out of business; all he has to do is change his mark and he can continue operating. The restitutionary award is a punitive remedy that strips the gains obtained by the infringer over the period of infringement, and thereby provides a powerful and appropriate disincentive to intentional wrongdoing. In the patent context, in contrast, an injunction threatens to put the defendant out of business and thereby gives the plaintiff an enormous bargaining advantage over the defendant. Armed with the threat of an injunction, the patent plaintiff can demand that the defendant hand over the gains he received from infringement in order to be allowed to stay in business. Given this, injunctions should be awarded less frequently in patent infringement lawsuits than in trademark infringement lawsuits. To be consistent with the theory of remedies set out here, injunctions should be awarded primarily in cases of unambiguously intentional infringement—because in those cases a punitive remedy provides the appropriate disincentives (i.e., taking away gains from theft). In the more general patent dispute, however, infringement may occur innocently, given the lack of notice with respect to many patent claims. In these more general cases, injunctions may not be appropriate, as the Supreme Court recognized in *eBay v. MercExchange*.[43]

Trade Dress

The trade dress cases reflect the economic principles we have examined in the trade name cases. Just as the law protects marks, it also protects the special design that a seller may adopt in order to distinguish his product from others.

This is an area in which the law has had to tread carefully. On the one hand, trade dress can be an even more important element in product identification than trademark. Anyone who looks for a particular brand of cola or of toothpaste or any other product comes to identify the brand with a specific color, design, and look. The way the product is packaged tends to be a consistent look that is intended simply and readily to convey an identification that the consumer can use as visible shorthand for the brand itself. The distinctive Tiffany blue box is identified with Tiffany jewelry and other Tiffany products. When other producers consciously imitate the trade dress of a competitor whose goods are sold in the same market, this can have the exact same effects as classic trademark infringement. Stores that have their own brand often design product packaging to mimic that of a successful brand and place the two next to each other, sometimes even alternating packages of different sizes of the store and name-brand products. Consumers then will purchase a product thinking it is the brand they are looking for, only to discover that the look-alike is a different brand from a different producer. The same considerations that support trademark protection, thus, can also support trade dress protection.

There is, however, an aspect of trade dress protection that must be carefully circumscribed if it is not to become an invitation to abuse. If a seller can use trademark law to prevent other sellers from adopting anything similar to his product design, he might find protecting that aspect of his enterprise preferable to seeking a patent. After all, it takes a substantial amount of money to obtain a patent, and the patent will be limited to twenty years. Once you have adopted a special mark or design, you do not have to invest anything into obtaining trademark protection (beyond registration), and the protection lasts forever. And, depending on how broad the scope of protection afforded trade dress, trade dress protection can be a broader deterrent to other sellers from entering the market with identical substitutes to your product. A liberal rule of protection for trade dress would lead to widespread monopolization of design-specific markets.

The law has dampened the potential for abuse by denying trade dress protection for any functional aspects of the seller's product, where function is understood broadly to cover utilitarian features.[44] The functionality exception reflects the law's effort to minimize the static costs of exclusion from trade dress protection. Still, because the exclusion costs are sufficiently higher in the context of trade dress than in ordinary trademark, the courts are warranted in providing the narrowest protection possible consistent with the prevention of fraudulent conduct.[45]

Of course, one could argue for liberal protection of trade dress on the ground that it would enhance incentives to create new products. But the overall experience of history goes against it. Many foreign countries have licensing regimes that effectively award monopoly rights to sellers who are friends of incumbent rulers.[46] Those regimes stay mired in poverty because the licensing rules block off innovation and competition. English common law rejected this approach to economic development in early cases such as *Darcy v. Allen*,[47] where the court stopped an effort to enforce a patent to sell playing cards in England. A liberal trade dress protection rule would reduce society's wealth by encouraging ever-expanding efforts to seek protection from competition.

Conclusion

Although the dilution doctrine has been criticized as an effort by courts to propertize trademarks, we think it is better understood as consistent with the trade-offs common law courts have long made between the static and dynamic costs of protecting the returns from effort and innovation. The modern dilution doctrine has evolved from the same utilitarian analyses underlying traditional unfair competition law and much of modern intellectual property doctrine. However, the statutory expansions of dilution doctrine are not necessarily defensible in our framework, because they do not always reflect a careful attempt to balance the costs and benefits of protection.

Our approach in this chapter has been to focus on the economic function of trademarks and the reasons for protecting them. Hotelling's analysis of competition sheds useful light on the costs and benefits of protecting trademarks. The optimal allocation of consumer search costs is unlikely to arise from the competitive process. Firms will attempt to grab the most desirable marks and to shunt new rivals to the boundary of the market. New entrants will tend to adopt marks as similar as possible, in their effects on consumers, to those of successful incumbents. Trademark law has evolved in the courts largely in response to these incentives.

8

Making IP Rights Work—Or Not

Between the Lines and Across Borders

Intellectual property rights are generally experienced as discrete topics: an inventor will go to a patent lawyer to protect his invention; a firm seeking to protect the identity of its brand will register its trademark; an author or publisher will look to copyright law for its protection; a company will look to trade secret law to protect important private information against disclosure to and use by its rivals. All of these areas share roots in property law, though some owe a great deal to tort, contract, and unfair competition law as well. But they generally are not thought of in practice as a group.

The different types of intellectual property rights, however, present related issues and at times intersect, requiring rules that draw boundaries between intellectual property rights regimes. All of them increasingly are located in global contexts, with international rules affecting the security of these rights. And all of them share as well the prospect that derogations in one intellectual property rights regime will diminish the protection of other rights, while strengthening one set of intellectual property protections will reinforce other rights. Finally, holders of all of the intellectual property rights discussed in earlier chapters share a similar defensive posture today, as both academic and practical developments have presented challenges to the basic underpinnings of intellectual property rights even as the express support for those rights has expanded. Some of the criticisms leveled at present law—and some of the recommendations for improving the law—suggest rather modest alterations that easily can be defended as conforming the law to the theoretical justifications for protecting intellectual property rights; in the language we've been using throughout this book, those are changes that improve the balance between static and dynamic costs. Some proposals, on the other hand, while put forward in terms of enforcing recognized limitations on intellectual property rights or of designing rights to reflect better the essential trade-offs between expanding use of innovations and encouraging innovations, threaten to unravel the structure of intellectual property protections.

This chapter explores several pivotal issues in modern intellectual property rights enforcement, starting with the boundary issues separating categories of intellectual property rights. It then moves to a different set of boundary issues, those presented by international law and the cross-border opportunities for infringing (or expanding) intellectual property rights. The chapter concludes with a brief exploration of issues that are at the forefront of current discussions about the way intellectual property rights work along with the risks and benefits of some better-known proposals for altering intellectual property rights.

International Property Rights' Boundaries

As we have seen, each intellectual property regime is designed in a way that balances the costs to society of protecting the particular type of information for longer or shorter times, in stronger or weaker ways, and with or without access to particular remedies. Because the different types of information are best protected in different ways—because the balance of static and dynamic costs differs for the different regimes—it is important to keep the boundaries between intellectual property regimes secure. To take one example, if the information that underlies a useful innovation (say a formula for a product) gained protection under copyright, would any writing that duplicates the formula violate the intellectual property right for the life of the author plus seventy years? Each of the different intellectual property rights regimes is set up as a collection of particular features for good reason. Even if one or another feature isn't exactly ideal, the basic designs fit fairly well with the measure of social good we've been using.

But some innovations don't fit obviously in one category. Consider, for instance, creative, decorative, or ornamental design elements that are attached to or incorporated in useful products. What regime should protect them? Patent? Copyright? Neither? Both?

Under U.S. law, design patents protect novel ornamental elements that are affixed to or part of useful products. The thought was that it made sense to have all aspects of innovation related to the same product protected under a single framework. Design patent protection does not extend for as long as copyright protection and costs more to obtain, but it provides more robust protection—for example, it protects against not just copying but also independent creation of the same (or very similar) design. Design patent rules do not completely track provisions for utility patents (for instance, having a term of fourteen years from the date of a patent grant rather than twenty years from filing) but provide benefits associated with patent that exceed those available under copyright. It is not obvious, however, that the innovation that design patents cover is best protected by the robust tools of patent law. In some circumstances, designs can also be protected by copyright, which may be a better fit with the sort of creative exercise involved in designing ornamental or decorative features for products (in terms of the modesty of the innovation fitting a more modest form of protection); but allowing designs to be covered simultaneously under both legal regimes could produce a complex of protections well beyond what is ideal for product design.

For many design features, the value of the design is tightly time limited. Tastes change, and the ability to ensure that a special design feature that requires creativity and investment to produce is not copied too completely, too quickly, has social value, but not the same sort of value that is associated with the protection of more durable sorts of inventiveness and creativity. Further, when the actual products for which design patents have issued are considered, it appears that yet another intellectual property regime may be in play. Some of the most durable designs covered by design patents—such as the classic Coca-Cola bottle—represent creativity of a very different sort than, say, the invention of a new computer and generate value in a different way. The principal value for many of these designs is more in the nature of an identifier akin to trademark or trade dress. Like the Tiffany blue box (a color trademark), the real significance is signaling to the consumer that this is a product from a particular source. The potential overlap with so many different intellectual property regimes with different rules presents opportunities for inconsistent outcomes, highlighting the importance of clear rules marking the boundaries between regimes.

Boundary issues have also been a long-running problem in the world of computing and will only increase as hardware and software become less distinct as computation becomes an increasingly ubiquitous feature of products (not just computers, but phones, cars, watches, switches, and so on). This and other evolutions of technology make it less easy to cabin creative-expressive from inventive-practical activity. Since 1980, software has been protected by copyright in the United States, despite the obvious connection to a useful product. Software is designed to make computers work, but the product cycles tend to be short and the special contributions to creativity often are relatively small differences or advances over prior work. The distinctive expression is important to how computers not only function but also to their look and feel to users. While not classic expressive creativity, new software does take what can be an enormous investment. Copyright protection safeguards against copying by reverse engineering and does this without time-consuming requirements for securing protection (which would necessarily attend software patents) in ways that are more consistent with the time-value of the creation. Software may not have looked initially like an obvious fit with copyright, but the regime has provided a reasonable set of protections without exaggerating the scope of what would constitute infringement. The question remains, however, whether in some circumstances alternative protection through patent for exceptionally novel advances in software makes sense. As more products are governed by the way hardware and software interact, the question of what is the right framework for software protection—where the boundary should be between patent and copyright—will necessarily recur in new settings.

Yet another boundary issue arises in the choice between trademark and copyright for protecting literary characters. As the law has evolved, both regimes have been given roles for safeguarding the creative investment that produces memorable characters from Sam Spade to Harry Potter. Copyright protects not only the exact words describing characters but also the detailed aspects of the character's nature, at least if the description given is detailed enough (a distinction going back at least as far as Learned Hand's 1930 opinion for the Second Circuit in *Nichols v. Universal Pictures Corporation*).[1] While authors are free to develop in later works the characters they create in one work without violating copyright, others who take the more well-defined and distinctive attributes of the character for their own works risk a finding of infringement. At the same time, the fact that much of the nature of a character consists of ideas as much as expression leaves a great deal out of the protected zone.

There is, however, separate protection for literary characters under the heading of trademark or literary service marks. The essential idea is that it diminishes the value of the creative enterprise to, for example, use the name Superman for a very un-super character, or Batman to depict a character who is quite unlike the well-known comic hero, or to trade on the fame of Sherlock Holmes in ways at odds with Sir Arthur Conan Doyle's image of that character. The dilution of that brand is protected by trademark rather than copyright. In this case, the two regimes of trademark and copyright provide complementary protection to different aspects of the creative enterprise. While the current rules mark out sensible lines of protection for each body of law, there always is a risk of expanding protection in the combined sets of rules to the point that it interferes with such a broad swath of follow-on creative enterprise that its costs exceed the value of the protection. The risk of overprotection—or of underprotection—inevitably increases when different bodies of law address related aspects of a single creative process.

Where a given form of creativity lies at the boundary of different intellectual property regimes, the goal is to select a mode of protection that clearly applies to the particular form, that provides a positive balance between static and dynamic costs, and that avoids the administrative costs associated with trying to divide different parts of the protection function among different legal schemes. At the same time, it is not advisable to create a large number of specific legal systems for protecting hull design, or cartoon characters, or some other particular intellectual property format. The cost of having numerous specific regimes will increase as technology evolves, requiring new legal forms as the creative enterprise produces types of innovative product that do not readily fit an existing specific regime. In other words, living with the boundary issues presented by the current set of protective regimes is probably less costly—even if a particular type of innovative work will not be readily assignable to only one intellectual property system—than having a series of new specific systems.

Beyond the Borders

International Piracy and Counterfeiting

Although courts, legislatures, and administrative agencies in each country can do a tolerably good job of working out the rules for each form of intellectual property and of locating the boundaries that separate them, that is not enough to secure good outcomes in a global economy. As trade and communication have expanded, opportunities for compromising intellectual property rights have expanded apace. Patent protection does little good if products can be reverse engineered and manufactured in nations that don't respect foreign patent rights. Copyright does little good if piracy is rampant in nations that have no stake in ensuring that foreign copyrights are protected. Trademark law does little good when marks are copied with impunity elsewhere and passed off as the legitimate goods.

In today's marketplace, copying is far easier than ever before. The problem is not confined to photocopying publications or downloading copies of musical performances or making unauthorized reproductions of movies and other entertainment media or of software. All of these violations of copyright increasingly can be accomplished cheaply and often with high-quality copies. But copying exists as well in auto part designs, in trademarked luxury goods, and in medicines.

Some of these are high-quality copies that are made cheaply with stolen designs and at times with stolen materials as well. Others are tragically defective. In Africa, copies of vaccines often are sold with little or none of the necessary active ingredients, leading to hundreds of thousands of unnecessary deaths each year.[2] While far more common in Africa, the problem of ineffective or harmful drug counterfeits affects advanced nations as well. In the United States, for example, almost one hundred Americans died in a few months in the winter of 2007–2008 from reactions to a blood-thinning medicine, heparin, manufactured in China using a sulfate compound in place of the active ingredient for heparin.[3] The substitute ingredient cost only one percent as much as the real thing—and it caused deaths instead of saving lives.

In some nations, copying is a lucrative business that is pursued because the benefits are largely captured within the country while the costs are mainly visited on rights-holders and others outside the country. In other instances, intellectual property rights are infringed privately but endemically by individuals trying to get something for less money, more quickly, or more easily than would be the case there if intellectual property rights were respected. And sometimes the lines blur between turning a blind eye to criminal enterprises and failing to suppress rampant, small-scale (but in combination, economically important) piracy.

Reports have linked large-scale drug counterfeiting operations to terrorist groups such as al-Qaeda, the Irish Republican Army, ETA, and Hezbollah as well as to organized crime organizations from Russia, China, Colombia, and other nations.[4] Worldwide, counterfeit or pirated products account for more than $600 billion in sales per year, or roughly 7 percent of the world market.[5] In China and Russia pirated software reportedly accounted for 90 percent of all software in use as recently as 2005, with similar astronomical rates of piracy in the fields of music and motion picture recordings (DVDs).[6] Nor was the problem confined to the obvious sources: consider that when the Chinese government announced a crackdown on the use of pirated software, its primary commitment was reducing piracy rates for the government's own computers.[7] Beyond that, the nature of piracy in a world of increasingly inexpensive copying and global communications presents major intellectual property rights-holders with a growing and changing menu of problems to address. Despite successes in reducing the suspected rates of piracy in China and Russia, global rates of piracy and losses from it continue to rise.[8]

Piracy of American firms' software and entertainment, of course, isn't just a problem in places like China or Russia or Vietnam. Core intellectual property industries in the United States sustain large financial losses each year from piracy at home. Even though the violations occur at a lower rate than in many other nations, the total value of losses is huge. Consider, for instance, a report by the Business Software Alliance concluding that while the United States has the lowest piracy rate for computer software of any nation—with roughly 20 percent of the software in use being pirated—it generated more than $9 billion in losses to software firms in 2008.[9] That figure was more than one-sixth of total losses worldwide and more than one-third higher than the losses attributed to China, which held second place in that ranking.[10]

Much of the focus of enforcement of U.S. intellectual property rights is on infringement of those rights at home. The investment in enforcement is seen in everyday events, such as the reminder that the cola you ordered has a particular trade name (as in, "we serve Coke" or "we serve Pepsi products"—responding to ongoing efforts by major brands to prevent restaurants from passing off other products as theirs). The concern over domestic infringements is seen as well in highly publicized crackdowns on unauthorized photocopying on college campuses or on sharing of copyrighted music compositions over peer-to-peer networks like Grokster (as part of a process of reproducing those works). But the problems associated with violations of intellectual property rights cannot be addressed solely by focusing on domestic enforcement.

International Accords

Although the scope of international piracy and counterfeiting today may be unparalleled, the underlying problem of international recognition of property rights—especially rights in property so peculiarly vulnerable to taking in remote settings as intellectual property—is not new. That is why nations most concerned with protecting their citizens' intellectual property rights have long agreed on common rules to safeguard those rights.

One of the first international agreements to protect intellectual property was the Paris Convention for the Protection of Industrial Property, dating from 1883, which set up a system of mutual recognition and respect for member nations' patent and trademark rights based on the concept of "national treatment."[11] Three years later, the Berne Convention for the Protection of Literary and Artistic Works set up a different arrangement for international protection of works protected by copyright or its rough analogue, *droit d'auteur*.[12] The Berne accord provided both a national treatment leg and a minimum set of protections that have to be given to foreign rightsholders, regardless of the existing domestic law.

While both the Paris and Berne conventions have played important roles in promoting international respect for intellectual property rights rooted in the laws of other nations, both schemes rely on other countries (meaning the nations' political leaders) to recognize their mutual interest in agreeing to protect intellectual property. From one vantage, that shouldn't present a problem. Even nations that produce relatively little legally protectable intellectual property of their own should be interested in supporting foreign intellectual property rights. After all, intellectual property rights-holders feel confident exporting products that embody those rights to nations that respect them, which supports access to more cutting-edge products in those foreign markets. The other side of that coin is that disrespect for intellectual property rights, as for other property, leads to a withdrawal of products that reflect high investment in the sorts of R&D that can be readily appropriated (including many types of intellectual property, though not including some of the information protected by trade secret law).[13] For those reasons, nearly all nations should be interested in participating in the Berne and Paris regimes.[14]

Two factors, however, have compromised that promise. The first is that political leaders often are advantaged by promoting policies that are not fully congruent with their nation's best interests. Any but the most utopian theories of governance understands that individual politicians act in ways that reflect their own self-interest. That self-interest often correlates with the interests of well-placed or well-funded groups or intensely interested individuals who favor policies that don't fit what we would regard as cogent proxies for public good. It doesn't have to be that way—private good and public good can go hand-in-hand. But political processes typically skew public decision-making in ways that depart from broader public welfare, judged by any respectable test. Public choice analysis, social welfare accounts, interest group theories of government—all of these explanations of how government works reach the same general conclusion.[15]

As these theories predict, the public interest in respect for intellectual property rights (primarily in order to gain greater access to products that embody the innovations protected by intellectual property rights) is unlikely to be fully reflected in public policies. Intense interests of groups that want access to products now at low prices—prices predicated on the marginal costs of production without the already "sunk" costs of R&D—can produce political pressure to depart from a policy of respect for intellectual property rights that is more beneficial to an importing nation in the long run.

Similarly, businesses (read: politically active business executives and workers' representatives) can make it attractive to politicians to lower protections for foreign competitors' intellectual property. Lowered protection for intellectual property rights—for instance, by allowing domestic competitors to appropriate a successful foreign firm's trademark or to use patent rights without compensation or to copy a protected design—effectively raises the cost to a foreign business of entering the market. The business then has to consider whether the risk to its intellectual property portfolio is worth the expected gains from sales in the particular market. Often, the risk is great enough that firms withhold their most advanced products. But that decision is just what the local competitors hope for; it puts them on a more even footing with the overseas rival. That may be helpful to a particular local business, but it almost always reduces national welfare by far more than the gain to the protected business.[16]

The political case for protecting intellectual property rights is very much like the case for open trade. Generally, open trade benefits a nation. Having access to the broadest range of products from around the world benefits consumers directly and serves national interests.[17] But the benefits are spread widely across the population, while the harm to individuals and businesses disadvantaged by the competition are more concentrated and visible. That's why politics almost everywhere is tilted too much against openness to imports.[18] There doesn't have to be any direct quid pro quo from import-competing interests to make politicians understand that they can secure political gains from selected interventions to restrict trade. The result is too much trade restriction.[19]

The same result holds for restricting protections of intellectual property rights, for much the same reason. In many countries domestic political forces tilt government decision-making to providing too little protection of foreign-held intellectual property rights. While the benefits of greater protection for intellectual property tend to be diffuse and relatively invisible, immediate costs associated with respect for foreign intellectual property rights often are highly concentrated and visible. Not only does that make it easier to mobilize political forces in opposition to intellectual property protections; it also provides a reason to believe that political players without a prior view on the matter will be more readily persuaded to favor cutting back foreign intellectual property rights than expanding them.

The political advantage to taking intellectual property from foreign rights-holders explains much of the controversy today over the international enforcement of intellectual property rights. It also explains the historic reluctance of the U.S. government to join certain international intellectual property accords during the time when the United States was a net importer of intellectual property. Indeed, while the United States acceded to the Paris Convention in 1883, it did not accede to the Berne Convention until 1989 (more than one hundred years after its negotiation and initial entry into force for signatory nations) and has been late to the party for other international intellectual property accords as well.[20] Although current U.S. holders of intellectual property rights understandably view it as irrelevant that the American government for many years took positions hostile to international enforcement of (some) intellectual property rights, the American history here also understandably is one that less developed nations see as signaling that the nation's present rights-friendly posture is borne of self-interest, not principle.[21] Worse, the lesson drawn by some foreign leaders from America's history on this score is that less developed nations are well advised to give short shrift to claims from foreigners for intellectual property protection until that is essential to protect a large body of their own intellectual property.

The second factor inhibiting effectiveness of arrangements like the Paris and Berne conventions is this: international agreements limited to a specific subject, such as protection of rights associated with foreign patents or trademarks or copyrights, rarely have serious enforcement provisions. Many, indeed, have no clear enforcement provision at all. Those that do typically are restricted to enforcement options closely tied to the subject matter.

As a practical matter, a voluntary agreement among sovereign nations dealing with patent rights is not going to be enforced through mechanisms having to do with troop placement or numbers of nuclear-armed missiles any more than a missile reduction treaty would be enforced by permitting more greenhouse gas emissions. A common result is that the real enforcement mechanism is the threat to withdraw from the treaty arrangement or to suspend reciprocal treaty rights of a nation found to be in violation of the particular accord. When the violating nation has little stake in the subject matter of the accord—at least little direct stake for the political leaders charged with effectuating the treaty—those mechanisms are of extremely limited value. That is one of the reasons that many scholars regard "international law" as something distinct from the ordinary conception of "law" as a set of binding rules, obedience to which can be compelled—or failing that, transgressions punished—for individuals and entities within the rules' ambit.[22]

In keeping with this system, violations of the Paris accords are theoretically matters for determination and sanction by the International Court of Justice (ICJ). Compliance with decisions of that body, however, is effectively a matter of national indulgence. Nations, including the United States, are reluctant to commit to rules that directly and fully implement adverse decisions of international bodies such as the ICJ. Even when a national government favors implementation of an adverse ICJ ruling, the absence of such rules may frustrate that end.

The recent experience of the United States in the *Medellín v. Texas* case is exemplary.[23] The U.S. government endeavored to give effect to an ICJ decision requiring consular notification regarding criminal proceedings against foreign nationals that potentially carried capital punishment. The underlying treaty provision, however, was deemed non-self-executing, and in the absence of either self-execution (admittedly a poor phrase in the context of a capital punishment case!) or national legislation implementing the provision, the Court concluded there was no ground in U.S. law to overrule state law (and state court determinations) on the basis of an ICJ decision. While the ICJ later declared that this violated international rules regarding treaty implementation,[24] it is not an uncommon result in domestic adjudications where treaties are invoked.

The Berne Convention had even weaker enforcement provisions—in fact, it did not specify a legal enforcement mechanism. When the effective sanction for violation of an international accord is withdrawal of rights to reciprocal protection under the accord (in this case, the protection of copyrights for that nation's citizens), that provides only the weakest incentive for public officials in nations with very little domestic intellectual property to respect treaty obligations. That explains why the more significant deterrents to disrespect for such obligations have been extra-legal mechanisms, such as jawboning by nations with larger economic or military muscle.[25] For political leaders of nations with little to protect under a copyright treaty, there still may be advantage to keeping favor of more powerful nations concerned with this issue.

The absence of express legal means for treaty enforcement, however, requires the political leaders of copyright-sensitive nations to decide when it is worth deploying limited "chits" to secure compliance with copyright treaty obligations. If the U.S. military establishment wants a base located in a nation with weak intellectual property protections, does the U.S. government forgo an opportunity to secure greater intellectual property protection in order to gain favorable action on the base? If the foreign service establishment wants to have support on an initiative respecting protection of consular officials, does it have a better chance of gaining that support if it doesn't press for full compliance with copyright obligations? These are the sorts of considerations that necessarily weaken the prospects for using the tools available to larger powers to actually secure full respect for internationally accepted intellectual property rights.

TRIPS: Marrying Intellectual Property Rights to Trade
The practical weakness of international treaty protections for intellectual property rights in a world of global trade and cheap copying led nations with substantial intellectual property portfolios in the 1980s and 1990s to press for a different solution. Intellectual property rights-holders recognized that widespread political sensitivity to maintaining access to export markets presented an opportunity: they proposed bringing the intellectual property rights regime inside the international trade regime. Eligibility for favorable trade treatment (which, in the political world, means lower tariffs on or barriers to exports) then would depend on agreement to abide by certain minimum standards for intellectual property protection.

While that change would provide an obvious inducement for nations with less interest in and respect for intellectual property protections to sign on to the agreement, more developed nations doubted that this would be enough—and the strong resistance from less developed nations to the proposed addition of an intellectual property leg to the trade stool confirmed that. The solution adopted was to require accession to the intellectual property accord, named the Agreement on Trade-Related Aspects of Intellectual Property (TRIPS), as a condition for membership in the World Trade Organization (WTO), gateway to the global trade system.[26] The result, from 1994 on, has been to broaden membership in the club of nations nominally committed to intellectual property rights protection and willing to sign up not just to a promise of equal treatment for all but also to a set of basic intellectual property standards.

More important, the change from single-purpose intellectual property conventions to a set of protections for all types of intellectual property integrated into the world trade regime has provided a better prospect for real enforcement of intellectual property rights. Critical to the negotiation of the TRIPS agreement was its assimilation into an enhanced enforcement (dispute resolution) process for the WTO.[27] The enforcement process continues to present disputes on a nation-to-nation footing (in contrast to the ability of individuals and commercial enterprises to initiate dispute-settlement proceedings under agreements such as the North American Free Trade Agreement (NAFTA) or the Convention on the Settlement of Investment Disputes between States and Nationals of Other States (the ICSID Convention).[28] That fact implicates some level of continued political trade-off in decisions on enforcing TRIPS provisions. At the same time, the creation of a separate enforcement process under the trade law aegis changes the calculus somewhat, making it more likely that rights will be enforced than if that depended entirely on negotiation within an open-ended bilateral frame.

As even the few statistics offered earlier in this chapter on the scope of international intellectual property derogations indicate, the TRIPS framework—however helpful it may be—has not ended problems of international intellectual property piracy and counterfeiting. In fact, even if TRIPS has helped slow the rate of growth in this burgeoning business, it has not (at least not yet) brought about a contraction in international infringements of intellectual property rights. Decisions within the WTO-TRIPS dispute resolution framework—on issues in Chinese law that insufficiently address problems of piracy and counterfeiting there, for example, or on India's failure to protect pharmaceutical and chemical products—reveal just the tip of this particular iceberg. Intellectual property rights-holders continue to be concerned about the extent to which their investments in innovation are at risk, asking for additional protections in bilateral treaties and increased pressure on intellectual-property-importing nations to enforce intellectual property rights.

Despite the fact that international piracy and counterfeiting continue to expand, the creation of even a modest set of potentially effective responses from intellectual property rights-holders against international infringements has proved disquieting to a range of public and private voices: nations that are intellectual property importers; intellectual property rights skeptics; outright opponents of strong intellectual property protections; advocates for specific, short-term derogations from intellectual property rights in order to further other goals; and antagonists of the basic property rights system on which intellectual property rights build. That is part of the story taken up below.

Problems and Solutions: Updating or Undoing Intellectual Property Law

In addition to the ongoing tug of war between those with immediate interests in expanding or contracting particular intellectual property rights, the current intellectual property landscape is notable for the intensity and variety of arguments among a wider array of observers over the proper shape of intellectual property rights. Some of the arguments ask whether the present laws setting parameters for intellectual property rights need adjusting in light of particular features of legal systems within which enforcement of those rights takes place. Some of the arguments ask whether we need to reconceptualize parts of the intellectual property system if we are to properly balance the social interests that system is supposed to serve—to replace some of what we now do to encourage innovation with different mechanisms better designed to strike the right balance between static and dynamic costs. And some of the arguments make pleas for exceptions to the current rules in ways that threaten to unravel the entire system of intellectual property rights.

System Design and Legal Process

While many intellectual property rights advocates focus on the expanding scope of piracy and counterfeiting, critics of the present system note that protections for intellectual property rights-holders have expanded over recent years. Copyright terms have lengthened; patentable subject matter has expanded; new protections against trademark dilution have been legislated.

More troubling for some rights skeptics, the sheer number of protected works has grown exponentially over the past several decades. Professor Lessig, among others, makes much of the interference that the burgeoning numbers of protected works cause, explaining, for example, the impediments put in the way of a team producing a retrospective on Clint Eastwood's career.[29] The same issues are faced by movie producers who must secure clearances for all of the songs, products, and references that might impinge on someone else's right. Arrangements can be devised that reduce the costs associated with the rights-clearance process. Small-value, high-volume inter-actions for rights associated with performance of copyrighted music have been worked out through copyright collectives such as the American Society of Composers and Producers, for example.[30] But the current situation leaves some potential users of copyrighted work frustrated at the administrative cost of dealing with so many clearances.

The problem posed by the volume of protected works is similar on the patent side for some products. With some rapidly advancing technologies, it is common for products to incorporate hundreds of components, any one of which might be similar to one covered by a patent. If relatively insignificant components that do not represent major advances (but that arguably infringe patent rights) are incorporated into complex products, each patent holder potentially could hold up the distribution of the larger products—and poten-tially extract sums far in excess of the ex ante value of the component's contribution.

The ultimate outcome of litigation between Research in Motion (maker of Blackberry mobile phones, heavily used by the U.S. government) and NTP, Inc., is often invoked as the paradigm for this problem.[31] NTP sued RIM for patent infringement, won in federal district court, and obtained an injunc-tion that would have shuttered Blackberry service in the United States. Although the injunction was suspended during negotiations between the litigants, the judge made clear that he was not going to deny injunctive relief just to avoid the problems that it would cause Blackberry users. NTP won a huge settlement (almost twenty times the amount the judge fixed as the rea-sonable value of royalties for the infringed patents), even as its patents were being reviewed and rejected as invalid by examiners in the U.S. Patent and Trademark Office.[32] The difference represents the value of continuing Black-berry service; that is a value that anyone able to secure injunctive relief pre-sumably could extract.

The concern over this sort of hold-up prospect has (at least in part) moti-vated changes in the remedies available to patent holders in the United States. In *e-Bay Inc. v. MercExchange, L.L.C.*,[33] the U.S. Supreme Court over-turned a lower court decision that had been based on the presumption that injunctions should be available for patent infringement except in unusual cases. The Court instead instructed judges to weigh the traditional factors used to decide whether to issue injunctions in all sorts of cases:

> That test requires a plaintiff to demonstrate: (1) that it has suffered an irreparable injury; (2) that remedies available at law are inadequate to compensate for that injury; (3) that considering the balance of hardships between the plaintiff and defendant, a remedy in equity is warranted; and (4) that the public interest would not be disserved by a permanent injunction.[34]

That instruction signaled a change in the way many courts handled injunctions in patent cases.[35]

The Court might have used the case, which involved patents on the "buy now" process for online auctions, to address problems with business method patents.[36] Although the line between business method patents and other patents can be thin, overall the class of business method patents—patents describing new ways of performing particular business functions rather than of producing a new product or compound—broadly differs from standard patent fare.

Business method patents have several characteristics that raise questions about their suitability for patent protection. They tend to describe practices that are relatively low on inventiveness, that directly help the businesses that use them, that are sensitive to the way in which they are implemented as much as to the concept, and that if subject to patent protections could seriously interfere with an array of common sense business practices. Consider, for example, a patent described as "a method and system for administering a loyalty marketing program (i.e., frequent buyer program) by using a government-issued identification card, such as a driver's license, as the frequent buyer redemption card."[37]

Giving injunctions against conduct that resembles such practices is apt to generate high costs without comparable off-setting benefits. Injunctions in these cases combine the sort of holdout costs identified in the small component-complex product case and costs associated with too broad an ambit for patentable subject matters.[38]

Recent court decisions seem increasingly sensitive to this imbalance in costs and benefits.[39] In particular, a decision from the Court of Appeals for the Federal Circuit substantially cut back on the scope of innovations eligible for business method patents.[40] The Supreme Court, in *Bilski v. Kappos*,[41] however, reversed the lower court decision, finding that there was no basis in the text of the law for treating business method patents differently from other patents; but the decision emphasized aspects of the ordinary tests for patentability, such as novelty and nonobviousness, that, applied critically, could result in far fewer successful applications for business method patents.

Even if sound statutory construction, the Court's decision creates the risk that its analysis will spill over to other areas—in other words, that future decisions seeking to avoid the harms associated with business method patents will apply restrictive tests for novelty and nonobviousness elsewhere. Similarly, concerns over the use of injunctions in settings like the RIM-NTP conflict or the dispute in *e-Bay Inc. v. MercExchange* threaten to expand into other contexts where the same concerns are not present.

One place where the concern over injunctions has not affected decisions on patent remedies is the U.S. International Trade Commission (ITC). The ITC has jurisdiction over complaints about patent infringements embodied in products imported into the United States. These complaints present essentially the same questions as district court patent litigation: the validity of the patent, construction of its claims, and whether the patent is infringed by the accused products. The ITC, which now decides 7 to 10 percent of all patent cases in the United States, does not have authority to award damages to patent owners but does have authority to issue "exclusion orders," which are a form of injunctive relief. The ITC has rebuffed contentions that, following *e-Bay*, it should shift from a presumption in favor of exclusion orders to something resembling the Supreme Court's four-factor test, and the Federal Circuit has confirmed that view.[42] Given the frequency with which patent disputes involve imported products, this sets up a two-track system, where patent owners will seek damages in the district courts and injunctive relief in the ITC.

At the end of the day, the system of intellectual property rights enforcement must be seen as part of the broader legal system. If the legal system efficiently parses good claims from bad, provides proper incentives for filing legally sound claims, and deals sensibly with remedial issues, the risk of holdups and the costs associated with litigation can be minimized. Flaws in any of these areas, on the other hand, will exacerbate problems within the intellectual property rights system.

Limits in Theory and Practice: Pools, Prizes, and Prescience
One of the persistent questions in the realm of intellectual property law—perhaps the central theoretical issue for design of intellectual property rights—concerns the way to conceive the balance between the incentives for innovation and the costs of awarding property rights. We have repeatedly adverted to the division between the dynamic and static effects of the law, which is one way of thinking about this issue. Other scholars have taken different approaches. Some have suggested that the starting point should be a presumption that creators are entitled to the same sort of rights to their property in all fields, whether the property is an invention, a painting, a musical composition, or a crop of wheat produced by the individual's labor and ingenuity. Some have questioned the whole notion of property rights in information and ideas. And many who are trained in or conversant with economics have framed the issue as locating the ideal trade-off between creation and production.

The idea underlying this last way of looking at the question typically is put this way: a reward is needed to secure novel inventions and artistic creations, but production that uses the innovative idea should be organized so as to permit sales at the marginal cost of production.[43] That is, the team of scientists at Pfizer, for example, should be encouraged to come up with new, life-saving drugs like Lipitor, but then ideally anyone should be able to produce the drug so that it can be sold at exactly the cost of the materials and labor (excluding the R&D costs). This is the understanding that, explicitly or implicitly, underlies a large and growing body of suggestions for changing the terms of intellectual property laws.[44]

John Duffy has thoughtfully discussed this set of writings in the broader context of the historic debate between Harold Hotelling and Ronald Coase over the proper way to think about public utility regulation.[45] Duffy points out the connection between modern proposals for intellectual property rights and Hotelling's argument for government subventions designed to relieve utilities of their fixed costs and permit marginal cost pricing of their operations. Coase persuasively rebutted Hotelling, urging that the government subsidies would have worse consequences than prices that exceed marginal cost. In declining-cost industries, those prices will be the norm and market forces will function in ways that constrain their ill effects, leaving government regulation of utilities a more limited role. Duffy rightly observes that Coase's argument decisively carried the day in the field of public utilities but has largely been ignored by recent writings in the intellectual property field.

This is most evident in calls to use innovation prizes in place of patents to induce investment in innovation, which then theoretically would allow production of the innovation to be priced at marginal cost. There are numerous versions of this proposal, many from quite thoughtful scholars. Some incorporate clever mechanisms to reduce incentive problems that accompany the simplest prize proposals. But all generate costs from substitution of central price setting for market price setting. That is the critical problem introduced by the use of prizes. After all, prize amounts have to be fixed in a way that will induce the appropriate investment in pursuing innovation. Information needed to do this almost never will be available to a central authority, certainly not in advance of the innovation's disclosure.

The patent system works on the principle that individuals whose own time, money, and energies are at stake will make better decisions on the optimal investments in innovation if the prize for success is whatever a market for the innovation will return than if the prize is a governmentally determined sum. There are good reasons to doubt that innovators will pick the socially optimal amount to invest, given the risks associated with innovative work, the winner-take-all returns from patent races, and the uncertainty regarding the progress being made by others competing in R&D. Yet, the current system does not generate the same risks of rent-seeking and associated resource misallocation problems, which add enormously to the costs of prize system alternatives. As Professor Duffy recognizes, the same considerations that were decisive in Coase's views prevailing over Hotelling in utility regulation should support greater reliance on markets and individual decision-making in the world of intellectual property as well.[46]

Another set of proposals is even more problematic. Several commentators have called for increased use of patent pools, arrangements that allow two or more rights-holders to share control over their patents and royalty revenues from the patents. The typical patent pool addresses a situation in which numerous patents potentially could block research or commercial activity that all of the patent holders want to facilitate though none wants to give up their patent rights. The patent pool is a solution to that problem.

The simplest case resembles the classic "Prisoner's Dilemma," a staple of game theory.[47] In the Prisoner's Dilemma, two prisoners are given the following choice. If neither talks, there is insufficient evidence to punish them for a serious offense but both will be prosecuted for, and likely found guilty of, a relatively minor offense (carrying a probable one-year sentence). If one talks and the other does not, the helpful prisoner will get no jail time while the recalcitrant prisoner will receive the maximum punishment, a ten-year sentence. If both talk, they will both receive consideration for their cooperation and be recommended for reduced, three-year sentences. Obviously, the ideal solution for the prisoners is for both to remain silent (guaranteeing at most a one-year sentence and, depending on the variant of the problem presented, perhaps no punishment at all), but they are forbidden from communicating with one another. Without any ready mechanism for agreeing on a mutual, cooperative strategy, each one is better off talking to forestall a draconian punishment.

In the patent realm, without cooperation, there has to be costly negotiation regarding the rights to proceed with activity that might later be found to infringe someone else's patent. Where a large number of relatively low-value patents held by two firms potentially could derail their important research or commercial ventures, the two firms face essentially the same problem as the prisoners. Neither firm would unilaterally give up its patent rights without an agreement; but if both hold to their rights, neither will be able to engage in the potentially more valuable activity that makes use of the rights. In this setting, the firms are likely to agree to pool the relevant patents so that both could use them.

The real-world problem comes when the set of potentially blocking patents is larger and so is the number of patent holders. As the set of players and patents grows, the possible asymmetries in both value of the patents and returns to their use grow as well. Patent pools can work within some bounds but will not be helpful if the values become too heterogeneous.

Recent proposals for overcoming this problem in order to facilitate research, development, and utilization of important advances, especially in health-related fields, have suggested government-sponsored patent pools as the answer.[48] However, these pools, which would not be voluntary, would not overcome a Prisoner's Dilemma so much as they would constitute the exercise of eminent domain powers. These forms of patent pools engender the static costs associated with the need to value appropriately the rights transferred in advance or, alternatively, the dynamic costs of essentially appropriating part of the rights' value. Inevitably, the proposals also would encourage rent-seeking activity, lobbying government to create pools to take property prized by politically influential groups. Those costs would inflate the social losses from these initiatives, both in their direct expenses and in the secondary distortions of investment they produce.

Compulsory Licensing: The Camel's Nose[49]

The sort of problems associated with various property rules, like the hold-out problem discussed above, are addressed in various ways with respect to different types of property. For real property, the hold-out problem arises when there is a compelling public need for an aggregation of properties held by a large number of owners (think, for example, of a community that has decided to set aside land for a reservoir or a military base).[50] The Anglo-Saxon legal solution is the law of eminent domain, which allows governments to take private property in exchange for reasonable compensation.[51]

Although reasonableness is subject to judicial assessment, there is a strong incentive for the government officials (and for the interest groups that often are moving forces behind projects invoking eminent domain powers) to provide too little compensation.[52] If the sale is voluntary, the owner and buyer set the price at which both believe they are receiving good value. If the sale is compelled, the buyer sets the price unilaterally, hardly an inducement to pay what the seller would want. Imagine the difference between getting to set the purchase price for your next new car at what you think is a reasonable price as opposed to having to persuade the car dealer.

The exclusive right to control the terms of access to property (including its sale) remains a critical defense against conduct that impinges on the best uses of the property and the incentives for investing in its discovery, development, and upkeep. For that reason, there has been great concern over the bounds the law sets around the occasions for invoking eminent domain. While these bounds have been loosened over the past half-century, some tightening has occurred in the past twenty years,[53] and the Supreme Court's most recent failure to continue that trend sparked a firestorm of popular protest justices won't soon forget.[54]

Intellectual property law also provides a very limited scope for interventions that limit the rights-holders' control over use of the property. Most of these interventions go under the heading of "compulsory licensing," a term rooted in concern that a patent owner would gain rights to a new technology but then not put it into use (or put it into such limited use that it effectively was the equivalent of not "working" the patent). Failure to "work" the patent essentially voids the trade-off underlying patent protection, which uses exclusive rights as the inducement to innovate and put the innovation into productive use. For that reason, a failure to work is viewed as akin to a breach of contract, providing a ground for government intervention to compel the patent holder either to begin production of goods using the patent or license someone else to do so, a compulsory license. Yet even in these circumstances, before permitting compulsory licensing, the law invariably requires some showing of need and that the patent holder has unreasonably declined to address the issue.[55]

A variant of this ground for invoking compulsory licensing addresses settings in which inventions of critical public interest are withheld from public use. In U.S. law, both the Atomic Energy Act and the Clean Air Act contain provisions that arguably fit this description. The Atomic Energy Act provides the possibility of compulsory licensing for patents that the U.S. Atomic Energy Commission (now subsumed within the U.S. Department of Energy) deems of special importance to the creation or utilization of nuclear material if the government also determines that the mission of the Act cannot be achieved without the license.[56] In the more than fifty years since the legislation was enacted, however, the government has never invoked it to grant a compulsory license. Section 308 of the Clean Air Act likewise provides a theoretical, but never-used, authorization for compulsory license of patents essential to accomplishing the environmental goals of the Act and for which no alternative technology exists.[57]

In both instances, the critical nature of the technology is not enough. Both provisions require a showing that the patent has been withheld from the use at issue. Although withholding a patent from a specific critical use is not as drastic as a complete "failure to work" a patent—the traditional requirement for compulsory licensing—it is close. The limited nature of the compulsory licensing provisions and, even more, the government's failure to utilize them to impose such licenses over long periods of time generates minimal risks to innovation incentives (low dynamic costs) and has not apparently given rise to significant costs in preventing critical uses of relevant patents (static costs).

Another circumstance in which the law provides for compulsory licensing occurs where there is a collective-action problem, as can happen at times in the copyright realm. The problem, discussed earlier in this chapter, occurs when there are many holders of intellectual property rights that are only modestly valued for particular uses and many potential users, so that the costs of identifying the relevant rights-holders and negotiating terms for use can exceed the value of the use. Both groups—rights-holders and potential users—gain from creating a way to reduce these transaction costs. Form contracts and entities that allow pooling of rights ("copyright collectives" like ASCAP) can help solve this problem. Still, a few laws contain compulsory licensing provisions to address these situations. U.S. law, for example, contains compulsory licensing provisions for certain audio recordings and for broadcast television programs that are retransmitted over cable television.[58]

These compulsory licensing provisions rest on substantial economic justifications and are circumscribed in ways that maintain the balance of costs that generally characterizes major aspects of intellectual property law. International law, by and large, has followed the same course as domestic law respecting compulsory licensing for intellectual property. In fact, international law historically has been careful to place limits on even the modest grounds for compulsory licensing recognized domestically. So, for example, the Paris Convention states that "a compulsory license . . . based on failure to work the patented invention may only be granted pursuant to a request filed after three or four years of failure to work or insufficient working of the patented invention and it must be refused if the patentee gives legitimate reasons to justify his inaction."[59]

The TRIPS accord continued this restrained approach to compulsory licensing. The agreement only mentions compulsory licensing once, flatly prohibiting compulsory licenses for trademarks.[60] Two other articles in the agreement (Articles 30 and 31) provide very narrow windows for governments to make exceptions to the exclusive rights of control enjoyed by patent holders, closely mirroring the exceptions in U.S. law. As might be expected from provisions drafted in large measure by representatives of nations heavily invested in production of (and protection of) intellectual property,[61] the articles stress the need to respect exclusive-control rights, to safeguard the economic interests of rights-holders, and to deploy carefully prescribed procedures for assuring that the exceptional instances in which the rights are restricted conform to the legal standards and provide adequate notice to rights-holders and opportunity for them to secure their interests.[62]

Although representatives of less developed nations went along with TRIPS as the necessary price for other parts of the Uruguay Round Agreements, from the outset many of them were interested in finding ways to cut back the accord's protections for intellectual property.[63] They were joined in this by a loose coalition of opponents of intellectual property rights, opponents of private property rights, and health activists eager to acquire drugs to fight certain diseases—largely HIV/AIDS, tuberculosis, and malaria—at prices that reflect only the very low cost of production, not the very large embedded R&D costs (estimated at roughly $1 billion per new drug).[64] Pharmaceutical manufacturers routinely provide drugs to less developed nations at a fraction of the cost charged in wealthier nations, but for those on the front lines of public health battles the cost can never be low enough.

When the Doha Round of trade negotiations began, obtaining exceptions to TRIPS patent protections was high on the activists' list of goals. They succeeded in getting language passed at the Doha Ministerial meeting in 2001 that recognized the existence of "flexibility" under TRIPS to address critical public health needs. The declaration asserted that TRIPS allows nations to issue compulsory licenses and to determine the grounds for granting them.[65] Some activists have characterized this as either changing the TRIPS (not something within the capacity of a ministerial meeting) or as confirming that the agreement all along had incorporated the right for any nation to issue compulsory licenses essentially for any reason.[66] The first nation to put that theory into practice was Thailand, followed shortly by Brazil, both issuing compulsory licenses for HIV/AIDS drugs and for drugs related to coronary-artery diseases.

The steps taken by Thailand and Brazil show the problem of pressing beyond the initial restraints of international law into an area of flexibility in recognizing or ignoring protections for intellectual property. At the outset,

all of the drugs subject to compulsory license were available in Thailand and
Brazil. No charge was made that the drug patents were not being worked or
even that the manufacturers had not made sufficient quantities of the drugs
available. Nor does extreme poverty or a need to control a health epidemic
explain the actions. These nations are, respectively, the thirty-third and
tenth largest economies in the world;[67] neither is among the least developed
nations; and both have extremely effective programs to contain the spread of
HIV/AIDS and extend the lives of those living with this disease.[68]

Evidently, something different is in play. In Thailand's case, the licenses
were issued in conjunction with a dramatic increase in military spending
and a cut in public health spending. The compulsory licenses were defended
as saving roughly $24 million—less than 2.5 percent of the increase in mili-
tary spending. The message in both cases was clear: the governments of
Thailand and Brazil wanted to reorder spending priorities and wanted some
of the cost to be born by drug manufacturers. But lowering the cost of patented products has never been recognized as a legitimate reason for
infringing the patents. Indeed, if that were enough, there would be no security at all to patent protections. That, of course, is the reason that both proponents and opponents of intellectual property rights see the Thai and
Brazilian actions as critical to the future of TRIPS.

Compulsory licensing can be defended in particular circumstances as
necessary to overcome collective-action problems or to prevent hold-out
problems. But if it is accepted as a legitimate mechanism for lowering the
cost of intellectual-property-intensive goods, this exception to the general
rule of exclusive control over property could become the vehicle for unrav-
eling the entire set of global intellectual property protections.

The defense offered for actions such as Thailand's and Brazil's is that the
dynamic cost is modest, because rich nations can supply the incentive to
innovate, as they account for the bulk of the short-run returns for pharmaceuticals (and for a good number of other products). This defense proves too
much. Any infringement of property rights is apt to be small relative to the
total amount invested in establishing the right. But allowing this to excuse
takings gives rise both to an inevitable free-rider effect (as the costs get piled
more and more onto the residual demanders of the product) and a corollary
falloff in incentives to invest in property as the total returns for investment
decline. Without perfect price discrimination, which is almost never possible,

the exclusion of revenues that might cover a portion of R&D from some users will reduce the overall returns to investment in R&D. Since total returns to R&D closely mirror total returns to other forms of investment, there is no real surplus to be captured by the compulsory licensing approach. Instead, there is simply a race to be first to take what is available without paying the price. Given the normal incentives for government leaders, there is every reason to expect that there would be too much compulsory licensing and too little investment in innovation.

Conclusion

The different types of intellectual property right, with different scopes and lengths of protection, are related in many ways but also need to be cordoned off from one another to provide the best fit between legal rules and the circumstances they were designed for. In some instances, the divisions among legal regimes are less easily maintained, but by and large the courts have done a respectable job of working things out. The courts also have been sensitive to problems that arise from changes in interpretation of the law or from changing technology and have moved to correct these problems.

That has not eliminated all the sources of objection to the law nor has it eliminated prospects for undermining the law. The scholarly literature today brims with explanations of problematic aspects of the law and proposals for correcting them, almost all starting from the supposition that intellectual property rights are too strong, putting too much control in rights-holders' hands. Many of the critiques have at least a kernel of truth in pointing out the defects, theoretical or real, of the current rules. Most, however, propose solutions that move us further away from, not closer to, the public good.

The greater problem lies in the opposite direction. Especially in a more global economy, opportunities exist for limiting the effective scope of protection offered by intellectual property laws. Although the framework for international protection of intellectual property rights has evolved to address that concern, most notably through the incorporation of avenues for addressing intellectual property protection under the WTO's aegis, substantial concerns still exist. Intellectual property piracy and counterfeiting are prevalent in many nations; and even where respect for intellectual property laws is highest, rights-holders still suffer substantial losses.

The international legal rules remain relatively porous in practice, and legal institutions directed at other ends—particularly those concerned with competition law—have the capacity to undo much of the fabric of the current intellectual property rights regimes. As we will see in the next chapter, the conflict between intellectual property rules and competition law is not as extreme as sometimes imagined, but thoughtful application of the law is critical if it is to serve as a check on illicit practices rather than on investment in innovation.

9

Antitrust and Intellectual Property

Is There a Conflict?

It seems obvious at first glance that there is a conflict between the antitrust laws and intellectual property laws. The conflict story is easy to set out and runs as follows. Antitrust laws aim to promote competition in order to enhance the welfare of consumers. Intellectual property laws, in contrast, aim to suppress competition in order to encourage innovation. Given these different aims, the two sets of laws necessarily conflict with each other and courts must decide which laws take precedence in particular cases.

While this conflict story is familiar, there is an alternative view that has been expressed in recent years which holds that the conflict is largely superficial. Both sets of laws, it is said, aim to enhance the total supply of goods and services; for this reason, both are essentially procompetitive.[1] Under this theory, the conflict story is simply a short-run snapshot of the tension between antitrust and intellectual property that arises when antitrust laws are applied without regard for the competitive nature of innovation efforts. In the long run, the tension dissolves because both legal regimes enhance the variety of goods on the market and the choices available to consumers; both aim at similar ends, and their application does not have to be a source of conflict.

This short-run versus long-run theory of the relationship between intellectual property and antitrust appears to have gained widespread acceptance and is the basis, apparently, for a less hostile treatment of intellectual property rights today by antitrust enforcers than was observed in the past.[2] Of course, the less hostile treatment of intellectual property may reflect a more general shift toward less aggressive enforcement of anti-monopolization theories in the United States since the mid-1970s.[3] This more general shift in enforcement attitudes may be due to influences unrelated to theories of intellectual property, such as the growth of import competition in the American market.

Under the framework advanced in the previous chapters of this book, the tension between antitrust and intellectual property largely dissolves, but for reasons that differ greatly from the short-run versus long-run theory. Antitrust law and intellectual property law are compatible, we believe, because they ultimately are grounded on the same substantive trade-offs between static and dynamic costs—the very trade-offs examined in detail in our previous chapters. In an ideal common law system, much of the conflict between intellectual property and antitrust would be understood to be largely superficial.

Of course, we are far from an ideal common law system today. For that reason, antitrust and intellectual property laws may be applied in ways that are in tension, and that tension may even grow over time. Our purpose here is to explain how best to think about this tension,[4] and ultimately to resolve it.

Intellectual Property Law versus Antitrust Law: An Example

The concepts of antitrust law cannot be discussed intelligibly without some examination of the market failure that antitrust aims to correct. The starting point for this chapter, hence, is an examination of the sort of market to which antitrust law and intellectual property law both apply.

Let us consider an example that illustrates the tension between intellectual property and antitrust. Suppose a firm obtains a patent on a widget and that the patent gives the firm monopoly power—that is, the power to set the price for the widget above the competitive level. If the firm did not have a patent, the widget would be quickly copied by rivals and the market would turn competitive.

Assume the firm's cost per widget (i.e., the average cost) is $1 and, to simplify matters, that the average cost is the same as the incremental cost for each widget. In other words, every single widget supplied to the market requires an additional outlay of $1 by the firm to cover production and selling (e.g., marketing, transportation, contracting) costs. If the market were competitive, the price of the widget would be driven down to its average cost, $1. Let us assume that demand conditions are such that twenty-two widgets would be sold to consumers each week when the widget price is at the competitive level of $1.[5]

We assume that there are no fixed costs in this example. That means that the firm incurs no current costs (e.g., paying for electricity to light the widget plant) that are independent of the number of widgets supplied to the market. Although there are no fixed costs, we assume there are sunk costs—specifically, the costs that were incurred before the widget production began. In this example, it is obvious what those sunk costs are—the costs of the R&D that went into designing the widget and obtaining a patent for it.

Given that the firm has a monopoly guaranteed by a patent on widgets, the firm will be able to determine the market quantity and price for widgets. Assuming the firm sets out to maximize its profits, it will keep supplying additional widgets to the market as long as the incremental revenue from an additional widget exceeds the incremental cost of $1.

What is the incremental revenue from an additional widget? If the firm sells an additional widget, it can do so for no more than the maximum price that the market will allow. That price is determined by the demand schedule for widgets—i.e., the schedule of quantities demanded for each widget price. Thus, suppose the firm is already selling one widget per week, at a price of $3.90; and suppose that in order to sell two widgets per week the price must be reduced, consistent with the widget demand schedule, to $3.80 per widget. If the firm increases its sales to two widgets per week, the incremental output would be one widget per week. Looking only at what that one widget sells for, the additional weekly revenue from the one additional widget sale would be $3.80. But notice that the firm must also reduce the price on the first widget that it sells in the same week. When it was selling only one widget per week, it could set the price at $3.90. When it sells two per week, it has to sell them both at $3.80. So the additional revenue from increasing widget sales by one unit is $3.70 ($3.80 minus the $0.10 that it no longer earns on the first widget sold each week). The schedule of incremental revenue amounts is therefore less than the maximum price that the market will bear at any time.[6]

Since the firm makes a profit every time the incremental revenue exceeds incremental cost, it will keep supplying widgets to the market until incremental revenue is just about equal to incremental cost. Let's assume that occurs when the price is equal to $2.25 per widget and the weekly quantity sold is eleven. Since the cost per widget is only $1, the firm makes a profit of $13.75 per week.[7]

The wealth consumers gain by going to the market is the difference between the maximum they are willing to pay and the amount they actually pay, multiplied by the quantity they purchase. This is called consumer surplus. Under the assumptions of this example, the consumer surplus generated is $9.62 per week when the price is $2.25 per widget and the quantity sold is eleven.[8]

Antitrust Perspective

From an antitrust perspective, the market outcome described above is less than desirable. It would be better for consumers, and society overall, if the price were set at $1.00 per widget. Society is wealthier when the widget price is $1.00 because, although widget producers make less profit, consumers gain more in return. Specifically, the $13.75 profit from selling widgets at a price of $2.25 becomes part of the consumer surplus if the price is set at $1.00. Consumers also gain additional surplus because widget sales expand from eleven to twenty-two. The additional surplus from expanded sales is simply the surplus that is forgone (sometimes called "the deadweight loss") when the widget-patent monopolist restricts output and raises its price to the monopoly level. In this example the amount of the forgone surplus due to monopoly—the amount of value that could have been produced but is not captured by either the producer or the consumers of the product—is $6.87 per week.[9] If the price is set at the competitive level of $1.00, consumer surplus would be $33.00 per week.[10]

There are two consumer surplus measures that are of potential interest here. One is the entire consumer surplus when the price is set at the competitive level of $1.00, which is $33.00. The other is the residual consumer surplus that is left over after the firm sets the monopoly price. The residual surplus is only $9.62 per week.

From the antitrust perspective, monopolization leads to a loss in society's wealth of $6.87 per week. This is the net benefit to consumers from sales that could be made but are forfeited by the firm's decision to set its price at the monopoly level. Alternatively, the static monopolization cost to society, measured as weekly flow, is $6.87 per week.

In addition to this loss in society's wealth there is a transfer of surplus that could have gone to the consumer but goes to the seller in the form of profits. That amount is the firm's profit, which is $13.75 per week. Society does not lose this amount even though consumers do.

To get a sense of the full magnitude of these sums, we should consider the time factor. The duration of the innovating firm's monopoly is twenty years. The forgone consumer surplus of $6.87 per week lasts over the full patent term. To evaluate the full magnitude, we have to translate the forgone surplus of $6.87 per week in the twentieth year back to an equivalent sum in today's dollars—and the same for the nineteenth year and so on. By discounting each future amount to an equivalent value today, we can arrive at a "present value" for the forgone surplus due to the patent monopoly. We will spare the reader the calculation and simply give the result. Assuming the patent lasts for the full twenty-year term, the costs and values associated with sales stay constant over time, and that the interest rate is 5 percent, the present value of the forgone surplus, which is the *total static cost* to society from the patent monopoly, is $4,451.21.

Intellectual Property Perspective

From the intellectual property perspective, the market outcome just described is by no means "less than desirable." The intellectual property approach focuses on the residual surplus enjoyed by consumers and the profit earned by the monopoly firm.

Suppose the firm, in order to produce the widget, has to incur a sunk R&D cost that, when amortized, amounts to $13 per week for the life of the patent. It would not have produced the widget if it could not secure a profit of at least that amount. So the firm's real profit is not $13.75 per week, but $0.75 per week. Moreover, consumers would not have the residual surplus of $9.62 per week if the widget market had not been developed through the incentive provided by the patent grant.

From the intellectual property perspective, consumer welfare is enhanced by $9.62 per week. In the absence of the patent, the firm would never have brought the widget to the market. Although the total surplus could be as much as $33.00, assuming the firm brings the widget to the market, there is no guarantee that the firm would have developed the widget market. The assumption that underlies the intellectual property perspective is that the firm would not bring the widget to the market if it could not get patent protection.

The total welfare enhancement from the patent is the sum of the consumer welfare enhancement and the additional profit earned by the innovating firm. Taking full development costs into account, the weekly profit of the innovating firm is only $0.75. Thus, the welfare enhancement from the patent is $10.37 per week.

The *dynamic cost* of disallowing intellectual property rights is simply the reduction in welfare that would result if patents were not awarded (and the firm therefore did not bring the widget to the market). Thus, the sum of the residual consumer surplus, $9.62 per week over the patent term, and the net profit from investment, $0.75 per week over the patent term, represents the dynamic cost to society of denying intellectual property protection to the innovating firm—or, alternatively, the dynamic benefit from intellectual property protection.

Again, it will be helpful to examine the full magnitude of the dynamic benefit. The dynamic benefit, translated to a stock rather than a flow, is the present value of $10.37 per week for the twenty-year patent, which amounts to $6,718.93.

This stylized example actually might understate the dynamic benefit that intellectual property rights confer. The dynamic benefit may be much larger than the sum of the residual consumer surplus and the net profit of the innovating firm. If no other firm would have ever developed the widget market, then the dynamic benefit is equal to the sum of the residual consumer surplus over the patent term, the net profit over the patent term, and the entire consumer surplus during the period of competition after the patent expires. If no other firm would have ever developed the widget market, the present value of the entire consumer surplus after the patent term is $12,935.21. Thus, the entire dynamic benefit could lie anywhere between a low of $6,718.93 and a high of $19,654.14.

Reconciling Antitrust and Intellectual Property Viewpoints

Which one of these positions is correct: Is social welfare reduced by the patent to the tune of $4,451.21 (the present value of $6.87 per week during the patent term)? Or is it increased by some amount between $6,718.93 and $19,654.14? The answer depends on underlying assumptions. And once we delve further into the assumption we will see additional difficulties in picking a single right answer.

Let's start with two examples that rely on the most extreme assumptions (one extremely negative to the intellectual property right, the other extremely positive). Suppose the amount the firm invests into designing and creating the widget is much less than $13 (amortized weekly flow); indeed, suppose it is zero. If so, none of the profit secured by the patent is necessary to bring the product to the market. The firm would have brought the widget to the market even without a patent. Under this assumption, the patent is simply enabling the firm to scoop out part of the wealth that would have gone to consumers. All of the profit earned by the firm is simply transferred from the surplus that would have otherwise gone to consumers. There is no social gain from the patent at all; it reduces society's wealth by the full static cost of $4,451.21.

In other words, if the market for widgets would have been developed even without a patent going to the innovating firm, then the patent monopoly is a pure cost to society. This would be true if the innovating firm would have brought the widget to the market without the patent, or if other firms would have brought the widget to the market without a patent. For example, if the patent design is obvious, or not novel, it is very likely that it would have been brought to the market anyway. Putting aside the question of a time lag in its introduction, the dynamic benefit of the patent award would then be zero.

On the other extreme, suppose the firm would not invest in creating the widget and bringing it to the market unless it could get a profit of at least $13.00 per week (the cost of the upfront investment in R&D, amortized over the twenty-year time frame). Suppose, in addition, that the design is so novel and nonobvious that no other inventor ever would have discovered it. In this case, there would be no widget market in the absence of patent protection for the innovating firm. The dynamic benefit of the patent is the sum of the residual consumer surplus, the net profit of the innovating firm, and the entire surplus post-expiration, which totals to $19,654.14. Note that the dynamic benefit could be as great as four times the dynamic cost in this example.

There is no static cost in this second extreme case. Although it is common to think of intellectual property as creating static costs, it does not in the case in which the patent award is necessary for the product market to be created. To talk of static costs in this case is to be guilty of the "Nirvana fallacy"—of criticizing an outcome because it does not match some theoretical ideal, which is unattainable anyway.

Static costs from intellectual property protection are real costs if they are avoidable while still obtaining the benefits of intellectual property. But where the patent is absolutely necessary to develop the product market, there are no static costs—only dynamic benefits.

Now let us consider an intermediate case to see what is left of the notions of dynamic and static costs. Suppose the innovating firm incurs a cost in developing the widget that translates to an equivalent debt stream of only $0.99 per week. In order to recoup its profits and to have an incentive to develop the widget market, the firm needs a profit of only $1.00 per week for the life of the patent. Moreover, assume, again, that no other firm would bring the widget to the market during the patent term if the innovating firm chooses not to.

Patent protection is necessary in this example to induce the innovating firm to bring the widget to the market. Without protection, the innovating firm would earn a profit of zero from the widget and would therefore not incur the development costs (which will generate a debt stream of $0.99 per week).

However, even though patent protection is necessary to develop the market, the level of protection goes beyond the minimum necessary to generate the widget market. For example, if the innovating firm were to sell twenty widgets per week at a price of $1.06, it would make a weekly profit of $1.20 over the patent term, which would make it worthwhile to the firm to develop the market.

It is in this intermediate scenario where we begin to see simultaneous validity in the concepts of dynamic and static costs. In the extreme case in which the market would have been developed anyway, there are no dynamic costs from denying patent protection. In the extreme case where the market would not be developed unless the firm earned the monopoly profit, there are no static costs from granting patent protection. It is only in the intermediate case (of the examples considered) in which the patent protection is more than sufficient to induce the firm to develop the market that a genuine static and dynamic cost trade-off is observed.

When there is a genuine trade-off between static and dynamic costs, it makes sense, as a matter of policy, to ask whether antitrust rules should be used to limit the innovating firm's power over price. In other words, even if we permit the innovating firm to gain patent protection, we might still ask whether antitrust laws should be applied to the firm, after it gains the patent, in order to reduce the static costs of monopolization. This is a sensible policy only if the antitrust laws do not reduce the innovating firm's profits below the level necessary to induce the innovation.

What sort of antitrust policies might be useful in this case? Any policies that reduce the pricing power of the innovating firm could be useful (within appropriate limits). Suppose, for example, the innovating firm uses price discrimination to maximize the profits from its patent monopoly. If those profits are far in excess of the minimum necessary to induce the innovation, antitrust law could enhance society's wealth by prohibiting price discrimination. Or, alternatively, suppose a tie-in arrangement permits the firm to price discriminate among widget buyers. An antitrust prohibition on tying might potentially enhance social welfare by prohibiting the tie-in. Even a compulsory license that permits a rival to enter the market might enhance welfare by reducing the innovating firm's pricing power.

We have not exhausted the scenarios in which a genuine dynamic and static cost trade-off might arise. To take one alternative, suppose the innovating firm incurs a development cost that translates to a debt stream of $13 per week over the patent term. The firm needs to earn the full monopoly profit over the patent term in order to bring the widget to the market. But suppose that within five years of the innovating firm's introduction of the widget, other firms will have become sufficiently familiar with the technology to develop a competitive widget market.

Granting the patent to the innovating firm leads to the dynamic benefit today of $10.37 per week. But that is a real benefit for only five years at most. After five years have passed the patent imposes static costs of $6.87 per week. We observe a genuine dynamic and static cost trade-off in this example. The question is whether a $10.37 benefit for five years is greater than a $6.87 cost for the remaining fifteen. That depends on the rate of interest.[11]

The difference between this example and the earlier one is that the dynamic and static cost trade-off is temporal or sequential in this example but simultaneous in the first example. In the sequential trade-off example, when the patent is awarded there are no static costs. But static costs arise five years after the award. Antitrust law restrictions on the innovating firm's pricing power could not be used to improve social welfare. The innovating firm needs to earn the full profit in order to bring the widget to the market. Antitrust restrictions that threaten to deny the firm the full profit will destroy the market.

Still, it may be socially desirable in an individual case simply to deny the patent on the ground that the static cost is too large relative to the dynamic benefit. Depending on the discount rate, society may be better off waiting five years for the competitive widget market to develop than granting a patent today and permitting a firm to monopolize the market for twenty years. This is the scenario in which a test for novelty or nonobviousness permits patent authorities or courts to consider the temporal trade-offs between static and dynamic costs.

It should be obvious that we can combine the simultaneous and sequential trade-off scenarios just considered. Suppose the innovating firm needs only one dollar of profit per week to recover its development costs. And suppose that within five years, rival firms will develop the same new product (widget). Antitrust law could be used to enhance society's welfare, just as in the earlier example.

These examples have offered an optimistic vision of the power of antitrust to enhance social welfare. In each of the examples, we noted that antitrust restrictions could work to enhance social welfare as long as it did not go too far by denying the innovating firm the return that it needed in order to recover its development costs. That is an important assumption. In general, courts cannot observe the level of profit a patentee must make in order to recover development costs plus a competitive or reasonable return. Inevitably mistakes will be made. The question is whether the costs of errors that result in denying firms the minimum return will be greater than the costs of inaction. We will return to this question.

Law

We have so far explored the concepts of static and dynamic costs more closely than in previous chapters. The foregoing examples suggest a need to distinguish the simultaneous trade-off case from the sequential trade-off case. In the simultaneous case the profit protected by the patent award is more than sufficient to induce the innovating firm to develop the market. In the sequential case the profit is just sufficient to encourage development, but a trade-off is still observed because a competitive market could have arisen (soon after the patent award) in the absence of the patent. In the simultaneous case it seems appropriate, as a theoretical matter, to consider using antitrust law to restrain the patentee's exploitation of monopoly power.

However, for antitrust law to be capable of enhancing society's welfare it must be able to restrain the patentee's exploitation in a way that improves upon intellectual property law. That is far from certain. The two major reasons for this are that intellectual property law already incorporates many of the concerns of antitrust, and that antitrust law, as traditionally understood in the United States, does not severely constrain innovating firms from exploiting their intellectual property protection.

Intellectual Property Law and Static Costs

Our previous chapters have argued that intellectual property law contains doctrines that constrain the static costs (e.g., monopolization costs) of property rights. We have explored these constraints in the context of patent, copyright, trademark, and trade secrets law. The existence of these constraints implies a smaller scope for antitrust to improve upon the outcome of intellectual property law on its own.

Consider, for example, patent law. The sequential static-versus-dynamic-cost trade-off scenario arises when the new product or process introduced by the innovating firm is one that would have been introduced in a competitive setting. Yet the novelty and nonobviousness tests are designed to deny patents in these cases. Given the existence of patent law doctrines that already do the work needed to eliminate the costs associated with an unnecessary monopoly, there is absolutely no scope for antitrust law to improve upon intellectual property within this set of cases.

The simultaneous trade-off scenario arises when the patent award for the new product or process imposes static costs and delivers dynamic benefits at the same time. This is because the profit protected by the award is more than the minimum amount necessary to encourage the innovation awarded by the patent. Patent law incorporates doctrines that limit the static costs that might be created in the simultaneous trade-off scenario. For example, patent law constrains static costs by adopting a general principle against awarding patents for abstract ideas and processes, and by excluding certain broad categories from patent protection (such as mathematical formulas). These rules prevent anyone from obtaining monopoly control over building-block concepts that have a wide variety of applications, including large numbers of both foreseeable and unforeseeable applications.

Unlike many areas of common law, patent law deals with special cases. The problems of tort law are sufficiently generic that they arise in many settings, and as a result tort law has developed numerous elastic rules that courts apply across a wide swath of cases. Patent law has not generated such a set of rules. The principles are general and the decisions involve a case-specific (i.e., product- or process-specific) balancing of static and dynamic costs. General categories excluded from patentability have arisen in this process. Outside of those general categories, the law of each case appears to be unique, in the sense that it reflects a court's assessment of the cost trade-offs for that particular instance.

The legal assessment of the trade-offs between static and dynamic costs already implicit in patent law severely diminishes the scope for antitrust to improve upon the outcomes from intellectual property law. Put another way, the most obvious cases where the static costs of monopolization are large relative to the dynamic benefits from innovation already have been taken off the table by patent law. The same goes for much of intellectual property law in general.

Antitrust Law and Dynamic Benefits

In addition to intellectual property law's incorporation of concerns modernly associated with antitrust analysis, antitrust law itself has not evolved with the sole purpose of constraining or eliminating the static costs of property rights in ideas and information. This provides another reason to be doubtful of the scope for antitrust law to improve on the welfare consequences of intellectual property law.

Antitrust law's ill fit to intellectual property settings stems from two fundamental aspects of antitrust doctrine: the concept of market power and the distinction between exploitation and exclusion.

Market Power

It is well understood that the anti-monopolization provision of Section 2 of the Sherman Act does not apply unless the firm has "market power," that is, the power to set price above the competitive level without the constraint of competition. The concept of market power is a difficult one. Like the uncertainty principle of physics, it becomes more difficult to comprehend as its measurement becomes more advanced.

It is common among antitrust authorities today to say that a firm has market power if it can impose a significant price increase for a substantial period of time without losing so many consumers or inducing so much entry from rivals that the price increase becomes unprofitable.[12] This "pricing test" approach is incomplete because it is lacking the notion that the ability to earn an above-competitive level of profit is a core element of market power. Under the price test, a firm that develops, after substantial investments, an especially low-cost method of selling office supplies (reducing cost to the consumer as well as the seller) could be found in possession of market power if it is capable of increasing its prices by 5 percent without causing most of its customers to switch to other sellers.[13] But unless the firm can increase its price enough to earn an above-competitive level of profit (that is, after covering the costs of investments in its sales process as well as operating expenses) over a period sufficiently long to permit entry to occur, the firm really does not have the power to price without competitive constraints.

Although we have treated the patent grant as giving a monopoly to the innovating firm in our example at the start of this chapter, patents do not necessarily lead to monopoly power or to market power. A patent is a property right rather than a monopoly right. In some cases, the patent will generate a substantial market in which the holder has a genuine monopoly. However, in the vast majority of cases, patents will neither lead to monopolies, nor even to commercially successful ventures. Of those instances in which the patent leads to a commercially successful venture, the patent usually will give the holder a property right to the stream of profits from some device or process that is equivalent to but differentiated from effective substitutes. In these instances, the patent permits the holder to exclude competition within the precise scope of the patent, but the holder will earn at best a competitive rate of return on investment.

Whether applying a price test or a more conservative approach that looks for evidence of power to earn an above-competitive return, antitrust law will not, as a general matter, constrain a firm's exploitation of intellectual property protection unless the firm has market power. Since the vast majority of patentees will not have market power, antitrust law should have a fairly limited application to intellectual property. We say "should" here because several special doctrines have developed in antitrust law specifically for cases involving patents. These doctrines have been controversial and have stood on shaky ground precisely because they have sometimes appeared to fly in the face of more general antitrust concerns. The Supreme Court's decision in *Independent Ink*,[14] jettisoning the presumption that a patent generates market power, is an important step in the direction toward reconciling special patent-antitrust doctrines with more general antitrust law.

If *Independent Ink* can be taken to signal an effort to rationalize antitrust and intellectual property law, the general trend should be toward the application of antitrust to intellectual property only when there is a credible claim that the intellectual property protection has created significant market power. These instances will be relatively rare. The infrequency with which intellectual property protection leads to market power implies a rather limited scope for antitrust as a tool for minimizing the static costs of intellectual property.

Exploitation versus Exclusion
One of the great paradoxes of antitrust law, at least in the United States, is that it provides a legal safe harbor for a firm that exploits its monopoly power by setting the monopoly price. In other words, the clearest expression of the harm that the antitrust law is supposedly designed to prevent or constrain— the exploitation of monopoly power—has long been held perfectly lawful under Section 2 of the Sherman Act. Antitrust law prohibits the acquisition or maintenance of monopoly power (i.e., monopolization) through means of *exclusion* that have been deemed especially harmful by courts, but it does not prohibit the mere *exploitation* of monopoly power.

The implication of this basic doctrine of antitrust is that there are legal limits on antitrust's ability to constrain the static costs of monopolization in connection with intellectual property. A monopoly obtained through intellectual property protection is not a violation of antitrust law—it is not a case of unlawful acquisition or unlawful maintenance. One exception is the case in which the patent is obtained through fraud, in which case any attempt to use the patent to exclude competition will violate Section 2.[15] But in the general case in which the firm honestly gains a monopoly through a patent, its acquisition of monopoly power does not violate the Sherman Act. This implies that by setting its price at the monopoly level the firm can exploit that monopoly power without violating the Sherman Act.

The case of setting the monopoly price is an easy one of legality. More complicated cases arise when we consider whether the firm with a patent-based monopoly can engage in acts that might be considered exclusionary on some theory, such as refusing to license a patent, or engaging in product tying. In these more complicated cases, antitrust law has sometimes intervened to limit rights that are normally associated with intellectual property. Although the interventions have been modest for the most part, some of them are inadequately reasoned and unlikely to stand the test of time.

Consider the refusal to license a patent. Among the ways to reduce the static monopolization costs of a patent grant, the most obvious would be simply to require the patentee to license the patent to a rival. Once the technology is licensed to a rival, the patent holder would no longer be unconstrained by competition within the scope of the patent. From a narrow static-cost vantage, this would be good for consumers. The downside is equally obvious. If the new competition reduces the return below the minimum necessary for the firm to recover its development costs, taking into account the time value of money, then the firm's future patenting incentives will be damaged, as will be the incentives of other firms that are contemplating investment in innovation. The immediate beneficiaries of compulsory licensing will have less incentive to innovate in the future, too, once they recognize that it may be cheaper to sue for the compulsory license of some existing proven technology rather than invest in the creation of a novel substitute technology.

The compulsory licensing threat has become a serious one for firms largely in two settings. In the domestic market, when an innovating firm is part of a consortium that sets an industry standard, claims for a compulsory license may arise after the standard has been set. The other major risk is in the context of international markets, where foreign competition regimes have treated the compulsory licensing of intellectual property as an appropriate method of increasing competition. In *Microsoft v. Commission*,[16] for example, the EU Court of First Instance held that Microsoft abused its dominant position in the market for personal computer operating systems, in violation of Article 82 of the Treaty Establishing the European Community, by refusing to license interoperability information to rivals in the market for work group server operating systems.[17] *Microsoft v. Commission* is notable for its extension of an implicit duty to deal under Article 82 to a setting in which the dominant firm is attempting to protect or control its intellectual property.[18] Large firms operating in global markets face the risk that their rivals will petition foreign competition authorities in order to gain cheap access to patents and trade secrets through a compulsory licensing order. While this clearly reduces the static costs of monopoly power, the innovation effect is likely to be negative for dominant firms and may even be negative for the petitioning rivals.[19]

However, the general rule in U.S. antitrust law is that a patent holder is not required by law to license the patent.[20] Not only is this the rule in the special area of overlap known as patent-antitrust law; in the more general antitrust law, courts have strongly disfavored the notion of a duty to deal with a rival, a position made even clearer in recent years. In the *Trinko*[21] and *Linkline* cases,[22] the Supreme Court has held that a firm with monopoly power does not have a duty to deal with a rival firm absent prior conduct revealing an intention to exclude the rival from the market. On the assumption that courts will take seriously the project of reconciling general antitrust law with more specific patent-antitrust rules, the *Trinko-Linkline* view on the monopolist's duty to deal should be applied to antitrust-based claims for a compulsory license.

Another area in which antitrust law has intervened to constrain the exploitation of intellectual property is that of patent misuse. These theories are generally ill considered and will withstand the test of time only if courts refuse to reconcile antitrust and patent-antitrust doctrines. The other possibility, which is undesirable, is that the courts will repudiate economic analysis as the conceptual basis for antitrust analysis.

One type of patent misuse, for example, is the *Brulotte v. Thys*[23] doctrine that the patentee cannot collect royalties under a license beyond the expiration of the patent. This was viewed by the Court as an anticompetitive effort to extend the duration of the patent monopoly. But once the patent has expired, any rival can enter into competition with the patentee—and the information underlying the patent has been publicly disclosed already. *Brulotte* is an excellent example of the disjunction, largely based in early patent-antitrust law, between special patent-antitrust doctrines and more general antitrust law. Under the more general antitrust approach, the expiration of the patent would put an end to any patent-based market power. At that stage, a decision to continue charging a fee to a licensee would have no serious implications for antitrust law.[24] Under a rational approach to the patent-antitrust intersection, the *Brulotte* doctrine would be reversed.

Moreover, the *Brulotte* doctrine may well have the perverse effect of reducing consumer welfare by making it more difficult for a patentee to license. A potential licensee may be a more efficient producer and yet unable, because of financing constraints, to pay a large royalty. An agreement to reduce the rate and extend the duration is simply a financing or risk-sharing agreement, commonly seen in credit markets.[25]

Finally, it is not hard to find lawyers who will suggest ways to get around the *Brulotte* decision. For example, many agreements simultaneously set the terms for licensing both the patent and complementary know-how information held as trade secrets (see Chapter 6). It is perfectly legal to license the secret know-how information for a much longer period than the patent term. For many patentees and potential licensees, only a little bit of ingenuity is required to evade the restriction imposed by *Brulotte*.

Another type of patent misuse involves the selling of a patented product on condition that the buyer also purchase an unpatented product as well—that is, tying of an unpatented product to a patented product.[26] It is also a misuse if the patentee imposed such a requirement in the licensing agreement.[27] The general antitrust law on tying, however, has come around to recognizing the fact that tying often has procompetitive effects.[28] In *Independent Ink,* the Court said that in order to find a violation of antitrust law based on a tie-in, the defendant must be shown to have market power in the tying product.[29]

The legal theory that it is patent misuse simply to tie patented and unpatented products has been narrowed in recent years through statute and case law.[30] In 1988, the patent statute was amended to limit the patent misuse theory of tying to only those instances in which the patentee has market power.[31] Still, even in its narrower form, this is again an example of a special patent-antitrust doctrine that makes little sense in light of modern antitrust

192 LAWS OF CREATION

law. The general trend of the antitrust tying case law has been toward a rule-of-reason analysis. As patent antitrust becomes reconciled with general antitrust, the rule of reason test should be applied to tying in the patent context as it is more generally; as courts begin to recognize efficiency defenses in tie-in cases under the rule of reason, the same principles should be extended to patent tie-ins.

The per se prohibitions of patent misuse doctrine are inconsistent with intellectual property law and increasingly inconsistent with modern antitrust law. As antitrust law evolves, we expect patent misuse doctrines to be reconciled with antitrust[32] and eventually replaced with rule-of-reason analyses—and with better results.

Evolution of Law and Error Costs

Antitrust law is an oscillating area of federal common law because it is subject to pressures from the legislature and from enforcement agencies. The oscillations have led to the adoption of per se prohibitions and the later abandonment of those prohibitions.[33] Intellectual property law, in contrast, has been more stable because it is subject to intervention from only one potentially destabilizing force: the legislature.[34] Still, antitrust, in spite of its oscillations, has tended toward a greater application of the rule-of-reason test over time. Antitrust courts generally have moved away from per se prohibitions and toward balancing tests.

The conflicts between antitrust and intellectual property law should be viewed in light of their evolutionary tendencies. Because of those tendencies, the conflicts between these bodies of law are somewhat less than might otherwise have been. In addition, the conflicts are likely to diminish over time.

Antitrust law and intellectual property law are less in conflict than one might predict on the basis of their general goals. One major reason is that both are the results of rather minimalist statutory foundations.[35] The Sherman Act says very little about what courts are supposed to do in deciding cases under the statute. For the most part, antitrust law has developed as a type of federal common law. The rule of reason has evolved as courts have found a need to make trade-offs between the anticompetitive and efficiency consequences of the conduct challenged under the statute.

Most of intellectual property law has also started off with a minimalist statutory architecture. Under Article 1, Section 8 of the U.S. Constitution, Congress was authorized to "promote the progress of science and useful arts, by securing for limited times to authors and inventors the exclusive right to their respective writings and discoveries." In implementing this constitutional provision, the legislature enacted sparsely worded patent and copyright statutes. Trade secrecy and trademark law developed initially within the common law, before statutes were passed to ease enforcement of common law rights. Because intellectual property has developed largely within the common law rather than the statutory process, it has generated doctrine built upon rational case-specific trade-offs between anticompetitive and efficiency concerns (i.e., encouraging innovation) all along.

When you step back and look at the trade-offs, explicit and implicit, that have governed legal decisions in both antitrust and intellectual property, the tension between these two areas of law largely disappears. In both areas, courts have for the most part intelligently traded off efficiency and anticompetitive effects in fashioning legal rules. Intellectual property law has had the advantage in this process because it has not been entrusted in part to politically-responsive public officials (or officials directly subject to their control) for enforcement. As a result, intellectual property courts have been able to make decisions without the pressure to alter legal rules in order to facilitate public enforcement efforts.

Indeed, from a broader historical point of view, the argument that antitrust and intellectual property are in conflict is to some degree misinformed. The U.S. Constitution *limits* the federal legislature's power to award patents to instances in which the award promotes progress in the sciences and useful arts. Patents have not always been so limited. In *Darcy v. Allen*[36] a court invalidated the queen's grant of a patent on the importation and sale of playing cards, because it recognized that it served no purpose other than to enrich the queen's friend Darcy. Governments around the world claim the power to limit markets to licensed sellers, and the English monarchy was no different in its outlook at the time of *Darcy*. The common law of intellectual property, taking *Darcy* as an early contribution, has involved a process of narrowing the scope of the government's power to control entry into markets. The government's authority has been limited to those instances in which the power to prevent competition might have a positive payoff for society. From this broader historical perspective, patent law has been a constraint on the monopolization of markets rather than a cause.

As patent antitrust becomes reconciled with the rest of antitrust law and as antitrust moves toward increased use of rule-of-reason tests (for instance, in areas such as resale price maintenance and tying),[37] the conflicts between antitrust and intellectual property law will become less noticeable. Antitrust law will intervene in order to constrain the static monopolization costs of intellectual property rights, but less frequently and with more reasoned discretion than required under the existing patent misuse doctrine.

In thinking through the grounds for antitrust intervention, courts are likely, as they have increasingly in antitrust, to take error costs into consideration. Recall from our model at the start of this chapter that the only instance in which antitrust can offer a possible improvement in social welfare over intellectual property law operating alone is when the law has protected an innovating firm in securing a profit well in excess of the amount needed to induce the firm's innovation. This is a difficult case to identify. There are few signs that a court can use to tell that it is dealing with a case in which the innovator's profit can be reduced without denying him a reasonable return on R&D costs.

Even if the court happens to identify such a case, it is unlikely to do so consistently. Recognizing the high risk of error, potential innovators will treat the possibility of antitrust intervention as a cost of innovation. Innovation incentives will be reduced and society will suffer to that extent. The empirical question is whether society is better off squeezing a bit more consumer surplus from the patent-based monopolies that arise and in exchange getting fewer patented inventions. This is a question of choosing more competition "within a patent" versus more competition from new patents.

Which choice leaves society better off is an empirical question to which no one has the answer, even though people can make informed guesses. Antitrust courts in the United States have shown a tendency of late that suggests favoring competition among different products or innovations. The starting point is the Supreme Court's decision in *Continental T.V. v. Sylvania*,[38] which permitted manufacturers to designate exclusive territories for dealers on the theory that interbrand competition generally would contribute more to consumer welfare than would additional intrabrand competition. The

Sylvania doctrine reflects an implicit Schumpeterian judgment that the cost of discouraging dynamic competition is greater than the benefit of squeezing the last penny from static competition.

The scope for enhancing consumer welfare from antitrust intervention is already limited given the structure of intellectual property law and of antitrust law. Intellectual property law has already sought in many of its applications to limit the static costs of monopolization. Antitrust would have to work with a scalpel-like accuracy to further reduce static costs without also dampening innovation incentives. But the likelihood of erroneous decisions is a well-understood feature of antitrust litigation.

A mistake in the direction of inaction permits a lawful patent-based monopoly to earn a higher return than the minimum necessary to reward its innovation. But even in this case, the most successful patents generate monopolies that are limited in scope and in duration; and substitute technologies can enter to compete away monopoly profits. A mistake in the direction of too much enforcement hurts innovation incentives. In view of the already limited scope for antitrust to improve upon intellectual property doctrine, and the imprecision of antitrust, the costs of mistaken intervention on antitrust grounds probably exceed the costs of mistaken inaction.

Reverse Payment Settlements

One of the most controversial issues in the intersection of antitrust and intellectual property is the settlement of infringement litigation, especially infringement litigation involving pharmaceutical patents. Given the nature of the industry, the plaintiff in these disputes is typically a large pharmaceutical company and the defendant is a generic seller. The settlement can take many forms, but one common type is an agreement by the generic to remain off the market until expiration of the patent, or to delay entry into the market to some later date ahead of patent expiration. Commonly, the plaintiff pharmaceutical firm makes a payment to the defendant generic seller in exchange for the promise to delay entry—often referred to as "pay for delay" agreements.

These settlements have been criticized on the ground that something seems fishy when a plaintiff pays a defendant to settle a lawsuit. In the vast majority of settlements in litigation, the defendant pays the plaintiff. It is the defendant who is being sued and would like the lawsuit to go away. Why would the plaintiff have a defendant summoned to court only to pay him? Because the payment runs in the reverse direction from the litigation claims and from what is most often observed in litigation, some courts and commentators have suggested that the reverse-payment settlements are anti-competitive agreements cloaked as settlements.[39]

Two issues generated by reverse payment settlements should be kept distinct. One is the agreement by the defendant generic to delay entry. That is, in essence, an agreement to abide by the terms of the injunction sought by the plaintiff. The second issue is the direction of the payment—from the plaintiff to the defendant. An agreement to abide by the terms of the sought-after injunction could be made along with a payment in the normal direction (defendant to plaintiff). Similarly, a reverse payment could be observed in a lawsuit in which the defendant does not agree to abide by the terms of an injunction. The controversy involves the combination of the injunctive settlement and the reverse payment.

The injunctive settlement is by no means special to patent infringement litigation. Such a settlement can arise in connection with any lawsuit in which the plaintiff asks the court to enjoin some conduct of the defendant.[40] Consider, for example, a nuisance lawsuit, where a class of plaintiffs seeks to enjoin the operation of a smoke-belching factory. The lawsuit could settle with an agreement by the factory to cut down its smoke emission, or to shut down entirely. The reverse (payment) injunctive settlement is unusual in the nuisance context, but there is no reason why it could not occur. It is possible that the gain to the plaintiffs from the injunction is so great that they would be willing to pay the factory to cut down its production of smoke. Or suppose one homeowner sues to enjoin a neighbor from playing his music too loud. The plaintiff homeowner might decide that he is better off paying the neighbor for an agreement to turn the noise down rather than to take his chances with a jury. There would be nothing sinister about the injunctive settlement or the reverse payment settlement in any of these cases.

The injunctive settlement and the reverse payment both become more suspect in the context of competition-blocking litigation—any lawsuit in which the plaintiff seeks to prevent the defendant from competing with it in the same market. Patent infringement is a classic example of competition-blocking litigation. Another example is an antidumping investigation, which we will treat as a type of litigation. Typically, a plaintiff will not seek to block competition in a competitive market; there is nothing to be gained by excluding one of a thousand entrants into the market. But if a firm enjoys a monopoly or operates in a cartel, there is much to be gained by excluding a new competitor. Any legal action that blocks a new competitor immediately raises the risk that consumers will be harmed.

The antidumping scenario is easier to analyze because these proceedings are designed to suppress price competition in a manner akin to price-fixing cartels. Antidumping actions typically are initiated when a domestic producer or group of producers complains to the U.S. Commerce Department that a foreign competitor is dumping—that is, selling at "unreasonably low" prices—in the United States. Although there are justifications for antidumping regimes that may be plausible in special circumstances, most arguments for these laws collapse on close inspection.[41] As a rule, when a firm complains about the unreasonably low prices of a competitor, the complainant is trying to block competition.[42] The Commerce Department often dutifully responds with a preliminary dumping finding against the foreign seller—the starting point of a process involving that department and the U.S. International Trade Commission. Antidumping investigations frequently end with the imposition of new tariffs on imports that suppress the most effective sources of price competition.

This sets the stage for occasionally ending antidumping proceedings with something very similar to a reverse payment settlement. The domestic complainants drop their prosecution, and, in exchange, the foreign seller increases its price to the same level as that of the domestic seller (where there are multiple domestic firms, this may be viewed as equivalent to a cartel arrangement). This is, in essence, an agreement in which the complainants pay the respondent in the form of a share of the cartel profits while the respondent agrees to stop competing with the complainants.

It simplifies matters to consider reverse settlements in the antidumping context because there is typically no issue of innovation or market development, as in the patent context. Although there are some exceptional circumstances that can support these actions, by and large antidumping is crony capitalism at its worst. Domestic cartels prefer not to face competition from foreign sellers, so they go to the government to get a legal barrier put in the way of their foreign rivals.

In theory, if the administrative costs of antidumping proceedings exceed the losses imposed on consumers and on foreign rivals over the period in which competition is blocked by a settlement, society could benefit from a settlement agreement that raises prices in exchange for an end to the antidumping proceedings. However, in most cases, the gains to consumers from competition will be greater than the costs of antidumping proceedings. In other words, most antidumping settlements are bad for society.

Within the set of antidumping settlements, reverse payment settlements are likely to be among the most harmful. The reason is that when a foreign seller (defendant) needs to be paid off to settle, it will be because the money it forgoes by agreeing not to compete (as part of the settlement) is much greater than the amount it expects to lose as a result of the proceeding. But the amount that the defendant forgoes is potentially available as surplus to consumers in the long run. A settlement in which the defendant agrees not to compete most often will deny society a larger pot of money than the defendant saves by not litigating. Antidumping settlements that block competition, thus, are likely to be bad for society, and reverse settlements are likely to be especially bad.

The case of antidumping provides an insight into the concerns of competition authorities over reverse settlements generally. In the case in which the agreement to settle is a naked restraint of trade, the reverse settlement is a strong signal that the restraint is harmful to society.

The patent infringement setting is different from the antidumping scenario. In the antidumping scenario, the only gain to society from a settlement is the avoidance of the administrative costs of an antidumping proceeding. In the patent setting, there are more important gains to society. A settlement quiets title with respect to the patent and avoids the risk of an erroneous finding of patent invalidity—a serious risk in a fact-intensive inquiry turning on technical judgments about prior art decided by judges who are not technologically trained. A settlement also enables the patent holder to continue to reap the rewards from market development. These are substantial benefits that the patentee plaintiff will be willing to pay for. They will also redound to consumers.

Unlike the antidumping scenario, in the patent infringement setting it is not at all clear that the litigation expense savings from settlements are likely to be dwarfed by the welfare costs of settlements. The reason is that the welfare costs of a settlement in the patent context may be negative—that is, the settlement may be beneficial to society overall. The risk of an erroneous finding of noninfringement is a cost that discourages innovation. A settlement that removes that risk enhances innovation incentives. In general, the greater the likelihood that the patent is valid, the greater the incentive cost of an erroneous finding of noninfringement and the more the plaintiff should be willing to pay for the settlement. This effect is magnified as the error rate among the decision-makers for litigated cases rises.

In the patent context, a reverse settlement in and of itself is not a sign of a pure cartel agreement with no upside for consumers. Such a settlement still could signal a cartel agreement that harms consumers, to be sure. But it could also be a sign that the underlying technology is valuable and the risk of an erroneous finding of noninfringement is significant. Both of these cases will generate the same observations of reverse settlements. Unfortunately, there is, as yet, no well-developed rule-of-reason test that would permit a court to distinguish anticompetitive reverse (payment) patent settlements from pro-innovation reverse patent settlements.

There is law governing settlements in the patent context, though what exists is, for the most part, noninterventionist. Courts will find reverse settlements anticompetitive when there are "suspicious circumstances" such as (1) the absence of a real dispute, (2) the absence of a real competition-related dispute, or (3) the presence of a settlement agreement that prohibits competition to a further degree than could have been accomplished by the plaintiff's lawsuit (i.e., the patent).[43] Courts have tried to distinguish disputes with a weak or fraudulent basis from real disputes over competition. They have also tried to distinguish settlements that stay within the scope of the plaintiff's claim from those that seem to reach beyond it to block competition more extensively. In short, the case law seeks to distinguish legitimate settlements from essentially fraudulent settlements.

The attempt to distinguish legitimate from fraudulent settlements is a noninterventionist approach because it does not involve the court prohibiting settlements on the basis of the existence of a substantial reverse payment, or on the basis of an assessment of the validity of the plaintiff's patent. The merits of the case are considered at the boundaries and not its core under the current law. While the bases for drawing the relevant judgments are not susceptible of great precision, they are generally the sorts of assessments that judges are accustomed to making.

The noninterventionist approach of current law on patent settlements must be compared to the alternatives. One alternative is a per se prohibition. Another alternative is a rule-of-reason standard. A per se prohibition would discourage innovation by treating legitimate pro-innovation settlements the same as anticompetitive settlements. The rule of reason test, in contrast, applied in the patent settlement context, would turn on factors that courts have trouble identifying, let alone measuring. The risk of error under such a rule-of-reason approach would be substantial. To see the difficulty in implementing a rule-of-reason test, consider the factors that should be examined. A settlement is desirable, on rule-of-reason grounds, if the sum of the litigation cost savings, market-development benefits, and innovation benefits exceeds the static welfare costs of blocking competition. It would be an enormous undertaking for a court to attempt to quantify and balance these costs and benefits. As in other fields, shortcuts might develop that would limit the ambit of judicial inquiry and align it better with judges' strengths, but the current noninterventionist approach seems at least as consistent with minimizing error costs than any of the alternatives.[44]

In many of the instances in which intellectual property and antitrust rub against each other, one finds that intellectual property law has already incorporated the concerns of antitrust. This is not so in the area of patent settlements, because intellectual property law has not developed a specific common law governing settlements. However, the established patent-antitrust law on settlements largely addresses the most troubling risks generated by such settlements. For antitrust law to improve upon the current noninterventionist common law on patent settlements, it will have to be applied with a degree of accuracy that has not been associated with it before.

Statutory Law, Proposals, and Unintended Consequences

Not content to leave the issue to existing antitrust law, or to its future common law development, legislators have recently proposed bans on reverse payment settlements in pharmaceutical patent litigation. Reverse settlements are presumed to be anticompetitive because they typically involve an agreement to delay the entry of a generic drug, though the entry still occurs, in many cases before the expiration of the challenged patent.

Legislators have charged that these settlements deny consumers access to cheap generic drugs.[45]

It follows from our earlier discussion that the case for banning reverse settlements of pharmaceutical patent infringement disputes is weak. The settlements are not necessarily opposed to the interests of consumers; and in some cases consumers may be better off, both in the short term and in the long term, as a result of a reverse settlement. A reverse settlement that permits entry of the generic before patent expiration delivers the generic to consumers sooner than they would have obtained access if the patentee had continued litigating and prevailed. The settlement removes the uncertainty for the generic producer as well as for the patent holder.

In the medium to longer term, the reverse settlement can provide additional benefits to consumers. In some instances, entry of a generic causes the pioneer firm to lose so much market share that it is no longer willing to continue promoting the drug or to further develop it, since the costs would be borne by the pioneer with the benefits reaped by the generic. If the settlement enhances the incentives of the pioneer to continue promotion, testing, and development, consumers may be better off even though access to the generic has been delayed. And the availability of less expensive alternatives to costly litigation also increases incentives to invest initially in the discovery process that produces pioneer drugs.

Critics of reverse settlements charge that they can be used to facilitate a price-fixing conspiracy.[46] Suppose the pioneer firm has a weak patent. The firm would file a patent infringement action not because it thought it would prevail, but because it thought it could use the patent as a basis for dividing the market with the generic seller. If this is true and if the pioneer is not engaged in any serious promotion or additional investments in the product, then consumers gain nothing from the market division agreement.

We cannot rule out this worst-case scenario, but the question raised by the proposed legislative ban is whether this is the most likely scenario. While the question is ultimately an empirical one, the argument proves too much. Indeed, if weak patents held by firms making little investment were the most likely scenario, then it would provide not only an argument for banning reverse payment settlements but a presumptive argument against pharmaceutical patents in general.

The worst-case theory is hard to square with the empirical evidence. Bessen and Meurer find that pharmaceutical patents are far more valuable than the litigation costs associated with their protection.[47] If pharmaceutical patents were generally weak, Bessen and Meurer would have found the opposite result. The Bessen-Meurer finding implies that the worst-case scenario envisioned by critics of reverse settlements is a relatively infrequent and unlikely occurrence. Banning all reverse settlements in pharmaceutical litigation on the basis of a relatively rare set of instances in which low-quality patents were used to facilitate collusion would be letting the tail wag the dog.

Still, the argument of those proposing a ban on reverse settlements cannot be fully understood without some consideration of existing legislation. The settlements that have generated controversy have occurred in connection with the Hatch-Waxman Act.[48] Under Hatch-Waxman, a generic seller can file an "abbreviated new drug application" (ANDA),[49] which permits the generic maker to bypass rigorous testing requirements imposed by the FDA if it can show that the generic is the equivalent of the pioneer drug. If the pioneer drug is still under patent protection, the generic seller must file a "paragraph IV" certification,[50] which states that the pioneer drug patent is invalid or that the generic is not infringing. At that point, the pioneer firm has forty-five days to file an infringement action.[51] After the pioneer files the infringement action, the statute permits the generic to enter the market if the litigation is not resolved within thirty months.[52]

The Hatch-Waxman statute is complicated, and we have only touched the surface of it. The most important feature of it for our purposes is the 180-day exclusivity period granted to the first generic seller to file an ANDA with respect to a particular patented drug.[53] The statute prohibits the entry of any additional ANDA applicant for 180 days after the first generic appears on the market.[54] The purpose of the exclusivity provision was to solve a "free-rider" problem in the generic market. The first generic to enter the market often has to fight off an infringement action from the pioneer. If it wins the infringement action, it opens the door to any new generic seller to enter the market. One of the risks that had traditionally dampened generic entry was the likelihood that after costly entry—costly because of patent infringement litigation—the generic seller would then face competition from later entering generics that did not bear the cost of patent infringement litigation. Hatch-Waxman attempts to enhance the incentive of the first generic entrant by giving it a 180-day exclusivity period to reap the rewards from attempting entry first.

This exclusivity period is at the core of the more sophisticated critiques of reverse settlements in pharmaceutical patent litigation. When a pioneer and generic settle an infringement action with an agreement to delay entry, no other ANDA generic can enter until that exclusivity period runs following first generic entry.[55]

The exclusivity period introduces a special incentive into the settlement negotiations between a pioneer pharmaceutical firm and the first generic entrant. The pioneer is aware, given the exclusivity, that an agreement to delay entry forecloses competition from other generics until the first generic enters, and guarantees a duopoly for 180 days after entry. This is an unintended consequence of the statute and a potentially valuable feature to both the pioneer and the generic. It creates a safely protected amount of consumer surplus that can be shared between the two parties, an amount that increases with the duration of the period in which entry is delayed.

This peculiar feature, generated by the Hatch-Waxman statute, does not by itself imply that all reverse settlements in pharmaceutical patent litigation are bad for consumers. The reasons we suggested these settlements may be good for consumers still hold true despite the special incentive to delay introduced by the statute. And recall that delay may still be better for consumers in the short run than a lawsuit that ends with an injunction against the generic seller.

In all events, it is a mistake to lose track of the fact that a settlement practice that offers increased returns to the generic firm may induce greater investment by generics seeking to be the first entrant and also, so far as the overall benefits of the settlement are positive, increase investment incentives for pioneers. It is similarly shortsighted to lose track of the benefit that exclusivity may generate. Removing the exclusivity period would reduce the rate of first generic entry. Similarly, banning the reverse settlement would also reduce the rate of first generic entry.

Given a choice between banning reverse settlements and banning exclusivity, the most sensible decision would be to ban (or reduce) the exclusivity period. Both decisions would reduce entry by the first generic. However, banning the reverse settlement removes a general approach to resolving patent disputes that could be beneficial to firms and to consumers even in settings in which the 180-day delay factor is trivial. The least harmful response to the delay incentive would be to act surgically against the specific statutory provision (the exclusivity provision) that has created the delay incentive. Of course, it is not at all clear that even this surgical approach would lead to a socially desirable result.

The reverse settlements phenomenon is another illustration of the trade-off tension between static and dynamic costs in intellectual property settings. The additional incentive created by Hatch-Waxman for the pioneer firm to pay for a settlement that delays generic entry can impose static costs on society, but these costs should be weighed against the static and dynamic benefits from these settlements.

Patents and Collusion

We have used the static and dynamic cost trade-off as the lens through which we view the conflict between intellectual property and antitrust. From the antitrust perspective, patents reduce social welfare by creating monopolies. From the intellectual property perspective, patents increase social welfare by encouraging innovation of products or processes that otherwise would not occur.

The trade-off approach reflected in intellectual property law leads to straightforward issues involving the award and exploitation of rights, such as patents. Should there be a patent for an abstract process, or for a process innovation that appears to be obvious? The trade-off questions observed in intellectual property law reappear at the intersection of intellectual property and antitrust. Should the patent holder be permitted to engage in any act that increases the profits from the patent and at the same time reduces competition? The reverse payment settlements controversy provides a modern illustration of the trade-off problem when intellectual property meets antitrust.

Perhaps the most traditional illustration of the trade-off problem in the intersection of intellectual property and antitrust involves the use of patents as facilitating mechanisms for collusion. Since patent licensing or cross-licensing agreements may involve some degree of cooperation among competing firms, such agreements could easily cloak collusive agreements, just as settlements of patent infringement suits can also be used to cloak collusion.

Indeed, many of the issues we discussed in connection with reverse payment settlements are played out in this setting too.

Start with the single-firm, single-process patent. Suppose firm *A* discovers a new way to make widgets that reduces its cost by half. Suppose in addition that firm *A* licenses the process to firm *B*. In the absence of the patent, firms *A* and *B* are equally efficient. However, given differences in their operations, the patent reduces firm *B*'s costs by two-thirds (substantially more than the reduction in firm *A*'s costs). Firm *B* can now cut its price for a widget to a level that drives firm *A* into bankruptcy. In this scenario, innovation followed by licensing would be one way for firm *A* to hoist itself on its own petard.

One solution to this problem is for firm *A* to license the process and require that firm *B* set its widget price above a certain floor that permits firm *A* to remain competitive. This solution imposes an immediate static cost; it reduces competition "within the patent." However, there is a countervailing dynamic benefit: the option to restrict the licensee's pricing protects the return from the patent and thereby encourages innovation and the licensing of patents to more efficient firms.

The price-fixing solution was examined early on in *E. Bement & Sons v. National Harrow,*[56] where the Supreme Court approved minimum price terms in licensing agreements. The Court recognized that the patent law is designed to give a monopoly to the patent holder and that the greater power to control exclusive access to the innovation included the lesser power to put restrictions on a licensee. Since then, the law has introduced constraints on various competition-limiting patent licenses, but the rule of *National Harrow* remains valid.

Consider a variation. Suppose both firms *A* and *B* have patents, one for the production of blue widgets, the other for the production of red widgets. They form a pool that essentially permits the two firms to act as if they own both patents jointly. If the red and blue widgets are substitutes, this agreement could easily reduce welfare by monopolizing the market in widgets (or the submarket represented by red and blue widgets). Unless there is some efficiency basis for the pool, a cross-licensing agreement in this scenario is simply a cloak for a collusive agreement.

Of course, one could argue that the pooling of substitute patents may be socially desirable because it enhances the return from innovation. However, patents were not intended to provide a justification for every arrangement that increases the profits from innovation. A patent would not provide a legal justification for the patent holder to blow up the manufacturing plants of all firms that make competing products that do not rely on the patent. Blowing up rivals would enhance the returns from the patent, but this has never been understood to be part of the rights associated with a patent. The patent is simply a property right that allows the holder to maintain exclusive control over a particular product or process for a limited time.

Suppose instead that red and blue widgets are complements rather than substitutes. For complements, the case for pooling is different than in the substitutes scenario. Complementary products or processes must be used together. Any consumer wishing to purchase the bundle of complements is concerned only with the total price, not the price of a particular component. Each component seller, however, is concerned only with the price that he gets for his individual component. This creates a conflict in incentives that could justify pooling as a method of enhancing the welfare of consumers and producers.

Firm A has a patent on a new type of right shoe, and firm B has a patent on a new (and similar) type of left shoe. If they do not pool their patents, each will set the monopoly price for the type of shoe design that it controls. The resulting total monopoly price for the bundle will be the sum of the two individually set monopoly prices. If the patents are pooled, the pooled entity will price according to the market for the entire bundle. The resulting monopoly price will be lower than if two individual firms set prices for the individual components without coordination. Pooling can therefore enhance welfare when the patents are complementary; the welfare of consumers and producers is larger than in the absence of pooling.

Thus, the desirability of cross-licensing patents is a complicated issue. Where the patents are substitutes, there is a significant risk that the cross-licensing agreement is little more than a cloaking device for a cartel. Where the patents are complements, there may be a strong efficiency basis for cross licensing. Obviously, the case of cloaking should be an antitrust violation. The efficiency cases should be examined under the rule of reason, which is the view that the law adopts.[57] The difficulty lies in distinguishing these cases, and in examining complicated cross-licensing agreements that involve both complements and substitutes.

This returns us to roughly the same position we reached in our discussion of reverse payment settlements. If the intellectual property arrangement at issue (patent pool or reverse settlement agreement) is primarily a cloak for an anticompetitive agreement, then it should be held to violate antitrust law. If it has a legitimate basis, then antitrust law must be applied with caution, though the scope for antitrust intervention is admittedly somewhat broader here than in the reverse settlement scenario. Courts can establish evidentiary markers for pools that are likely to be cloaks for collusion—inclusion of substitute patents, prohibitions on entry—but in the case of a pool that involves complementary patents, the assessment of anticompetitive potential is a difficult enterprise.

The problem of patent pools suggests two senses in which antitrust comes into conflict with intellectual property. One is at the boundary of intellectual property and antitrust, where the rights-holder attempts to extend a right into a greater degree of market control (e.g., a cartel) than anticipated by the intellectual property laws. Here, the courts should be mainly interested in determining whether the holder is making an essentially fraudulent use of the right. The other sense in which antitrust law comes into conflict with intellectual property law is modeled at the start of this chapter—as a second level of analysis applied to an unquestionably legitimate right (e.g., a patent). The more expansive claims for antitrust—involving per se prohibitions of price restrictions in patent pools,[58] or proposals for a per se prohibition of reverse payment settlements above a certain monetary threshold—have tended to fall in this category. In this mode of analysis, where antitrust law "second guesses" intellectual property law, antitrust intervention requires a great deal of accuracy in order to improve the trade-offs already struck by intellectual property law, often far more than reasonably can be anticipated from litigation.

Conclusion

The statutory roots of antitrust law and of key parts of intellectual property law were set so that these fields would conflict with each other. But the common law that later developed from these sources is not in tension. The reason for this is that common law courts have implicitly and explicitly traded off static and dynamic costs in fashioning common law rules for intellectual property and, to a lesser extent, antitrust. The result is that much of intellectual property law appears to be designed to tolerate the static cost of monopolization only where the dynamic innovation benefits are substantial. This leads to a pessimistic assessment of the scope for antitrust law to improve upon the welfare consequences of intellectual property law. To be sure, antitrust must stand ready to condemn instances where intellectual property is used primarily to cloak a collusive agreement. But outside of this traditional function for antitrust, only the most wishful thinkers believe that more interventionist antitrust would generate a perfectly optimal trade-off between the static and dynamic costs of intellectual property rights.

10

Understanding Intellectual Property Law

Although parts of this book address details of the law, the main point is quite simple. Those of us who write and teach and talk about law, economics, and public policy need to regain a more balanced and reasonable perspective on the way our laws treat the world of ideas.

Two Views of Intellectual Property Rights:
Zero-Sum versus Positive-Sum

Despite the obvious contributions of innovations and creative works to improvements in our lives as well as the link between investments in such innovations and the rights protected by intellectual property laws, the concept of intellectual property as a type of *property* has increasingly come under attack in the academic literature. Academic writers typically see flaws in the thinking behind property-centric approaches. These include a failure by those who think in property terms to understand the unfairness of granting exclusive rights to those fortunate enough to claim them; the contribution of such rights to inequalities within and among societies; and, especially, a failure to appreciate the consequences of nonrivalry among users of ideas and expressive works (the quality that allows many people to enjoy and employ ideas and expressions without impinging on anyone else's ability to do so). A perspective (such as the one offered here) that seeks to explain the basic economic justifications for intellectual property rules, focusing on the utilitarian trade-off between dynamic and static costs, runs against the grain of modern scholarship.

More broadly, the modern academic view treats intellectual property law largely as a set of rules determined in a zero-sum conflict between rights-holders and members of the public. Beyond some modest realm, for one side to gain, the other side must lose. The individual is encouraged by this view to choose a side: either you are with the public or with the rights-holders. For some writers, the choice is put in even more loaded terms: either you side with those who are rooted in the past or line up with the vanguard of the future, freed of entangling rights.[1]

In contrast, the property-centric perspective advanced in this book views intellectual property rules as generally enhancing society's welfare. For the most part, courts, and often lawmakers, have made intelligent trade-offs when confronted with the static versus dynamic cost problem that underlies reasoned analysis of intellectual property rights.

As a result of these trade-offs, generated largely through hundreds of judicial decisions, intellectual property law has developed, and continues to develop, into a force that advances welfare in modern societies. Most of these decisions are empirical, in the sense that they involve a cost-benefit conflict that is unique to the matter at hand. Decisions of this sort hardly afford solid ground for a comprehensive set of rules that can be applied mechanically to future cases. However, occasionally a judge, like Justice Story in *Folsom v. Marsh*,[2] which created the doctrine of fair use in copyright law, will extract a general set of rules from a specific trade-off problem.

Statutes at times have set or reset the foundation—the initial conditions—from which the law of intellectual property has evolved. As we noted in Chapter 3, while the common law process is best suited for examining specific questions concerning the scope of a right, trading off static and dynamic costs in order to find the optimal resolution of a particular case, the statutory process has a clear advantage when there is a need to modify significant aspects of property rights in response to major changes in the technologies available to society or in society's preferences. Over hundreds of years, lawmakers have drawn on experience with different creative enterprises and widely shared views about how best to promote creativity to prescribe general rules for intellectual property.[3] Although some special statutory innovations undeniably reflected political interests, the set of common law and statutory rules that has emerged to govern Western intellectual property rights (especially in the United States) has worked well enough to support an ever-expanding array of innovative activities and industries.

Rights Skepticism

Given the success enjoyed by societies with broad intellectual property rights, why has the zero-sum view of intellectual property gained the popularity that it has? And why does its popularity seem most pronounced now, when the proportion of national income and growth tied to intellectual property is rising?

In part, the answer lies in the fact that, in fairness, the zero-sum perspective is more complicated than the label implies. While we think that a substantial amount of modern writing about intellectual property in this vein is mistaken in important ways, we also think that coming to grips with the prevalence of this writing requires more than merely addressing its arguments or setting forth contrary arguments. It is important to identify the sources as well as the risks of modern skepticism toward intellectual property rights.

Provenance and Classification

One source is the ambiguity about the roots of intellectual property laws and their proper place in the taxonomy of legal disciplines. The name "intellectual property" suggests that it is an offshoot of property law. But intellectual property skeptics resist property-centric approaches in part on the ground that intellectual property law just as easily could be viewed as subsidiary to other parts of our common law canon.

Many core intellectual property doctrines have to do with issues, such as breach and remedies in noncontract settings, that could be assigned to other disciplines as readily as to property law. Trademark law is concerned with behavior that misleads consumers, focusing on the degree to which duplication of a mark will confuse potential customers, an analysis familiar to business torts. Copyright law concerns the misappropriation of someone else's creative work—with the language of piracy suggesting that the conduct at issue is not just unfortunate but wrong in a more serious way. Given these characteristics, intellectual property could be treated as a branch of tort law, a view held by John Henry Wigmore, whose 1912 tort law casebook includes materials on patent, copyright, trade secret, and trademark law.[4]

While this ambiguity makes opposition to property-centric analysis somewhat more understandable, it should not be given excessive credit. Even if contestable, the instinct to treat intellectual property law as a species of property law has solid doctrinal roots: after all, intellectual property law disputes typically revolve first around the inquiry whether an individual has a duty to respect the right-holder's entitlement, such as a patent. In other words, the question whether a property right exists comes before an examination of the nature of the breach and the appropriate remedy. Further, the core element in intellectual property rights, like patent and copyright, is a right to exclusive use that is consistent with property rules.

In one sense, the ambiguity about where intellectual property belongs in the law school curriculum or in the organization of legal doctrines is irrelevant. Many fields of law are separated only by fiat, with the separations changing over time according to shifting views of which features are central to a given field or which organization of the curriculum is the best match for student or faculty interests. Intellectual property law has drawn on ideas and doctrines from different sources and resembles not one but many branches of the law. Property law may be an apt analogy, but it is not the only one.

The more important reason for embracing a property-centric approach is that it places dynamic cost considerations at the center of intellectual property rights analysis. Dynamic cost and benefit concerns are central because they orient analysis to the most important effects associated with intellectual property rules and because they also are the values that are most likely to be affected in a serious way by legal rules. Many static costs can and will be diminished by changes in behavior, an observation that has become commonplace since Ronald Coase's publication of "The Problem of Social Cost," more than fifty years ago.[5] Dynamic costs, however, are less likely to be dissipated by such adjustments. If the result of a particular rule choice is that intellectual property rights are less certain and, hence, less valuable, there will be less investment in bringing innovation to the stage where it can be covered by one of those rights. Finally, this analytical approach provides a salutary counterweight to the current trend of scholarship.

In a variation on the standard objection to proceeding as if intellectual property law were rooted in ordinary property law, some critics protest the conflation of intellectual property and other property law because, they argue, the scope of many intellectual property rights is less clear than rights in traditional property, such as land.[6] This is a more reasonable position, explored in some detail in Chapter 2. It rests in part on real differences between the ease in mapping land boundaries and the relative opacity of boundaries around some intellectual property rights, especially patent rights in contexts where there are many small innovations that are linked together in complex products. This juxtaposition, however, contrasts the clearest form of real property with the least readily defined type of intellectual property. The point has a kernel of truth, but the differences between intellectual property and other property are easily overstated. More important, even if true, this proposition does not establish that some other approach is preferable to the property-centric view, and it certainly does not provide a basis for the zero-sum thesis that intellectual property doctrine consists of rules favoring rights-holders at the expense of society in general.

Public Interest and Public Choice
Another source feeding the zero-sum, anti-intellectual-property position draws on experience with statutory reform. The copyright extension statute challenged in *Eldred v. Ashcroft*,[7] for example, has been cited as evidence in support of the zero-sum perspective toward the intellectual property world.[8] The statute was, in the eyes of its critics, a benefit to copyright holders and a taking from the public.

The antiproperty argument based on cases like *Eldred* assumes both that this is a typical case for legislation on intellectual property and that it is a clear case of self-interest triumphing over public interest. This view starts with the presumption that any extension of copyright term is a zero–sum transfer from the public to rights-holders. As we explained in Chapter 6, while there is a zero-sum character in the case of some existing works, this is not true for all such works and certainly is not true for the entire class of works that will be produced subject to the new term. A new extension of copyright terms transfers something of value from consumers to producers of copyrighted works, but the extension also supports investments that benefit consumers. Which effect is larger is an empirical question that remains to be tested.

Modern intellectual property rights skeptics are correct in pointing out that as codification of intellectual property laws has expanded, especially in the trademark and copyright fields, the rights of holders have tended to expand too. Codification consists of two main parts: statutory provisions modifying existing intellectual property protections, and statutory rules

designed to import court decisions into the statutory framework or to over-
turn court decisions directly. The modern drift toward codification has provided some additional clarity to intellectual property law, but it has also led
to an expansion of the rights of holders and corresponding diminishment of
the rights of others wanting to use intellectual property. Our defense of a
slightly expanded fair use doctrine (the safety-valve argument) in Chapter 7
was based in part on this gradual shift in copyright law.

If the modern skepticism toward intellectual property rights is based on
the observed effects of codification, then the skepticism is at least partly justifiable. But even in this event, we think the skeptics have correctly observed
a trend and then drawn the wrong conclusion.

Codification very likely has led, at least in some cases, to a transfer of
rights from the public to the holders of intellectual property. The reason is
predictable in view of the legislative process. Rights-holders tend to form
concentrated interest groups with large stakes in the intellectual property
rules that affect them. The public is a dispersed group that pays little attention to the intellectual property laws. Given this structure, the legislative
process is likely to tilt in favor of rights-holders.[9]

But it is a mistake to conclude from this structure that intellectual property law is largely a zero-sum game biased in favor of rights-holders. The
codification process is a recent phenomenon in the history of intellectual
property laws. Before the late 1940s, the statutory component of the patent
laws was relatively sparse and dealt largely with procedural matters (e.g., setting up the patent office). The critical details of intellectual property laws
with a statutory foundation (patent, copyright) have developed for the most
part through the common law process. The intellectual property laws with a
common law foundation (trademark, trade secrecy) have an even larger relative portion of their corpus attributable to the common law process. The
likelihood that the codification process in intellectual property law, a relatively short period in its history, will favor rights-holders does not imply that
the entire body of law is biased toward rights-holders.

Moreover, much of the codification that has occurred has attempted to
clarify rules that have developed through the common law process rather
than state new rules that favor rights-holders. The codification of fair use
doctrine is an example. Justice Story's exquisite analysis of the fair use question in *Folsom v. Marsh* could not possibly be captured within a statute.

Some part of the analysis will inevitably be lost in any effort to translate a judicial opinion into a statutory rule. In spite of this, the statutory fair use rule is not an extremely poor or absurdly biased version of the test laid down in *Folsom*. The statutory rule can be read to enhance the rights of copyright holders beyond what was provided in *Folsom*.[10] However, the statutory rule can also be read in a manner that is largely consistent with Story's analysis. That is a matter for courts to determine in their own applications of the fair use test.

So even if we take the codification process as providing evidence in support of the skeptical, zero-sum view of intellectual property law, that view is based ultimately on an exaggeration of the effects of codification. The codification process has not turned intellectual property law into a zero-sum game with rules tilted in favor of rights-holders. Even where there is initial statutory underpinning or subsequent codification, the law is largely based on the common law analysis of case-by-case trade-offs between dynamic and static costs. Throughout the previous chapters, we have shown a strong preference for the development of intellectual property law through this process.

Still, codification does present some dangers. The tendency to shift rights toward concentrated interest groups is one. The tendency for intellectual property scholars to interpret this shift as a sea change in the law (an interpretation used to undermine the law) is another. We should be clear that we are not opposed to codification under all circumstances. The legislative process is preferable to the common law process when it comes to significant, nonincremental changes in a legal framework, such as the establishment of new property rights or the abolition of existing rights. But the common law process is preferable when a decision has to be made requiring a cost-benefit trade-off in connection with the scope of a specific protection. The worrisome consequences of codification are observed largely when codification takes over the space of decisions that are better governed by common law courts.

Yet another observable danger of codification is reflected in the Supreme Court's analysis of business method patents in *Bilski v. Kappos*.[11] As we noted in our patent law chapter, the Court rejected the incentive-based trade-off analysis of the Federal Circuit (an analysis that had led that court to adopt a test that is highly restrictive toward business method patents) and instead relied primarily on a reading of the patent statute's text. The *Bilski* Court's approach to the patent doctrine, even if defensible as faithful to the statutory language, slights considerations that have been critical to the historical development of patent law. In so far as that approach is a consequence of codification, it can be taken as evidence that codification is unlikely to result in better law than case-by-case decision-making in the long term.

In the end, the codification process may serve to undermine the rights that intellectual property holders are seeking to secure through the legislature. As the zero-sum view gains ground, after having trained legions of law students, skepticism toward the intellectual property laws may become a powerful force that drives changes in those laws through the legislative process.

Indeed, as teachers of law, we have witnessed the increasingly common perspective that intellectual property law is a specialized field walled off from discourse with other fields of law because of the technical nature of the subject. This is a view that obviously was not widespread a century ago, given that Wigmore taught intellectual property as a part of tort law in 1912. But few law professors today would view that as appropriate, especially among those who specialize in intellectual property. The danger in the perception of specialization, which has been enhanced by codification, is that it encourages scholars to think that intellectual property is in some sense divorced from the rule-of-reason analysis of cost and benefit trade-offs that has formed the intellectual core of the common law.

Admittedly, the practice of intellectual property law sometimes requires a high degree of specialization. Patent lawyers have to work with scientists to translate plans into patent applications. But the teaching of intellectual property law to students does not necessarily call for the same level of specialization. The level of specialization required to teach intellectual property law is a function of the needs of students. Students who are introduced to the subject for the first time need to understand the general connection between intellectual property law and the analyses found in the ordinary common law opinions. Students introduced to intellectual property for the first time do not need to learn the translation of a particular branch of science into a patent application. For students who intend to specialize in the practice of intellectual property, or even to teach students who intend to specialize, a deeper level of connection with specific topics of practice may be required.

Changing Attitudes, Technologies, and Risks

The landscape of changes in the law and in academic attitudes toward the law cannot be limited to considerations like the way intellectual property law fits with other bodies of doctrine or other academic subjects, or the degree to which legislative enactments tilt toward or away from stronger intellectual property rights. Changes in modern academic writings on the subject may owe something to technological change as well.

The last half-century has seen a striking increase in the ease with which the fruits of innovation can be copied cheaply and accurately, a trend that has accelerated with advances in computing, digitization, lasers, and other technologies. When one of us (we're not disclosing which one) began practicing law, law offices housed many typists and proofreaders who spent hours typing, retyping, and checking documents. Some standard products, apart from the originals typed on machines that had changed little since the late nineteenth century, were hard to read, and "carbon copies" of typed manuscripts even harder to read. Motion pictures were on reel-to-reel film shown in theatres, and copying them required an elaborate process to reproduce the film and transport it physically from one location to another. In that environment, copying was difficult, expensive, and inaccurate.

In today's world, a push of a button, not special talents and large staffs, is all that is needed. Technology—often packaged in small, portable devices that are accessible around the globe—together with instant communications, cheap data storage, and low-cost means for manipulating data have made piracy easy and counterfeiting an international business. Perfect copies of documents, including signatures and watermarks, can be reproduced at low cost in seconds and made available instantly in remote locations. Movies can be replicated digitally and distributed electronically. The advent of three-dimensional copiers may soon bring the same ease of replication to physical objects. Advancements in the technology of copying and dissemination affect a potentially large number of enterprises, dramatically shifting the balance of reward between creators and copiers.

These changes suggest that there is a greater social benefit from protecting intellectual property. The easier copying is and the harder it is to protect against it, the greater the disincentive to invest time, energy, and money in producing inventions and creative works. Increasing legal protections may not fully offset these changes, but stronger protections are at least within the set of plausible responses, potentially improving incentives for creativity.

We recognize that whether changes in technology and practice make greater protection of innovation and creative work socially desirable is ultimately an empirical question. In the field of creative expression, there is arguably a trade-off in social welfare between a regime of deeper investments by established participants and one of shallower investments among a broader group of individuals. In the field of life-changing innovation, such as medical devices, the notion of such a trade-off seems far-fetched. Although the Nigerian film industry appears to thrive locally even in the absence of effective copyright protection, we are aware of no important centers of technological innovation that thrive in the absence of intellectual property protection. Intellectual property rights enable financiers to support the intensive investment (of time and effort) and specialization necessary to bring large-scale innovation to global markets. A reduction in protection necessarily implies shallower investments, which the example of filmmaking in Nigeria serves to illustrate. But any significant change in the scope of protection in response to the changing technology of copying will have to come, at least in part, through the legislature. We have reached a stage where technological change may require a reset in the foundations of intellectual property.

The rather muted academic response to this state of affairs, coupled with the rise of the zero-sum view, may reflect an instinct to promote more copying as it becomes cheaper to do it, because the social cost of protecting property increases as the total cost of using it approaches the marginal cost (which is close to zero). It's not just that the *next* copy of *Despicable Me* or *The Da Vinci Code* costs nothing to the author or producer once the initial creative work has been produced; the perfect copy itself now costs next to nothing. That raises the net value produced by the copying and, by extension, the net cost of preventing it. And this ignores any costs from oversaturating the market, which we will put aside for these purposes. The more serious problem with the static-cost-focused analysis is that it ignores the dynamic knock-on effects on creativity and innovation.

We have tread lightly around the issue of technology and copying. Our focus in this book has been to state (or restate) and to remind readers of the legal and economic basis for intellectual property laws, an argument sorely provoked by modern academic writing. To fully explore the problem of technology and copying would require an entirely new book. Still, there are some straightforward observations we can offer here.

Although technology has brought the cost of copying down to almost zero, that does not mean that the people who copy and that the people who acquire copies do so for free. Digital technology has made copying easy and apparently free, but only for those who first gain access to the technology. In other words, technology has created a digital amusement park of sorts, where all the rides are free but you have to pay a fee to get into the park. The entrance fee is represented by the prices charged for personal computers, smartphones, Internet service, and similar devices and services. What determines the entrance fee? The entrance fee is determined in part by the amount users are willing to pay to gain access to all of the free content made available by the technology. Of course competition drives the profits of computer makers down to low levels, but their overall market is determined in substantial part by the demand for free content. Examining the technology problem from this perspective reveals that it is really less about people getting things for free than about a redistribution of the rewards for creative activity. This technology-induced redistribution has shifted the reward from creators to copyists and to the makers of the technology that makes copying possible. Much of the business in the technology sector today appears to be a struggle over control of the rents from creative activity. When Apple negotiates with music labels over the prices charged for songs on iTunes, it enters the bargaining process with enormous leverage—because technology already allows the consumers Apple targets to get the music for free. Today the struggle between technological conveyors and content creators appears to be one in which creators are losing.

The law can take any of several approaches to the technology problem. One is to facilitate the efforts by content creators to redistribute the rents from content back toward themselves. This would entail enforcement of intellectual property rights by courts, as a minimal step. The law could go further within its existing framework by permitting mergers for the purpose of gaining bargaining power among content providers. Outside of these options, a license fee could be charged against each device or service that can be used for downloading free content, on the theory that it would eventually be used for this purpose. Although this would undermine the function of legal digital libraries, it would come to grips with the reality that many users bypass legal sources to get copyrighted content free from the Web. Indeed, Microsoft, before being stopped by the Department of Justice, charged computer makers a license fee for each personal computer made, whether or not Microsoft's operating system was installed, on the theory that it would very likely have Microsoft's operating system installed eventually. It was much cheaper to just charge the license for every device rather than monitor the installation of Microsoft's operating system. The same holds true today for the distribution of digital content; most owners of personal computers and similar devices will get access to a great deal of copyrighted content for free today. Finding a way to charge them up front for that eventuality would save a lot of negotiating time and costs. Finally, doing nothing, always an option, ensures that the technology sector will continue to grab the economic rents generated by content creators—at least until another technology comes along that would allow content creators to stop that.

As for this book's connection to the problem of technology and copying, we have offered the modest proposal that the existing legal framework provides at least part of the solution to the copying problem facing content creators today. But first, courts and commentators have to recognize the problem as a struggle over the distribution of rewards rather than a struggle between holdouts of the past and harbingers of the future.

Learning from the World: Relating to the World of Ideas

In looking at the range of intellectual property rules currently in place in advanced economies, and especially in the United States, we have made the case that a property-focused approach best addresses the trade-offs associated with any change in the scope of protection. We also have made the case that the existing legal rules are generally defensible within an analysis of their costs and benefits.

Obviously, the existing rules are not perfect; the careful reader will note that we have been less than Panglossian in our outlook. But admitting that the current framework is imperfect still leaves us far away from those engaged in a broad-based assault on fundamental propositions that support intellectual property. In closing this book, our most impassioned plea is for the people who think and write about intellectual property law, who teach about it and make policy for it, and who draft and interpret the laws, to be sensitive to the real-world context in which it must live.

Our intended audience for this book consists of intellectual property scholars; policy makers; students; commentators; and people interested in innovation, creativity, and invention—indeed, any person who wants to or is required to think broadly about the policies underlying our intellectual property laws. We hope that we can reach them in a moment or at a stage where they have not become committed to the skeptical view promoted in the current academic discourse.

Law has provided a great natural experiment. While there is considerable overlap in the basic elements of intellectual property laws across economically advanced societies, it is also true that legal institutions vary substantially across nations and even within nations. Our intellectual property laws have helped to create a society that is wealthier by virtually every conceivable measure than those of alternative legal regimes. To maintain the benefits of our laws for future generations, we should try to understand why they have worked. Freedom is a worthy goal, but making what others create and nurture "free" can be the most expensive change.

Notes

1. Understanding Intellectual Property Law

1. National Center for Health Statistics (U.S.), DHHS pub. No. 2008–1232, Health, United States, 2007: With Chartbook on Trends in the Health of Americans 69, 192 (U.S. Dept. of Health and Human Services ed., Hyattsville, Md.: Dept. of Health and Human Services, Center for Disease Control and Prevention, National Center for Health Statistics 2007) (1977), available at http://www.cdc.gov/nchs/data/hus/hus07.pdf.

2. See Bernard Guyer, et al., *Annual Summary of Vital Statistics: Trends in the Health of Americans During the 20th Century,* 106 Pediatrics 1307, 1307–17 (2000).

3. U.S. Patent No. 174,465 (filed Feb. 14, 1876) (issued Mar. 7, 1876). See, e.g., Ben Ikenson, Patents: Ingenious Inventions, How They Work and How They Came to Be 55–57 (Black Dog & Leventhal Pub. 2004).

4. Tim Kelly, *Twenty Years of Measuring the Missing Link,* 4, ITU, Oct. 2005, http://www.itu.int/osg/spu/sfo/missinglink/kelly-20-years.pdf; *The Missing Link, Report of the Independent Commission for World Wide Telecommunications Development,* 13, ITU, Jan. 1985, http://www.itu.int/osg/spu/sfo/missinglink/The_Missing_Ling_A4-E.pdf.

5. See John Locke, The Second Treatise on Civil Government 18–35 (Prometheus Books 1986) (1689) (see discussion in Chapter 2).

6. Arthur Young, Travels in France, July 30, 1787 & November 7, 1787, quoted in The Home Book of Quotations 1622 (Burton Egbert Stevenson ed., 10th ed., Dodd, Mead & Co. 1967).

7. Pierre Joseph Proudhon et al., What is Property?: An Inquiry Into the Principle of Right and of Government 11 (Benjamin R. Tucker, trans., Humboldt Publishing Company 1890) (1840). Proudon referred to property as "robbery," but the quote is commonly expressed using the word "theft."

8. See, e.g., Gerald A. Cohen, Self-Ownership, Freedom, and Equality (Cambridge Univ. Press 1995); Jennifer Nedelsky, Private Property and the Limits of American Constitutionalism: The Madisonian Framework and Its Legacy (Univ. of

Chicago Press 1994); Joseph W. Singer, *Sovereignty and Property*, 86 Nw. U. L. Rev. 1 (1991); Mark Tushnet, *An Essay on Rights*, 62 Tex. L. Rev. 1363 (1984).

9. On desert theories of resource allocation see, e.g., Serena Olsaretti, Liberty, Desert, and the Market: A Philosophical Study (Cambridge Univ. Press 2004); David Miller, Principles of Social Justice (Harvard Univ. Press 1999); Joel Feinberg, "Justice and Personal Desert," in Doing and Deserving 55–94 (Princeton Univ. Press 1970). An argument in the same general vein treats property as primarily the product of social institutions; see Liam Murphy & Thomas Nagel, The Myth of Ownership: Taxes and Justice (Oxford Univ. Press 2002).

10. John Christman, The Myth of Property: Toward an Egalitarian Theory of Ownership (Oxford Univ. Press 1994); Samuel Bowles & Herbert Gintis, Recasting Egalitarianism (Verso 1998); Egalitarianism: New Essays on the Nature and Value of Equality (Nils Holtug & Kasper Lippert-Rasmussen eds., Oxford Univ. Press 2007).

11. The major source of this viewpoint in legal philosophy circles is Rawls's theory of justice. See John Rawls, A Theory of Justice (Harvard Univ. Press 1971).

12. Oskar Lange & Fred M. K. Taylor, On the Economic Theory of Socialism 89–90 (Benjamin E. Lippincott. ed., 1st paperback ed., McGraw-Hill Book Co. 1964) (1936); Abba P. Lerner, The Economics of Control (MacMillan 1944).

13. George Soros, The Credit Crisis of 2008 and What it Means: The New Paradigm for Financial Markets (Public Affairs 2009); George Akerlof & Robert Shiller, Animal Spirits (Princeton Univ. Press 2009); Thomas Frank, The Wrecking Crew (Metropolitan Books 2008); Thomas Woods, Jr., Meltdown (Regnery Press 2009).

14. Mancur Olson, Jr., The Logic of Collective Action: Public Goods and the Theory of Groups 11, 29, 48 (Harvard Univ. Press, 2d ed. 1971).

15. On the overexploitation of common property, see, e.g., H. Scott Gordon, *The Economic Theory of a Common-Property Resource: The Fishery*, 62 J. Pol. Econ. 124 (1954); Garrett Hardin, *The Tragedy of the Commons*, 162 Science 1243, 1243–1248 (1968). For a brief intellectual history of the common property problem, see Henry E. Smith, *Semicommon Property Rights and Scattering in the Open Fields*, 29 J. Legal Stud. 131, 138 n.18 (2000).

16. The works within this genre range from technical analyses of planning to polemically charged pieces on the failures the market. On the technical side, see, e.g., Stephen A. Marglin, Approaches to Dynamic Investment Planning (North-Holland, 2d ed. 1967). On the nontechnical side, see Bowles & Gintis, *supra* note 10.

17. See, e.g., Ludwig von Mises, Human Action: a Treatise on Economics 257–59 (Ludwig Von Mises Institute, 3d ed. 1966) (1949); F. A. Hayek, *The Use of Knowledge in Society*, 35 Am. Econ Rev. 519, 524–526 (1945); Milton Friedman & Rose D. Friedman, Free to Choose 38–39, 134–35 (Harcourt Brace Jovanovich, 1980). But see, e.g., Lester C. Thurow, The Zero-sum Society: Distribution and the Possibilities for Economic Change 23, 105, 130 (Basic Books 1980).

18. Joint Economic Comm., 107th Cong., Russia's Uncertain Economic Future, S. PRT. 107–50, at 269, 271–272 (1st Sess. 2001).

19. See, e.g., Cass R. Sunstein, Free Markets and Social Justice (Oxford Univ. Press 1999).

20. See Adam Bryant, *On a Wing and a Fare: Deregulation Decoded,* N.Y. Times, Nov. 5, 1995, §4 at 5; Robert Crandall, *Charge More, Merge Less, Fly Better,* N.Y. Times, Apr. 21, 2008, at A26.

21. Richard A. Posner, A Failure of Capitalism (Harvard Univ. Press 2009).

22. In some European systems, there is also a moral rights basis for some intellectual property rights. See Chapter 3.

23. See, e.g., Wendy J. Gordon, *Render Copyright unto Caesar: On Taking Incentives Seriously,* 71 U. Chi. L. Rev. 75, 89 (2004).

24. See, e.g., *Prescription for Change, A Survey of Pharmaceuticals,* 375, Issue 8431, The Economist, Special Section 3–5 (2005).

25. Susan Fitzgerald, *Vaccine Pioneer Who Saved Millions Dies at 65,* Phila. Inq., Apr. 12, 2005 at A1; Michael Kremer & Christopher M. Snyder, *Why Are Drugs More Profitable Than Vaccines* 11–22 (Nat'l Bureau of Econ. Research, Working Paper No. 9833, 2003).

26. See, e.g., William M. Landes & Richard A. Posner, The Economic Structure of Intellectual Property Law 25–30 (Belknap Press 2003).

27. Letter from Thomas Jefferson to Isaac MacPherson, (Aug. 13, 1813), reprinted in Thomas Jefferson, Writings (Library of America, 1984) at 1286, quoted in David G. Post, His Napster's Voice, in Copy Fights: The Future of Intellectual Property in the Information Age at 114 (Adam Thierer & Clyde Wayne Crews, Jr., eds., Cato Institute 2002).

28. See, e.g., Richard M. Stallman, *Did You Say "Intellectual Property"? It's a Seductive Mirage,* 4 Policy Futures in Education 334, 334–336 (2006), available at http://www.gnu.org/philosophy/not-ipr.xhtml.

29. Richard M. Stallman, *Freedom—Or Copyright,* GNU Operating System, http://www.gnu.org/philosophy/freedom-or-copyright.html.

30. Richard M. Stallman, *Why Software Should Not Have Owners,* GNU Operating System, http://www.gnu.org/philosophy/why-free.html.

31. Lawrence Lessig, The Future of Ideas: The Fate of the Commons in a Connected World 247 (Vintage Books 2002).

32. Post, *supra* note 27, at 115.

33. Michele Boldrin & David K. Levine, Against Intellectual Monopoly (Cambridge Univ. Press 2008).

2. Rights to Property

1. This is the familiar account, though the record on land holding by American Indians has been recognized as more complicated for a long time; see, e.g., John C. McManus, *An Economic Analysis of Indian Behavior in the North American Fur Trade,* 32 J. Econ. Hist. 36 (1972); William Cronon, Changes in the Land: Indian,

Colonists, and the Ecology of New England (Hill & Wang 1983). For an economic account of the property patterns among American Indians, see Harold Demsetz, *Toward a Theory of Property Rights,* 57 Am. Econ. Rev. 347–359, at 352 (1967). Demsetz suggests that tribal land-holding (in contrast to individual land-holding) regimes were common in areas, and at times, in which the benefits of property systems were small relative to the burdens of maintaining them. This was so often the case that a common story developed based on the observation of tribal property claims.

2. See, e.g., Ronald H. Coase, *The Federal Communications Commission,* 2 J.L. & Econ. 1, 2–7 (1959); Thomas W. Hazlett, *The Rationality of U.S. Regulation of the Broadcast Spectrum,* 33 J.L. & Econ. 133, 135–36 (1990).

3. Thomas W. Hazlett, *Assigning Property Rights to Radio Spectrum Users: Why Did FCC License Auctions Take 67 Years?* 41 J.L. & Econ. 529, 529–30 (1998).

4. Adam Smith, Lectures on Jurisprudence 14 (Ronald L. Meek, David Raphael & Peter G. Stein eds., Oxford Univ. Press 1978). For a modern economic approach to property rights that is consistent with Smith, see Demsetz, *supra* note 1. Demsetz emphasizes the role of property in internalizing external costs and benefits. Although Smith did not refer to externality theory, his arguments are similar to Demsetz's—though simpler and less theoretically developed. Both theories explain how property regimes change in response to changes in technology and consumption patterns. The Demsetz paper touched off a wave of studies of the historical and cultural development of property rights—see, e.g., D. Bruce Johnsen, *The Formation and Protection of Property Rights Among the Southern Kwakiutl Indians,* 15 J. Legal Stud. 41 (1986); Martin J. Bailey, *Approximate Optimality of Aboriginal Property Rights,* 35 J. Law & Econ. 183 (1992). Carol Rose suggests that the narrative approach in these studies is necessary because standard economic analysis would have difficulty explaining the formation of a property regime; see Carol Rose, *Property as Storytelling: Perspectives from Game Theory, Narrative Theory, and Feminist Theory,* in Perspectives on Property (Robert C. Ellickson, Carol M. Rose, & Bruce A. Ackerman, eds., Aspen Law & Bus., 3d ed., 2002).

5. *Id.* at 14–20.

6. *Id.* at 16.

7. *Id.* For similar reflections concerning the role of commerce and property law, see Hernando De Soto, The Mystery of Capital: Why Capitalism Triumphs in the West and Fails Everywhere Else 69–103 (Basic Books 2000); Thomas W. Merrill & Henry E. Smith, *What Happened to Property in Law and Economics,* 111 Yale L.J. 357, 362 n.18 (2001).

8. We have conflated the issues of the existence of a property rule and the security of enforcement. A property rule can exist without being enforced. Similarly, a right to property can be enforceable in the absence of a legal rule protecting it. Our discussion assumes that property rules are enforced. Where rules are not necessarily enforced, the security (and the value) of property will be determined largely

by the likelihood of enforcement. See, e.g., Annette M. Kim, *A Market without the 'Right' Property Rights,* 12 Economics of Transition. 275–305 (2004).

9. John Locke, The Second Treatise on Civil Government 20 (Prometheus Books, 1986) (1689).

10. *Id.* at 20.

11. *Id.* at 29.

12. Robert Nozick, Anarchy, State and Utopia 175 (Basic Books 1974).

13. See, e.g., Adam Mosoff, *Locke's Labor Lost,* 9 U. Chi. L. School Roundtable 155, 156–63 (2002).

14. Hobbes's argument preceded Locke's by roughly a generation. See Thomas Hobbes, Leviathan 132 (Richard Tuck ed., Cambridge Univ. Press 1991) (1660). Locke does not refer explicitly to Hobbes in the text of the treatise, but it is clear that many of the arguments respond directly to those of Hobbes. For specific arguments on the limitations of government power, see Locke, *supra* 75–78.

15. For a similar analysis, see Frederick Schauer, *Categories and the First Amendment: A Play in Three Acts,* 34 Vand. L. Rev. 265, 280–81, 307 (1981).

16. Jeremy Bentham, Theory of Legislation 100, 111–13, 146 (Etienne Dumont & Richard Hildreth trans., Kegan Paul, Trench, Trubner & Co. 1864); Jeremy Bentham, A Manual of Political Economy 71 (G.P. Putnam 1839).

17. See David Hume, Thomas Hill Green & Thomas Hodge Grose, Essays: Moral, Political, and Literary 288–99 (Longmans, Green 1889).

18. Adam Smith, The Wealth of Nations 496–97 (Prometheus Books 1991).

19. For a thorough analysis of the productivity benefits of property rights, see Steven Shavell, Foundations of Economic Analysis of Law 12, 16, 20 (Harvard Univ. Press 2004).

20. See Robert H. Lowie, Primitive Society 206–10 (Liveright Publishing Corporation 1947); Richard A. Posner, *A Theory of Primitive Society, with Special Reference to Law,* 23 J. Law Econ. 1, 12–13 (1980).

21. *See, e.g.,* Richard Dawkins, The Selfish Gene 117 (Oxford Univ. Press 1976); see also Matthew Ridley, The Red Queen: Sex and the Evolution of Human Nature 213 (Harper Perennial 2003).

22. Smith, *supra* note 16, at 24, 86; David Hume, A Treatise of Human Nature 485, 514 (Lewis Amherst Selby-Bigge ed., Clarendon Press 1888); David Hume, The Philosophical Works of David Hume 257 (Little, Brown and Company 1854) (Originally from Harvard University); David Ricardo, On the Principles of Political Economy and Taxation (3d ed., 1821), reprinted in The Works and Correspondence of David Ricardo 128–49 (Piero Sraffa ed., Cambridge 1951); Richard A. Epstein, The Monopolistic Vices of Progressive Constitutionalism, 2005 Cato Sup. Ct. Rev. 11, 15. Merrill and Smith have emphasized the limited cookie-cutter nature of property rights as an illustration of their role in promoting trade; see Thomas W. Merrill & Henry E. Smith, *What Happened to Property in Law and Economics,* 111 Yale L.J. 357 (2001).

23. See Craig Richardson, The Collapse of Zimbabwe in the Wake of the 2000–2003 Land Reforms (Edwin Mellen Press 2004).

24. See, e.g., Paul Kennedy, *Political Barriers to African Capitalism,* 32 J. Mod. Afr. Stud., 191, 199 (1994); Joseph Schumpeter, Capitalism, Socialism and Democracy (Harper Torchbooks 1975) (1942); Walt Whitman Rostow & Michael Kennedy, Theorists of Economic Growth from David Hume to the Present: With a Perspective on the Next Century 323–24 (Oxford Univ. Press 1990); Mancur Olson, Power and Prosperity: Outgrowing Communist and Capitalist Dictatorships 6–14, 111–35 (Basic Books 2000).

25. See, e.g., Ronald H. Coase, *The Problem of Social Cost,* 3 J.L. & Econ. 1, 8, 15–16 (1960).

26. See Amartya K. Sen, Commodities and Capabilities 9 (Oxford Univ. Press 1999); Amartya Sen, *Capability and Well-Being,* in The Quality of Life 30–53 (Martha Nussbaum & Amartya Sen eds., 1993). A related critique of the utilitarian case for property rights focuses on whether there is a sensible way to talk about social value at all. The problem is especially clear when voluntary exchange is not available. The problems with making interpersonal utility comparisons are substantial and affect all social welfare calculations, even those based on the assumption that no one is made worse off (Pareto criterion). See, e.g., Amartya Sen, *Personal Utilities and Public Judgments: Or What's Wrong with Welfare Economics,* 89 Econ. J. 537 (1979). In a wide range of real world cases, however, this objection is mainly theoretical— some decision has to be made regarding the rules that will obtain for a society, and a credible assessment can be made of the rules that on balance will make society better off.

27. See, e.g., Ronald A. Cass, *Property Rights Systems and the Rule of Law,* The Elgar Companion to Property Right Economics 222–248 (Enrico Colombatto ed., Edward Elgar Publications 2003).

28. See, e.g., Thomas W. Merrill & Henry A. Smith, *Optimal Standardization in the Law of Property: The Numerus Clausus Principle,* 110 Yale L. J. 1 (2000).

29. Ronald H. Coase, *The Lighthouse in Economics,* 17 J.L. & Econ. 357, 363–65, 375–76 (1974).

30. See, e.g., Charles Fried, Right and Wrong (Harvard Univ, Press 1978).

31. Stephen R. Munzer, A Theory of Property 131 (Cambridge Univ. Press 1990). The argument is based directly on Kant; see Immanuel Kant, The Metaphysical Elements of Justice 52–52, 64–65 (John Ladd trans., 1965) (1797). The argument should be distinguished from the relatively recent one of Margaret Radin, who argues that some property interests should be protected because they "are closely bound up with personhood because they are part of the way we constitute ourselves as continuing personal entities in the world" Margaret Jane Radin, *Property and Personhood,* 34 Stan. L. Rev. 957, 959 (1982). Radin's argument is a normative theory for extending property protection to things that are deemed personal, or closely bound up with privacy and personality.

32. See NOMOS XXII: Property 174–76 (J. Roland Pennock & John W. Chapman eds., New York Univ. Press 1980).

33. Richard A. Posner, Economic Analysis of Law (5th ed., 1998); Michele Boldrin & David K. Levine, Against Intellectual Monopoly (Cambridge Univ. Press 2008); Ian Aryes & Paul Klemperer, *Limiting Patentees' Market Power Without Reducing Innovation Incentives: The Perverse Benefits of Uncertainty and Non-injunctive Remedies,* 97 Mich L. Rev. 985 (1999); Michael A. Heller & Rebecca S. Eisenberg, *Can Patents Deter Innovation? The Anticommons in Biomedical Research,* 280 Science 698 (1998).

34. Harold Demsetz, *Barriers to Entry,* 72 Am. Econ. Rev. 47–57 (1982).

35. They can be broader of course, see Posner, *supra* note 33, at 37–38; Heller & Eisenberg, *supra* note 33. Heller and Eisenberg have emphasized the "anticommons" effect of property rights. The idea is similar to the double-marginalization problem identified in antitrust law, or the familiar story of the toll road divided into two segments. Let one person own one segment of the toll road and another person own the other. Each will set the monopoly price, which results in far less consumption of the toll road services than if one firm set a single monopoly price for the entire road. In the same sense, excessive fragmentation of property rights, which tends toward an "anticommmons," leads to inefficient underconsumption of resources. However, the anticommons theory raises as many questions as it answers. In a competitive market, firms will bid for patent rights. Inefficient fragmentation will generate bids, especially from dominant firms, to consolidate patent rights. Excessive fragmentation will tend to be reduced by market forces. Moreover, owners of fragmented pieces will have an incentive to pool ownership stakes in order to lessen the inefficiency from fragmentation. For additional arguments, see Richard A. Epstein & Bruce N. Kuhlik, Navigating the Anticommons for Pharmaceutical Patents: Steady the Course on Hatch-Waxman, 2004, available at http://ssrn.com/abstract=536322.

36. Aryes & Klemperer, *supra* note 33.

3. Intellectual Property

1. See Kris Bisgard, Ctrs. for Disease Control and Prevention, U.S. Dept. of Health and Human Servs., Guidelines for the Control of Pertussis Outbreaks, at Chapter 1 (2000), http://www.cdc.gov/nip/publications/pertussis/guide.htm; *Pertussis—United States, January 1992–June 1995,* 44(28) Morbidity and Mortality Weekly Report (MMWR) 525, 525–29 (1995), available at http://www.cdc.gov/mmwr/preview/mmwrhtml/00038200.htm.

2. *Id.*

3. See Doug Jenkinson, Statistics about Whooping Cough (2005), http://www.whoopingcough.net/statistics.htm.

4. Infoplease.com, *Death Rates by Cause of Death, 1900–2005,* http://www.infoplease.com/ipa/A0922292.html; Kenneth D. Kochanek et al., *Deaths: Final*

Data for 2002, National Vital Statistics Reports (2004), at Table 11, available at http://www.cdc.gov/nchs/data/nvsr/nvsr53/nvsr53_05acc.pdf.

5. Centers for Disease Control, *Prevention and Control of Tuberculosis in U.S. Communities with At-Risk Minority Populations: Recommendations of the Advisory Council for the Elimination of Tuberculosis,* 41(RR-5) Morbidity and Mortality Weekly Report 1 (1992), available at http://www.cdc.gov/mmwr/preview/mmwrhtml/00019899. htm; Centers for Disease Control, Table 1: Tuberculosis Cases, Case Rates per 100,000 Population, Deaths, and Death Rates per 100,000 Population, and Percent Change: United States, 1953–2007, http://www.cdc.gov/tb/surv/2007/pdf/table1.pdf.

6. The national reporting system on Tuberculosis incidence began in 1953. See, e.g., Ending Neglect: The Elimination of Tuberculosis in the United States 26 (Lawrence Geiter ed., National Academies Press 2000), cited in *Trends in Tuberculosis Incidence—United States, 2006,* 56(11); Morbidity and Mortality Weekly Report 245 (Mar. 23, 2007), available at http://www.cdc.gov/mmwr/preview/mmwrhtml/mm5611a2.htm. Around the same time antibiotic drugs were introduced to treat Tuberculosis B, which led to a new method of controlling it, see Madelon Lubin Finkel, Truth, Lies, and Public Health: How We Are Affected When Science and Politics Collide 107 (Praeger 2007).

7. Marko B. Lens & Martin Dawes, *Epidemiological Trends of Cutaneous Malignant Melanoma: Mortality From Cutaneous Malignant Melanoma,* (2004) available at http://bcbsma.medscape.com/viewarticle/470300_3.

8. See Robert D. Atkinson & Randolph H. Court, *Computing Costs Are Plummeting,* Progressive Policy Institute (1998), http://www.neweconomyindex.org/section1_page12.html.

9. Ray Kurzweil, *The Law of Accelerating Returns,* KurzweilAI.net, Mar. 7, 2001, http://www.kurzweilai.net/articles/art0134.html?printable=1.

10. This basic defense of intellectual property has been recognized for a long time, though critics of intellectual property often lose sight of it. See Chauncey Smith, *A Century of Patent Law,* 5 Q. J. Econ. 44, 63 (1891).

11. We recognize, of course, that there are alternative ways that innovators can appropriate part of the returns from innovation; patenting is not the only avenue. But the effectiveness of the alternative strategies, such as trade secrecy, is often dependent on special circumstances. For a balanced review of the evidence on the importance of patents, compared with alternatives, see Jonathan M. Barnett, *Do Patents Matter? Empirical Evidence on the Incentive Thesis,* 178–211, in Handbook on Law, Innovation and Growth (Robert Litan ed., Edward Elgar 2011). We discuss trade secrecy as an alternative to patenting in Chapter 5.

12. For stories, see Sally Helgesen, Wildcatters: A Story of Texans, Oil and Money 56–70 (Beard Books 2003); Roger M. Olien & Diana Davids Hinton, Wildcatters: Texas Independent Oilmen 18–19 (2d ed., Texas A&M Univ. Press 2007).

13. Richard A. Posner, *The Social Costs of Monopoly and Regulation,* 83 J. Pol. Econ. 807–828 (1975).

14. On the economics of information and the social costs of property in information, see Kenneth J. Arrow, *Economic Welfare and the Allocation of Resources for Invention, in* National Bureau of Economic Research, The Rate and Direction of Inventive Activity: Economic and Social Factors 609–626 (Princeton Univ. Press 1962).

15. Our view is in contrast to that of Arnold Plant, an early economic critic of intellectual property rights, who argued that intellectual property rights *create* scarcity by restricting access to information; Arnold Plant, *The Economic Theory Concerning Patents for Inventions,* 1 Economica 30 (1934), *reprinted in* Selected Economic Essays and Addresses 35 (Routledge & Keegan Paul 1974). In the worst-case scenario, Plant's argument would be a fair description, and intellectual property rights would operate as a pure tax on economic activity. But the information that individuals will seek to gain property rights to will tend to be scarce, or difficult to produce, in the first place. The property right will encourage the production of, or search for, the information.

16. The ability to secure payment for the information, of course, depends on the expectation that the person buying access to it can profit from it, which either depends on substantial "first mover" advantages or on the ability to continue to limit access. One additional problem is that the owner of an idea may have an incentive to decompose the idea into components in order to gain a monopoly on each part. This returns us to the double-marginalization, or anticommons, problem addressed in some recent critiques of intellectual property; see, e.g., Michael A. Heller & Rebecca S. Eisenberg, *Can Patents Deter Innovation? The Anticommons in Biomedical Research,* 280 Science 698 (1998). The anticommons theory implies that the owner of a patent monopoly, in combination with vertically related patents, leads to a much greater loss in social welfare than implied by the standard monopoly analysis. An empirical test of the anticommmons hypothesis, using data from the biomedical research setting, rejected the hypothesis; see John P. Walsh, Charlene Cho & Wesley M. Cohen, *View from the Bench: Patents and Material Transfers,* 309 Science 2002 (2005).

17. The same point can be expressed in terms of natural law rather than utilitarian analysis; see, e.g., Benjamin G. Damstedt, *Limiting Locke: A Natural Law Justification for the Fair Use Doctrine,* 112 Yale L. J. 1179, 1199 (2003).

18. This aphorism has been attributed to Benjamin Franklin; see http://www.brainyquote.com/quotes/authors/b/benjamin_franklin_9.html.

19. See generally Alexander Meiklejohn, Free Speech and Its Relation to Self-Government (Harper Bros. 1948) (advocating unrestrained free speech and the First Amendment as the cornerstone to a democracy).

20. David Shelledy, *Access to the Press: A Teleological Analysis of a Constitutional Double Standard,* 50 Geo. Wash. L. Rev. 430, 432–33 (1982).

21. Michael L. Seigel, *A Pragmatic Critique of Modern Evidence Scholarship,* 88 Nw. U. L. Rev. 995, 1034, n.173 (1994); Karl R. Popper, The Logic of Scientific

Discovery 279 (rev. ed., Hutchinson 1972) (scientists' conjectures are not dogmatically upheld, but rather scientists strive to overthrow them); see also Daubert v. Merrell Dow Pharm., Inc., 509 U.S. 579, 593 (1993) (falsifiability is crucial to determining whether proffered evidence amounts to scientific knowledge).

22. See Whitney v. California, 274 U.S. 357, 377 (1927) (Brandeis, J., concurring) ("[T]he remedy to be applied is more speech, not enforced silence."); see also Richard Delgado, *First Amendment Legal Formalism Is Giving Way to First Amendment Legal Realism,* 29 Harv. C.R.-C.L. L. Rev. 169, 172 (1994).

23. This is by no means a fanciful scenario, witness the outcome from now disproved charges about silicone gel breast implants; see, e.g., David Bernstein, *The Breast Implant Fiasco,* 87 Cal. L. Rev. 457, 470–72 (1999).

24. See, e.g., Vincent Blasi, *The "Checking Value" in First Amendment Theory,* 1977 Am. B. Found. Res. J. 521 (1977); Ronald A. Cass, *The Perils of Positive Thinking: Constitutional Interpretation and Negative First Amendment Theory,* 34 U.C.L.A. L. Rev. 1405 (1987); Frederick Schauer, *The Second-Best First Amendment,* 31 Wm. & Mary L. Rev. 1 (1989); see also Kent Greenawalt, *"Clear and Present Danger" and Criminal Speech,* in Eternally Vigilant: Free Speech in the Modern Era 96, 107 (Lee C. Bollinger & Geoffrey R. Stone eds., Univ. of Chicago Press 2003).

25. Wendy J. Gordon, *Render Copyright unto Caesar: On Taking Incentives Seriously,* 71 U. Chi. L. Rev. 75 (2004).

26. Professor Henry Smith emphasizes another aspect of the relationship between the inputs to innovation and intellectual property rights that reward innovation. Smith argues that intellectual property rules can be understood as ways of improving the allocation of inputs to innovative activity. See Henry Smith, *Intellectual Property as Property: Delineating Entitlements in Information,* 116 Yale L.J. 1742 (2007). Ordinary market mechanisms will not suffice to get the allocation of resources useful for innovation right where their use in R&D efforts, but not in other activities, can provide social benefits that the purchaser of the inputs cannot capture. If, for example, there were property rights in automobiles but not in conceptualizing a different sort of automobile engine, engineers would be directed to spend too much time fixing technical production problems and too little time (from a social standpoint) on discovering new ways to power cars. Exclusive rights in the innovation in many instances provide the best route to balancing the social costs and benefits.

27. See, e.g., Edmund W. Kitch, *The Nature and Function of the Patent System,* 20 J. L. & Econ. 265, 266, 276–77 (1977); F. Scott Kieff, *Property Rights and Property Rules for Commercializing Inventions,* 85 Minn. L. Rev. 697, 710, 717–26 (2000).

28. See, e.g., Mark A. Lemley, *Ex Ante versus Ex Post Justifications for Intellectual Property,* 71 U. Chi. L. Rev. 129, 129 (2004).

29. We have surveyed theories of property rights in the previous chapter, and those theories clearly apply to intellectual property as well. For a survey of some property theories with a special focus on intellectual property, see William W. Fisher, *Theories of Intellectual Property,* in New Essays in the Legal and Political

Theory of Property (Stephen R. Munzer ed., Cambridge Univ. Press 2001). Of available theories, the utilitarian approach (cost-benefit analysis) is most easily informed by empirical evidence. For criticisms of the cost-benefit approach, see Madhavi Sunder, *IP3,* 59 Stan. L. Rev. 257 (2006); Tim Wu, *Intellectual Property, Innovation, and Decentralized Decisions,* 92 Va. L. Rev. 123 (2006); Alfred Yen, *Restoring the Natural Law: Copyright as Labor and Possession,* 51 Ohio St. L. J. 517 (1990).

30. World Economic Forum, The Global Competitiveness Report 2002–2003 at 603 (Peter K. Cornelius ed., Oxford Univ. Press 2003).

31. For a review of the empirical literature on economic growth and patents, see James Bessen & Michael J. Meurer, Patent Failure: How Judges, Bureaucrats, and Lawyers Put Innovators at Risk 73–94 (Princeton Univ. Press 2008).

32. Indeed, if judges think about the social consequences of their decisions, they will tend to expand the scope of intellectual property only when the social benefits appear to exceed the social costs. Arguments such as this have generated a literature arguing that common law is economically efficient. See generally Richard A. Posner, Economic Analysis of Law (7th ed., Aspen 2007). The common law-efficiency thesis is stronger than necessary for our purposes, and we do not rely on it in later chapters. It is enough, for our argument, that common law courts have an advantage relative to legislatures in assessing specific cost-benefit trade-offs.

4. Patent Law

1. See, e.g., Robert P. Merges, Patent Law and Policy 1–4 (2d ed., Michie 1997). Craig Nard & Andrew Morriss, *Constitutionalizing Patents: From Venice to Philadelphia,* 2 Rev. L. & Econ. 223 (2006); Pamela Long, *Inventions, Authorship, "Intellectual Property," and the Origins of Patents: Notes Toward a Conceptual History,* 32 Technology & Culture 846 (1991).

2. See E. Wyndham Hulme, *The History of the Patent System Under the Prerogative and at Common Law,* 12 L. Q. Rev. 141, 141 (1896), cited in Merges, *supra* note 1, at 6.

3. See Edward C. Walterscheid, *The Early Evolution of the United States Patent Law: Antecedents (Part I),* 76 J. Pat. & Trademark Off. Soc'y 697, 709 (1994), cited in Merges, *supra* note 1, at 4 (quoting Venetian patent law of 1474).

4. *Id.*

5. This is the standard set of requirements for product and process patents, but not for all categories of patent, such as design patents.

6. Mackay Radio & Tel. Co. v. Radio Corp. of Am., 306 U.S. 86, 94 (1939).

7. Gottschalk v. Benson, 409 U.S. 63, 67 (1972) (punctuation omitted).

8. This point deserves underscoring, because critics of intellectual property rights sometimes assume that pointing to higher costs of follow-on research (or, for copyright, follow-on expression) is reason enough to defeat or scale back intellectual property protections.

9. See, e.g., Alan Newell, *The Models Are Broken, The Models Are Broken!* 47 U. Pitt. L. Rev. 1023, 1025 (1986). Where a mathematical formula is of widespread significance—imagine a patent on the calculation of the diameter of a sphere or the volume of a cube—the administrative cost of pricing the formula is potentially quite large, perhaps larger than the value of the formula to many putative users. To the extent these administrative costs are borne by initial and follow-on researchers, they simply add to the dynamic costs of recognizing property rights in mathematical results.

Assertions that there are costs associated with pricing the use of an idea, like a mathematical formula, are by no means sufficient in themselves to prove that a property right in the idea is ill conceived. Of course, dynamic effects on follow-on research are important. But the costs associated with property rights in earlier research do not necessarily present large obstacles to later research. Where the benefits of a formula are substantial and immediate—where the users may be expected to capture a significant share of the value of the formula's use—concerns about discouraging follow-on research and discovery diminish. The formula becomes another cost that can be evaluated by the potential user in the same way that he would assess the value of using a higher powered but costlier computer.

In many instances, however, the benefits of using a formula will be difficult to capture, uncertain, and remote, to a degree qualitatively different from the case of physical goods. And as the share of potential societal benefit likely to be gained by the researcher declines, the deterrent effect of pricing the earlier research grows. And the more generally useful a mathematical formula is, the larger the cost to further research of limiting its use.

10. This point applies to basic research generally. Kenneth Arrow argued that in a profit-driven system the degree of underinvestment in research would tend to become greater as the research became more basic in nature; see Kenneth J. Arrow, *Economic Welfare and the Allocation of Resources for Invention,* in The Rate and Direction of Inventive Activity: Economic and Social Factors 609–626 (Richard R. Nelson ed., Princeton Univ. Press 1962), available at: http://www.nber.org/chapters/c2144.

11. See David Bodanis, E = mc^2: A Biography of the World's Most Famous Equation 93–113 (Berkeley Publishing Group 2000).

12. *Id.* at 182–83.

13. *Id.* at 83–84.

14. See Thomas S. Kuhn, The Structure of Scientific Revolutions 96–98, 106 (Otto Neurath ed., Univ. of Chicago Press 1962); Karl R. Popper, Conjectures and Refutations: The Growth of Scientific Knowledge (Basic Books 1962).

15. See Bodanis, *supra* note 11; Richard Rhodes, The Making of the Atomic Bomb (Simon & Schuster 1986).

16. 35 U.S.C. § 101 (2006).

17. 409 U.S. 63 (1972).

18. *Id.* at 70.

19. 405 U.S. 175 (1981). Between *Benson* and *Diehr,* there was another important decision, *Parker v. Flook,* 437 U.S. 584 (1978). *Flook* involved an attempt to patent a process for monitoring the catalytic conversion of hydrocarbons. The application was rejected by the Supreme Court on the ground that the *only* novel feature of the process was the incorporation of a mathematical algorithm. Perhaps the best way to think about *Flook* is to imagine that someone discovered a mathematical algorithm for pitching fastballs. Pitchers have been throwing fastballs for ages, so the algorithm could not be said to have introduced a new process or a new result. A patent application for the "new fastball process" would be rejected under the principles of *Benson* and *Flook*. The principles of *Benson* and *Flook* were applied to reject the business method application in *Bilski v. Kappos,* 130 S. Ct. 3218 (2010).

20. 405 U.S. at 175.

21. Application of Christensen, 478 F.2d 1392, 1393 (C.C.P.A. 1973).

22. Petisi v. Rennhard, 363 F.2d 903, 907 (C.C.P.A. 1966).

23. 56 U.S. (15 How.) 62, 112–113 (1853). See also Gottshalk v. Benson, 409 U.S. 63, 67 (1972).

24. Edmund W. Kitch, *The Nature and Function of the Patent System,* J.L. & Econ. 265, 265–290 (1977). For an alternative viewpoint questioning the Kitch thesis, see Robert P. Merges & Richard R. Nelson, *On the Complex Economics of Patent Scope,* 90 Colum. L. Rev. 839 (1990).

25. Kitch, *supra* note 24, at 268.

26. Yoram Barzel, *The Optimal Timing of Innovations,* 50 Rev. Econ. & Stat. 348 (1968).

27. See Mark F. Grady & Jay Alexander, *Patent Law and Rent Dissipation,* 78 Va. L. Rev. 305 (1992).

28. Scholars have noted the difficulty of setting out clear rules in patent law; see John F. Duffy, *Rules and Standards on the Forefront of Patentability,* 51 Wm. & Mary L. Rev. 609 (2009).

29. For years, U.S. authorities followed a "mental steps" doctrine invalidating patents depending critically on a "mental step." This doctrine was rejected by the Court of Customs and Patent Appeals in 1970. In re Musgrave, 431 F.2d 882, 889 (CCPA 1970).

30. See discussion *infra,* Chapter 8. Compare State St. Bank & Trust Co. v. Signature Fin. Grp., Inc., 149 F.3d 1368, 1368, 1375–77 (Fed. Cir. 1998), with Loew's Drive-In Theatres, Inc. v. Park-In Theatres, Inc., 174 F.2d 547, 552 (1st Cir. 1949).

31. See 35 U.S.C. §§ 101–103 (2006).

32. Brenner v. Manson, 383 U.S. 519, 519 (1966).

33. One important critique of the patent system is that patents are often written with a strategic view toward litigation rather than to communicate ideas in a straightforward way. This is not the same thing as fraud of course, but it still imposes a burden on the innovation process. See Sean B. Seymore, *The Teaching Function of Patents,* 85 Notre Dame L. Rev. 621 (2010).

34. See Titanium Metals Corp. of Am. v. Banner, 778 F.2d 775, 777 (Fed. Cir. 1985).

35. See Alan W. White, *The Novelty-Destroying Disclosure: Some Recent Decisions,* 12 Eur. Intell. Prop. Rev. 315, 318 (1990). [check citation – incl. author] For case law, see Robert Patrick Merges & John Fitzgerald Duffy, Patent Law and Policy 380–387 (4th ed., LexisNexis 2007).

36. See 35 U.S.C. § 102(b) (2006).

37. *Id.*

38. Although we have avoided the question whether date of invention or date of filing should be the optimal rule on priority, our discussion suggests that it is unclear a priori, especially in light of the statutory bars in the United States. The choice between date of invention and date of filing is often thought to have predictable distributional consequences. Suppose the world of inventors can be divided neatly into two types: corporate research departments and independent inventors. Large firms with research departments would appear to be advantaged by date of filing, while independent inventors should tend to prefer date of invention. Although it is commonly said, often by independent inventors, the costs of litigation over priority (in "interference" cases) might provide an advantage to large firms that can easily bear the litigation expenses; see Linda R. Cohen & Jun Ishii, Competition, Innovation and Racing for Priority at the U.S. Patent and Trademark Office (September 2, 2005), USC CLEO Research Paper No. C05–13, AEI-Brookings Joint Center Working Paper No. 05–22, available at SSRN: http://ssrn.com/abstract=826504.

39. Our description of the nonobviousness requirement as a type of cost-benefit inquiry suggests that courts are authorized, as general matter, to conduct a discretionary and heavily fact-dependent analysis. This appears to be the message of the Supreme Court's decision in KSR Int'l Co. v. Teleflex Inc., 550 U.S. 398 (2007), which rejected a more rigid approach adopted by the Court of Appeals for the Federal Circuit.

40. 35 U.S.C. § 103(a) (2006) (forbidding issuance of a patent where "the differences between the subject matter sought to be patented and the prior art are such that the subject matter as a whole would have been obvious at the time the invention was made to a person having ordinary skill in the art to which said subject matter pertains").

41. Sloan Filter Co. v. Portland Gold Mining Co., 139 F. 23, 26 (8th Cir. 1905); St. Regis Paper Co. v. Bemis Co., Inc., 549 F.2d 833, 838 (7th Cir. 1977); Span-Deck, Inc. v. Fab-Con, Inc., 627 F.2d 1237, 1244 (8th Cir. 1982); Hailes & Treadwell v. Van Wormer, 87 U.S. 353, 368 (1873).

42. Florsheim v. Schilling, 137 U.S. 64, 76 (1890); Hotchkiss v. Greenwood, 52 U.S. 248, 252–53 (1850); 35 U.S.C. § 103 (2006); KSR Int'l Co. v. Teleflex Inc., 550 U.S. 398 (2007) (a solution is obvious if it solves a known problem that is obviously solved by combining elements of prior art, even if it solves a different problem than did prior patents).

43. 52 U.S. (11 How.) 248, 267 (1850). The court referred to the invention requirement, rather than the nonobviousness term. However, the meaning of the invention requirement at that time was equivalent to our modern understanding of
nonobviousness.

44. Graham v. John Deere Co. of Kansas City, 383 U.S. 1, 16 (1966).

45. Robert P. Merges, *Commercial Success and Patent Standards: Economic Per-
spectives on Innovation,* 76 Cal. L. Rev. 803, 817, 823 (1988); Amanda Wieker, *Secondary
Considerations Should Be Given Increased Weight in Obviousness Inquiries Under §35
U.S.C. 103 in the Post-*KSR v. Teleflex *World,* 17 Fed. Circ. B. J. 665, 675 (2008).

46. Otto v. Koppers Co., 246 F.2d 789, 799–800 (4th Cir. 1957); Nickola v.
Peterson, 580 F.2d 898, 914 (6th Cir. 1978); Dickey-john Corp. v. Int'l Tapetronics
Corp., 710 F.2d 329, 346–347 (7th Cir. 1983); see also Herbert F. Schwartz, Patent
Law and Practice 90 (4th ed., BNA 2003). On critiques of the use of commercial suc-
cess as a proxy for nonobviousness, Merges & Duffy, *supra* note 35, at 718–724.

47. Seth Shulman, The Telephone Gambit: Chasing Alexander Graham Bell's
Secret 32–35 (W. W. Norton 2008). Anton A. Huurdeman, The Worldwide History
of Telecommunications 176–77 (Wiley-IEEE Press 2003).

48. Fred C. Kelly, The Wright Brothers: A Biography (Dover Publications 1989).
John David Anderson, Introduction to Flight (McGraw-Hill Professional 2004).

49. Ben Ikenson, Patents: Ingenious Inventions, How They Work and How They
Came to Be, 32–36 (Black Dog & Leventhal Publishers 2004).

50. See, e.g., Michael Abramowicz, *Perfecting Patent Prizes,* 56 Vand. L. Rev. 115,
183–190 (2003); Steven Shavell & Tanguy van Ypersele, *Rewards versus Intellectual
Property Rights,* 44 J. L. & Econ. 525, 542–543 (2001).

51. Moreover, while patent races can be problematic, the risk of overinvestment
that underlies concerns over patent races is easily overstated. Those who are investing
their own time, energy, and money in racing to secure a patent generally understand
the nature of the prize and the risk of being second to secure it. They can make reasoned assessments of how much the prize is worth, balancing the risks of failure
with the gains brought by success, both before starting the race and at many different steps along the way. Even though the sequential nature of investment decisions in such races can have the effect of inducing socially undesirable commitments
of resources to pursuit of patentable innovations, there is no persuasive evidence
that there is excessive investment in research directed at discovering patentable
inventions. That would require evidence that returns to investment in research are
systematically lower than returns to other economic activity. To the extent investment in innovation yields differential returns from investment in other activities,
the evidence seems to be modestly tipped the other way.

52. See, e.g., Diamond v. Chakrabarty, 447 U.S. 303, 309 (1980) ("Thus, a new
mineral discovered in the earth or a new plant found in the wild is not patentable
subject matter."); Alan L. Durham, *Natural Laws and Inevitable Infringement,* 93
Minn. L. Rev. 933, 947 (2009) ("Modern science allows researchers to modify nature

in subtle ways, but it is only in that modified form that the products of nature may be patented.").

53. Of course, there would be intense curiosity in some cases to see what the new creature looked like, which is a form of value from investing in exploration for these novelties. It is not the sort of value promoted by the patent law; it is much closer to the type of value encouraged by copyright. And, by and large, the specific commercial value of curiosity can be tapped by the finder without patent rights. The finder will be the first to describe the creature, to take photographs, and so on. All of these can find a commercial market for exposure to a broad audience of interested consumers, and copyright law will protect the particular expression of the finder.

54. 447 U.S. 303 (1980).

55. Merck & Co. v. Olin Mathieson Chem. Corp., 523 F.2d 156 (4th Cir. 1958).

56. Hotel Sec. Checking Co. v. Lorraine, 160 F. 467 (2d Cir. 1908).

57. State Str. Bank & Trust Co. v. Signature Fin. Grp., Inc., 149 F.3d 1368 (Fed. Cir. 1998).

58. In re Bilski, 545 F.3d 943 (Fed. Cir. 2008) (rejecting most business method patents under a test that requires the patent to apply to a machine or to transform an article); Bilski v. Kappos, 130 S. Ct. 3218 (2010) (rejecting Federal Circuit's machine-transformation test, and also rejecting specific patent application because of abstraction principle).

59. 130 S. Ct. 3218 (2010).

60. For a comprehensive description of the specific terms and conventions, see Robert C. Faber, Faber on Mechanics of Patent Claim Drafting (Practicing Law Inst., 6th ed. 2011); Patent and Trademark Office, Manual of Patent Examining Procedures (Government Printing Office, 8th ed. rev. 2010).

61. 517 U.S. 370 (1996).

62. See S. Jay Plager, *Abolish the Federal Court of Claims? A Question of Democratic Principle,* 71 Geo. Wash. L. Rev. 791, 797 (2003). See also Kimberly A. Moore, *Are District Judges Equipped to Resolve Patent Cases?* 15 Harv. J.L. & Tech. 1 (2001). Professor Schwartz argues that it is far from clear that experience is much help, given the difficulty of applying Federal Circuit rules on claim construction. See David L. Schwartz, *Practice Makes Perfect? An Empirical Study of Claim Construction Reversal Rates in Patent Cases,* 107 Mich. L. Rev. 223 (2008).

63. See 35 U.S.C. § 112 (¶1).

64. See 35 U.S.C. § 112 (¶6).

65. At the same time as means-plus-function expands the potential reach of patent rights, it also risks invalidation of the patent either for failing to disclose sufficient information in the specification or for claiming so wide a territory as to be obvious. See, e.g., WMS Gaming, Inc. v. International Game Technology, 184 F.3d 1339 (Fed. Cir. 1999).

66. Sanitary Refrigerator Co. v. Winters, 280 U.S. 30, 42 (1929). See also Graver Tank & Mfg. Co. v. Linde Air Prods. Co., 339 U.S. 605, 608 (1950).

67. See, e.g., Warner-Jenkinson Co. v. Hilton Davis Chem. Co., 520 U.S. 17 (1997).

68. One property related topic that we have not discussed in this chapter is that of remedies for violations. In eBay, Inc. v. MercExchange, L.L.C., 547 U.S. 388 (2006), the Supreme Court rejected the claim that an injunction is the presumptive remedy in a patent infringement dispute, holding that traditional equity principles apply. We discuss remedies in Chapter 7 (on trademarks).

69. For an important empirical assessment of the patent system, see James Bessen & Michael Meurer, Patent Failure: How Judges, Bureaucrats, and Lawyers Put Innovators at Risk (Princeton Univ. Press 2008). Bessen and Meurer find that the litigation costs outweigh the value of patents in many subject matters. A balanced and thorough review of the empirical literature is provided in Jonathan M. Barnett, *Do Patents Matter? Empirical Evidence on the Incentive Thesis*, 178–211, in Handbook on Law, Innovation and Growth (Robert Litan ed., Edward Elgar 2011). On the effects of patent laws, see Albert G. Z. Hu & Ivan P. L. Png, Patent Rights and Economic Growth: Cross-Country Evidence, CELS 2009 4th Annual Conference on Empirical Legal Studies Paper (Nov. 2009), available at http://ssrn.com/ abstract=1339730 (finding that patent rights foster innovation and economic growth); Sunil Kanwar & Robert E. Evenson, "Does intellectual property protection spur technological change?," 55 *Oxford Economic Papers* 235–264 (2003) (patents foster innovation); Bronwyn H. Hall & Rosemarie Ham Ziedonis, *The Patent Paradox Revisited: Determinants of Patenting in the U.S. Semiconductor Industry, 1979–95*, 35 Rand. J. Econ. 101–128 (2001) (mixed findings; patents spur strategic patenting, but also foster innovation); Lee Branstetter, Raymond J. Fisman & C. Fritz Foley, Do Stronger Intellectual Property Rights Increase International Technology Transfer? Empirical Evidence from U.S. Firm-Level Panel Data, World Bank Policy Research Working Paper No. 3305 (May 2004), available at http://ssrn.com /abstract=610350 (strong patent rights encourage transfer of technology); Linda Yueh, *Patent Laws and Innovation in China*, 29 Int'l Rev. L. & Econ. 304 (2009) (patent laws promote innovation in China); James S. Ang, Chaopeng Wu & Yingmei Cheng, Does Enforcement of Intellectual Property Rights Matter in China? Evidence from Financing and Investment Choices in the High Tech Industry, AFA 2011 Denver Meetings (Dec. 2010), available at http://ssrn.com/abstract=1571392 (using data on patent enforcement in China to show that patent laws encourage innovation); James W. Hughes, Michael J. Moore, & Edward A. Snyder, "Napsterizing" Pharmaceuticals: Access, Innovation, and Consumer Welfare, NBER Working Paper Series, No. w9229 (Sep. 2002), available at http://ssrn.com/abstract=334321 (using simulation to show that eliminating patent protection for drugs would reduce long-run consumer welfare); Patricia M. Danzon, Y. Richard Wang & Liang Wang, *The Impact of Price Regulation on the Launch Delay of New Drugs-Evidence from*

Twenty-five Major Markets in the 1990s, 14 Health Econ. 269 (2005) (price regulation delays launch of patented drugs).

5. Trade Secrets

1. See *Dispute Over Coca-Cola's Secret Formula,* N. Y. Times, May 3, 1993, available at http://www.nytimes.com/1993/05/03/business/dispute-over-coca-cola-s-secret-formula.html. The formula, known as "Merchandise 7X," has been a tightly guarded secret since Coca-Cola was invented in 1886. It has been disclosed only under a court order that stipulated additional protective measures to prevent inadvertent disclosure. See Coca-Cola Bottling Co. of Shreveport, Inc. v. Coca-Cola Co., 107 F.R.D. 288, 289 (D.Del.1985).

2. See http://www.kfc.com/about/secret.asp.

3. Although trade secret law—or the common law concerned with the protection of trade secrets—has for many years extended protection beyond the enforcement of contractual agreements, the noncontract-based part of trade secrecy law remains controversial to many scholars. See, e.g., Robert G. Bone, *A New Look at Trade Secret Law: Doctrine in Search of Justification,* 86 Cal. L. Rev. 241 (1998). Bone argues that trade secret law should be scaled back to protect only contractual agreements.

4. This is, of course, a matter of interpretation. For a long time tort law on trade secrecy has referred to the implicit contractual nature of some secrets. A violation of an implicit contract is indistinguishable from an ordinary tort.

5. Previous economic analyses of trade secret law have reached varying conclusions. Professors David Friedman and William Landes and Judge Richard Posner have argued that trade secret law appears to be an economically optimal supplement to patent law. See David Friedman, William Landes & Richard Posner, *Some Economics of Trade Secrets Law,* 5 J. Econ. Persp. 61–72 (1991). Later, Robert Bone marshaled several economic arguments against the optimality of trade secret law. See Bone, *supra* note 3. Landes and Posner offered a more cautious assessment of trade secret law in their book chapter on trade secrets. See William Landes & Richard Posner, The Economic Structure of Intellectual Property Law 354–371 (2002). See also Steven N. Cheung, *Property Rights in Trade Secrets,* 20 Econ. Inquiry 20 (1982).

6. One trade secret scholar described the doctrine as "a Centaurian creature, half 'confidential relationship,' half 'implied contract.'" Roger M. Milgrim, Milgrim on Trade Secrets. Business organizations v. 12, 12A, 12B. New York, NY: M. Bender, 1967. Vol. 1 § 3.01 Protection by Operation of Law. 3–8.

7. Cal. Bus. & Prof. Code § 16600 (West 2009). Edwards v. Arthur Andersen LLP, 189 P.3d 285, 291 (Cal. 2008) (ruling that section 16600 generally prohibits employee noncompetition agreements but noting an exception where restrictions are necessary to protect employer's trade secrets).

8. Although we focus on the dynamic and static cost trade-off here, for a general discussion of the history and economics of the law governing contracts in restraint of trade, see Michael Trebilcock, The Common Law of Restraint of Trade: A Legal and Economic Analysis (Carswell 1986). For a recent survey see Orly Lobel, *Intellectual Property and Restrictive Covenants* in Encyclopedia of Labor and Employment Law and Economics, (Kenneth Dau-Schmidt, Seth Harris & Orly Lobel eds., Edward Elgar Publishing 2009).

9. 24 Eng. Rep. 347 (K.B. 1711).

10. The effort to find a balance has led to the creation of multifactor tests in many state courts. See, e.g., Concrete Co. v. Lambert, 510 F.Supp. 2d 570, 579–80 (M.D.Ala. 2007) (naming four factors used by Alabama courts to determine the reasonableness of noncompetition agreements: (1) the employer has a protectable interest; (2) the restriction is reasonably related to that interest; (3) the restriction is reasonable in time and place; and (4) the restriction imposes no undue hardship).

11. See, e.g., Weigh Sys. S., Inc. v. Mark's Scales & Equip., Inc., 68 S.W.3d 299, 301–02 (Ark. 2002) ("A protectable 'trade secret' under the Uniform Trade Secrets Act has four general characteristics: (1) information, (2) deriving independent economic value, (3) not generally known, or readily ascertainable by proper means by others who can obtain economic value from its disclosure or use, and (4) the subject of efforts, reasonable under the circumstances to maintain its secrecy.") "'Trade secret' means information, including a formula, pattern, compilation, program, device, method, technique, or process, that derives independent economic value, actual or potential, from not being generally known to, and not being readily ascertainable by proper means by other persons who can obtain economic value from its disclosure or use, and is the subject of efforts that are reasonable under the circumstances to maintain its secrecy." Uniform Trade Secrets Act § 1 (4)(i)(ii) (amended 1985), 14 U.L.A. 538 (2005). These legal definitions are overinclusive, and many courts stress the factual nature of the inquiry. See, e.g., Network Telecomms., Inc. v. Boor-Crepeau, 790 P.2d 901 (Colo. App. 1990) (what constitutes a trade secret protected by Uniform Trade Secrets Act is a question of fact for the trial court). We claim that the judgment call courts make under these legal tests is typically determined by an implicit balancing of the static and dynamic costs.

12. Gary S. Becker, Human Capital: A Theoretical and Empirical Analysis, with Special Reference to Education 11–29 (2d ed., Columbia Univ. Press 1975); Edmund W. Kitch, *The Law and Economics of Rights in Valuable Information*, 9 J. Legal Stud. 683–723 (1980); Paul H. Rubin & Peter Shedd, *Human Capital and Covenants Not to Compete*, 10 J. Legal Stud. 93–110 (1981).

13. 160 A.2d 430 (Pa. 1960). See Kitch, *supra* note 12, at 704–705.

14. H. B. Wiggins' Sons' Co. v. Cott-A-Lap Co. 169 Fed. 150 (D. Conn. 1909). An earlier Massachusetts case stated the principle more broadly, describing goodwill generated through skill and attention as property. See Peabody v. Norfolk, 98 Mass. 452 (1868).

15. 18 U.S.C. § 1832 (2006).

16. 526 F.3d 1312 (11th Cir. 2008).

17. *Id.* at 1316.

18. The conviction of Williams and Dimson was for conspiracy to steal trade secrets, in violation of 18 U.S.C. § 1832(a)(1), (3), and (5).

19. 431 F.2d 1012 (5th Cir. 1970).

20. Alternatively, nuisance law could be applied in the case of a flyover that interferes with an individual's enjoyment of land. For a discussion of the early law on trespass and occupation of space above property, see John Henry Wigmore, Select Cases on the Law of Torts, with Notes and a Summary of Principles 560–563 (Little, Brown 1912). In Neiswonger v. Goodyear Tire and Rubber Co., 35 F.2d 761 (N.D. Ohio 1929), the court found that an airplane overflight within five hundred feet of the ground and in violation of federal air traffic rules implied a right of action on the part of the plaintiff, who had been injured as a result. The Goodyear blimp had passed over the plaintiff's farm at an altitude less than two hundred feet, which caused the plaintiff's horses to stampede, running over the plaintiff. While the court did not discuss trespass or nuisance law, its decision is consistent with the view that the plaintiff possessed rights protected by the common law (either trespass or nuisance). In some respects, *Neiswonger* serves as a precedent for *Christopher;* in both cases a violation of the airspace above the plaintiff's property led to an injury to the plaintiff.

21. See, e.g., Swetland v. Curtiss Airports Corp., 41 F.2d 929, 942 (1930).

22. In tort law, reasonable care is understood by many courts to require the court to compare the likely losses avoided by precaution against the burden of precaution, see United States v. Carroll Towing, 159 F.2d 169 (2d. Cir. 1947). Many courts use rather vague descriptions of the duty of reasonable care in trade secrecy. See, e.g., Computer Assocs. Int'l v. Quest Software, Inc., 333 F.Supp. 2d 688 (N.D. Ill. 2004) (noting that the Illinois Trade Secrets Act (ITSA) "requires only reasonable measures [to protect confidential information], not perfection"); Aries Info Sys., Inc. v. Pac. Mgmt. Sys. *Corp.,* 366 N.W.2d 366, 368 (Minn. App. 1987) (The possessor of a trade secret is not required to guard against unanticipated, undetectable, or unpreventable methods of discovery).

23. We say "established" to avoid the circularity of saying that reasonable care must be taken to avoid losing protection for failing to take reasonable care as required by trade secret law. We use the term "established" to refer to commonly applied trespass rules outside of the trade secrecy context.

24. Robert G. Bone, *Trade Secrecy, Innovation, and the Requirement of Reasonable Secrecy Precautions,* The Law and Theory of Trade Secrecy: A Handbook of Contemporary Research, (Rochelle C. Dreyfuss & Katherine J. Strandburg eds., Edward Elgar 2011). Bone argues persuasively that the traditional "notice" explanations are inadequate and relies on signaling and litigation-cost arguments as possible justifications. However, he concludes that the rule is difficult to justify.

25. Richard A. Posner, The Economics of Justice 262 (Harvard Univ. Press 1981).

26. Uniform Trade Secrets Act § 1 (2). See, e.g., On-Line Technologies v. Perkin Elmer Corp., 141 F.Supp. 2d 246, 257 (D. Conn. 2001) (dismissing a misappropriation claim against a third party competitor after trade secret owner failed to show that the competitor "knows or has reason to know" that information it purchased had been improperly acquired).

27. Trust and informal sanctions have been offered as explanations for the success of family-owned businesses; see Harvey S. James, "Owner as Manager, Extended Horizons and the Family Firm," 6 Int'l J. Econ. Bus. 41–56 (1999); Mike Burkart, Fausto Panunzi, & Andrei Shleifer, 2003. "Family Firms," J. Fin. 2167–2202 (2003). On the value of trade secrecy as an explanation for the existence and success of family firms, see Anuja Rajbhandary, Protecting Trade Secrets Through Family Businesses: A Case Study on Nepal 16 Int'l. Rev. L. & Econ. 483–490 (1996).

28. Jonathan S. Feinstein & Jeremy Stein, *Employee Opportunism and Redundancy in Firms,* 10 J. Econ. Behav. & Organ. 401–414 (1988).

29. KFC Corp. v. Marion-Kay Co., Inc., 620 F.Supp. 1160, 1163 (S.D. Ind. 1985).

30. David D. Friedman, William M. Landes & Richard A. Posner, *Some Economics of Trade Secret Law,* 5 J. Econ. Persp. 1, 61–72 (1991).

31. For an economic analysis, see James J. Anton & Dennis A. Yao, *Little Patents and Big Secrets: Managing Intellectual Property,* 35 Rand J. Econ. 1–22 (2004); Ignatius Horstmann, Glenn M. MacDonald & Alan Slivinski, *Patents as Information Transfer Mechanisms: To Patent or (Maybe) Not to Patent,* 93 J. Pol. Econ. 837–58 (1985).

32. This is a matter of debate in part because such an injunction has never been observed; see, e.g., Karl F. Jorda, *Patent and Trade Secret Complementariness: An Unexpected Synergy,* 48 Washburn L.J. Rev. 1, 27 (2008).

33. 35 USC § 102(g) ("A person shall be entitled to a patent unless . . . another inventor involved therein establishes . . . that before such person's invention thereof the invention was made by such other inventor and not abandoned, suppressed, or concealed . . ."). See, e.g., Young v. Dworkin, 489 F.2d 1277 (3d Cir. 1974). If you put the secret innovation into public use, even without disclosing the secret, your action could satisfy the requirement of prior innovation and public revelation. The information constituting the trade secret does not have to be revealed to invalidate the later patent. However, the fact that you have kept it secret means that you have a burden of establishing that the information incorporated in your innovation in fact is sufficiently close to the patent claims to constitute a prior public use.

34. 35 U.S.C. § 102 (b). See also Metallizing Eng'g Co. v. Kenyon Bearing & Auto Parts Co., 153 F.2d 516, 520 (2d Cir. 1946) (Judge Learned Hand affirmed the rule that an inventor who has waited more than one year to file forfeits his right to a patent, regardless of whether or not the invention was a secret or publicly known, "just as he can forfeit it by too long concealment, even without exploiting the invention at all.").

35. In other words, trade secrets exclude only those rivals who are less efficient at the combined process of innovation and production. Any rival who is less efficient, but who can still duplicate the innovation, will be excluded because he will be unable to compete against the incumbent. The rival who duplicates independently at higher cost (because he is less efficient) will need to make a greater return than the incumbent in order to break even. But if the incumbent reduces its price sufficiently, it will be able to continue to earn a profit and prevent the duplicator from breaking even. Realizing this, the potential duplicator will refrain from attempting to duplicate the secret independently.

36. A secret process that reduces supply costs is the most likely candidate for this theory. Any trade secret that improves consumer benefits is likely to be observed by everyone (e.g., in the form of an observably superior product). But innovative production processes can be kept secret. It follows that a trade secret that generates a long-lasting monopoly is likely to take the form of a process innovation. The exception to this will be found in new products that cannot be reverse engineered. The new product can create a monopolized market. In this case, the efficiency results from providing value to consumers that would otherwise not be supplied by the market.

37. It has been argued that trade secret law actually encourages dissemination of information by saving companies the costs of overinvestment in secrecy, and by allowing an inventor to disclose an idea secure in the knowledge that the other party cannot take the idea (violating the terms of the disclosure agreement) without having to pay compensation. "[Trade secrecy] therefore permits business negotiations that can lead to commercialization of the invention or sale of the idea, serving both the disclosure and incentive functions of IP law." See Mark A. Lemley, *The Surprising Virtues of Treating Trade Secrets as IP Rights,* 61 Stan. L. Rev. 311, 337 (2008).

38. Lemley, *supra* note 37.

39. In 2009, the U.S. Justice Department investigated high-tech firms' hiring practices: "Federal Antitrust Probe Targets Tech Giants, Sources Say," Wash. Post., June 3, 2009, available at http://www.washingtonpost.com/wp-dyn/content/article/2009/06/02/AR2009060203412.html. See also "Google Recruiter: Company Kept 'Do Not Touch' in Hiring List," Mercury News, June 4, 2009, available at http://www.mercurynews.com/business/ci_12514244?source=email.

40. See Annalee Saxenian, Regional Advantage: Culture and Competition in Silicon Valley and Route 128 (Harvard. Univ. Press 1994); Ronald J. Gilson, *The Legal Infrastructure of High Technology Industrial Districts: Silicon Valley, Route 128, and Covenants Not to Compete,* 74 N.Y.U. L. Rev. 575 (1999).

41. See, e.g., All Stainless, Inc. v. Colby, 308 N.E.2d 481, 485 (Mass. 1974).

42. On the difficulties, see, e.g., Bell Atl. Corp. v. Twombly, 550 U.S. 544 (2007).

43. On the evidence, see, e.g., Paul Almeida & Bruce Kogut, *Localization of Knowledge and the Mobility of Engineers in Regional Networks,* 45 Management

Science 905 (1999). One might be inclined to conclude, on the basis of the patent evidence, that prohibiting the enforcement of noncompete agreements encourages innovation as measured by patents. Of course, the evidence may reflect nothing more than a change in strategy; unable to enforce noncompete clauses, firms may adopt a strategy of protecting information through patents. One would then observe an explosion in patenting after a state adopts a policy of nonenforcement with respect to noncompete agreements, but that would by no means imply that the non-enforcement policy encourages innovation.

44. See, e.g., Jorda, *supra* note 31; Elizabetta Ottoz & Franco Cugna, *Patent-Secret Mix in Complex Product Firms,* 10 Am. L. & Econ. Rev. 142–158 (2008).

45. The complementarity thesis is suggested in the analysis of Anton & Yao, *supra* note 30.

46. Edmund W. Kitch, *The Nature and Function of the Patent System,* 20 J. L. & Econ. 265 (1977).

6. Copyright Law

1. Lawrence Lessig, The Future of Ideas: The Fate of the Commons in a Connected World 201 (Vintage Books 2002).

2. See, e.g., Erwin Chemerinsky, *Balancing Copyright Protections and Freedom of Speech: Why the Copyright Extension Act is Unconstitutional,* 36 Loy. L.A. L. Rev. 83 (2002); Wendy J. Gordon, *Render Copyright Unto Caesar: On Taking Incentives Seriously,* 71 U. Chi. L. Rev. 75 (2004); Lawrence Lessig, *supra* note 1; Neil W. Netanel, Copyright's Paradox (Oxford Univ. Press 2008); David Post, *His Napster's Voice,* in Copy Fights: The Future of Intellectual Property in the Information Age 114, 115 (Adam Thierer & Clyde Wayne Crews, Jr. eds., Cato Institute 2002); Richard Stallman, *Freedom—Or Copyright,* GNU Operating System, available at http://www.gnu.org/philosophy/freedom-or-copyright.html.

3. Some scholars, after reflecting on criticism of arguments they had made against copyright, have admitted analytical errors in their first efforts. See, e.g., Stephen Breyer, *The Uneasy Case for Copyright: A Study in Copyright of Books, Photocopies and Computer Programs,* 84 Harv. L. Rev. 281 (1970); Barry Tyerman, *The Economic Rationale for Copyright Protection for Published Books: A Reply to Professor Breyer,* 18 UCLA L. Rev. 1100 (1971); Stephen Breyer, *Copyright: A Rejoinder,* 20 UCLA L. Rev. 75 (1972) (conceding the weakness of arguments indicating that publishers could profit sufficiently from "first mover" advantages and from threats to underprice rival publishers to sustain their businesses at about the same level of activity without copyright). Breyer's initial position had been presaged by Sir Arnold Plant, *The Economic Aspects of Copyright in Books,* 1 Economica (new series) 167 (1934), reprinted in Arnold Plant, Selected Economic Essays and Addresses 57 (Routledge & Kegan Paul 1974). Moreover, only extreme copyright opponents endorse some anticopyright assertions, such as the claim that copyright "locks up

knowledge" (as if the knowledge, rather than a specific creative expression, was made the copyright holder's exclusive dominion). Nonetheless, both the cost and benefit side of the case against copyright—the concern over interference with creativity by those who might infringe copyrighted works and the assertion that copyright's worth in promoting valuable creative activity is unproven—are still debated.

4. See, e.g., Plant, *supra* note 3; Lyman Ray Patterson, Copyright in Historical Perspective 28–142 (Vanderbilt Univ. Press 1968); Paul Goldstein, Copyright's Highway: From Gutenberg to the Celestial Jukebox 32–34 (Stanford Law & Politics 2003). That does not, however, mean that there was no arguable social good rationale for the basic structure of monopoly copying rights. Goldstein, recounting the argument made in Tyerman, *supra* note 3, observes that monopoly rights, even in a time of limited technological capacity for copying, might be socially desirable as a means of promoting investment in a portfolio of publications of unknown appeal to the public. If there were no protection against others publishing the same work, follow-on publishers would pick only the most successful titles, leaving the first publisher to bear the costs of unsuccessful books without being able to capture the full value of successful ones to offset those losses. Goldstein, *supra,* at 19–20.

5. This sentiment was voiced by Justice Joseph Story, among others, who thought almost all literary giants sat squarely on the shoulders of their forbears in taking story ideas freely from prior works, going all the way back to the oral storytelling traditions that preceded famous first writings. See Emerson v. Davies, 8 F. Cas. 615, 619 (C.C.D. Mass. 1845).

6. 101 U.S. 99 (1879).

7. *Id.* at 104.

8. See, e.g., Herbert Rosenthal Jewelry Corp. v. Kalpakian, 446 F.2d 738 (9th Cir. 1971). While some cases flatly deny copyright protection, others explore the extent to which specific attributes of the expression may be protected against copying while more general aspects are not. See, e.g., Yankee Candle Co., Inc. v. Bridgewater Candle Co., LLC, 259 F.3d 25 (1st Cir. 2001). The argument that there is only one manner of expression for a particular type of idea is generally thought of as a defense to infringement rather than an exclusion of material from the ambit of copyright. That view is not uniformly adhered to, however. See, e.g., Atari, Inc. v. N. Am. Philips Consumer Elecs. Corp., 672 F.2d 607, 614–16 (7th Cir. 1982).

9. Cases reach a similar result for ordinary types of characters who play predictable parts, a rule of law often referred to as a mise-en-scene defense.

10. See, e.g., CCC Info. Servs., Inc. v. Maclean Hunter Mkt. Reports, Inc., 44 F.3d 61 (1994); Kregos v. Associated Press, 937 F.2d 700 (2d Cir. 1991).

11. That concern may explain cases such as Herbert Rosenthal Jewelry Corp. v. Kalpakian, 446 F.2d 738 (9th Cir. 1971) ("Obviously a copyright must not be treated as equivalent to a patent lest long continuing private monopolies be conferred over areas of gainful activity without first satisfying the substantive and procedural

prerequisites to the grant of such privileges."). Other cases distinguish between "hard" and "soft" ideas or between facts and value judgments. See, e.g., CCC Info. Servs., Inc. v. Maclean Hunter Mkt. Reports, Inc., 44 F.3d 61 (2d Cir. 1994). Those distinctions—beyond being disconnected from any clear textual command in the law—are plainly separate from concerns about imposing unreasonably high social costs by protecting essentially utilitarian ideas under a regime geared to promote innovative nonutilitarian expression. The distinctions generally rest on intuitions that are sensible—such as, that it is costlier to inhibit copying of factual information than of individual value judgments—but evaluating the policy basis for those distinctions or their justification under law (by no means identical questions) requires a more extended discussion. Note, as well, that the problem of protecting utilitarian ideas under the rubric of copyright (designed for nonutilitarian expression) is not a one-way street; there is a corollary problem of failing to protect innovation that combines expressive and useful attributes appropriately through patent and trade secret law. A well-known special case concerns the appropriate means for protecting innovative computer software programs. See, e.g., Computer Assocs. Int'l, Inc. v. Altai, Inc., 982 F.2d 698 (2d Cir. 1992); Apple Computer, Inc. v. Franklin Computer Corp., 714 F.2d 1240 (3d Cir. 1983), cert. dismissed, 464 U.S. 1033 (1984).

12. U.S. Patent 5,960,411.

13. While there are nearly 500,000 patent applications filed annually now in the United States, only 150,000–180,000 patents are awarded. That understates the effect of the novelty and nonobviousness requirements, as their existence as barriers to patent award no doubt discourages a substantial number of other filings as well.

14. See Mathew McCubbins & Thomas Schwartz, *Congressional Oversight Overlooked: Police Patrols Versus Fire Alarms*, 28 Am. J. Pol. Sci. 165–179 (1984).

15. Under section 411(a) of the 1976 Copyright Act, registration is a condition to instituting an infringement action for any U.S. work. See, e.g., Strategy Source, Inc. v. Lee, 233 F. Supp. 2d 1, 4 (D.D.C. 2002) (finding that "a certificate of registration is a jurisdictional prerequisite to filing an infringement suit in this Court, the only exception being where the Copyright Office has refused to issue the certificate of registration.").

16. H.R. Rep. 94-1476 (1976).

17. The Copyright Act protects only those original works that are "fixed in any tangible medium of expression," though section 101 provides a safe harbor for live performances that are fixed at the same time that they are broadcast. Fixation has been an issue in some live performance and computer cases. See, e.g., Prod. Contractors, Inc. v. WGN Continental Broad. Co., 622 F. Supp. 1500, 1504 (N.D. Ill. 1985) (holding that "the telecast of the parade is a work of authorship fixed simultaneously with its transmission only for purposes of copyright protection from videotaping, tape-delays, or secondary transmissions. This protection does not extend to prevent another simultaneous live telecast by another television or radio station.").

See Matthew Bender & Co. Inc. v. West Pub Co., 158 F.3d 693 (2d Cir 1998) (a more or less complete discussion of the fixation requirement, and whether a CD fits the definition of copy); Mai Sys. Corp. v. Peak Computer, Inc., 991 F.2d 511 (9th Cir. 1993), cert. dismissed, 510 US 1033 (1994) (holding that RAM does satisfy fixation requirements, despite temporariness of copy).

18. See, e.g., Boisson v. Banian Ltd., 273 F.3d 262, 270 (2d Cir. 2001) ("Absent evidence of copying, an author is entitled to copyright protection for an independently produced original work despite its identical nature to a prior work, because it is independent creation and not novelty that is required.").

19. See Sheldon v. Metro-Goldwyn Pictures Corp., 81 F.2d 49, 54 (2d Cir. 1936) ("[I]f by some magic a man who had never known it were to compose anew Keats's Ode on a Grecian Urn, he would be an 'author,' and, if he copyrighted it, others might not copy that poem, though they might of course copy Keats's.").

20. See, e.g., Feist Publi'ns, Inc. v. Rural Tel. Serv. Co., Inc., 499 U.S. 340, 346–47 (1991).

21. See, e.g., Reader's Digest Ass'n v. Conservative Digest, Inc., 821 F.2d 800, 806 (D.C. Cir. 1986); West Publ'g Co. v. Mead Data Cent., Inc. 799 F.2d 1219, 1223 (8th Cir. 1987), cert. denied, 479 U.S. 1070 (1987); Alfred Bell & Co. v. Catalda Fine Arts, Inc., 191 F.2d 99, 102 (2d Cir. 1951).

22. See, e.g., Atari Games Corp. v. Oman, 979 F.2d 242 (D.C. Cir. 1992).

23. See, e.g., Concord Fabrics, Inc. v. Marcus Bros. Textile Corp., 409 F.2d 1315 (2d Cir. 1969).

24. Alina Ng, *The Social Contract and Authorship: Allocating Entitlements in the Copyright* System, 19 Fordham Intell. Prop. Media & Ent. L. J. 413, 462 (2009) (arguing for a theory of copyright that includes a deserts-of-labor component as well as "a personality-based philosophy that justifies an author's entitlement to property rights in his or her creation because the work manifests the author's personality or self."); Joseph Scott Miller, *Hoisting Originality,* 31 Cardozo L. Rev. 451, 493–494 (2009) (attribution and other moral rights should only have to meet the current lower standard of originality, while economic rights should have a heightened standard of originality in order to be copyrighted). But see Roberta Rosenthal Kwall, *Inspiration and Innovation: The Intrinsic Dimension of the Artistic Soul,* 81 Notre Dame L. Rev. 1945, 1998 (2006) (Agreeing that moral rights and economic rights should be held to different standards, but arguing that works that are "rooted in the inspirational realm of authorship" are the only works that deserve both economic and moral rights protection, while other lesser works deserve only economic protection or "thinner protection.").

25. See, e.g., New York Times Co. v. Sullivan, 376 U.S. 254 (1964); Cohen v. California, 403 U.S. 15 (1971); New York Times Co. v. United States, 403 U.S. 713 (1971) (the Pentagon Papers case); Vincent Blasi, *The "Checking Value" in First Amendment Theory,* 1977 Am. B. Found. Res. J. 521; Ronald A. Cass, *The Perils of Positive Thinking: Constitutional Interpretation and Negative First Amendment Theory,* 34

UCLA L. Rev. 1405 (1986–1987); Daniel Farber, *Free Speech Without Romance: Public Choice and the First Amendment,* 105 Harv. L. Rev. 554 (1991); Frederick Schauer, *Language, Truth and the First Amendment: An Essay in Memory of Harry Canter,* 64 Va. L. Rev. 263 (1978); Frederick Schauer, *The Second-Best First Amendment,* 31 Wm. & Mary L. Rev. 1 (1989).

26. See, e.g., Ronald A. Cass, *Commercial Speech, Constitutionalism, Collective Action,* 56 U. Cin. L. Rev. 1317 (1988); Frederick Schauer, *Categories and the First Amendment: A Play in Three Acts,* 34 Vand. L. Rev. 265 (1981).

27. We have said little about administrative costs. To the extent copyright protects only against copying, not against similar artistic or creative embodiments of the same ideas, the administrative costs of determining whether something is protected will be slight. When protection is only against copying rather than inadvertent similarity, occasions when one needs to incur the costs of looking for the originator of an expression and determining whether a right to it needs to be obtained will be significantly reduced.

28. This is essentially the reasoning Oliver Wendell Holmes asserted in connection with the requirement of originality in Bleistein v. Donaldson Lithographing Co., 188 U.S. 238, 251–252 (1903).

29. As we discussed earlier in Chapters 3 and 4, and take up again later in this chapter, the incentive-effects argument also comprehends protection for the investments needed after creation of a work to ensure that the product of creative effort can be distributed or marketed in ways that best promote the value of the property. Protecting returns from investments in those post-creation activities raises the value of the intellectual property right, which in turn increases incentives to invest in the initial creative activity.

30. See Edward J. Damich, *Right of Personality: A Common-Law Basis for the Protection of the Moral Rights of Authors,* 23 Ga. L. Rev. 1, 6–8 (1988) (discussing droit moral in France, and how certain protection is based on an author's personal rights instead of economic protection); Robert J. Sherman, *The Visual Artists Rights Act of 1990: American Artists Burned Again,* 17 Cardozo L. Rev. 373, 380 (1995) ("In Europe, however, author's rights protection coexists with the economic aspects of copyrights—as they are separate, but related interests").

31. The connection is not only a source of inspiration for European systems based on *droit moral, supra* note 24, but also laws such as the Visual Artists Rights Act of 1990, Pub. L. 101–650, 104 Stat. 5089, codified at various sections of 17 U.S.C. § 101 et seq. See also Roberta Rosenthal Kwall, *How Fine Art Fares Post VARA,* 1 Marq. Intell. Prop. L. Rev. 1 (1997) (discussing how VARA statute took into account moral rights and protecting personal expression in U.S. copyright law).

32. One could argue, for example, that rights to prevent alteration of works, such as art work, which are grounded in moral rights theories, are inconsistent with the "first sale" doctrine in U.S. law (a largely judge-made doctrine, now codified in 17 U.S.C. §109). Although U.S. federal copyright law is largely utilitarian, provisions in

U.S. law also track moral rights claims. See, e.g., 17 U.S.C. §106A; Sherman, *supra* note 29, at 391. The first sale doctrine, which allows rightful possessors of copyrighted works to resell or dispose of that copyrighted work without the copyrighter's permission, does not affect a copyrighter's attribution rights, which are vested only in authors.

33. Of course, physical products equally can be part of "popular culture"—the Harley-Davidson's association with American highways and rebellion against authority, Coca-Cola as the symbol of a young nation that even in its drink was breaking new ground, the Ford Thunderbird and later the Mustang's assimilation to a new suburban lifestyle (more driving, but also the right to look young and hip behind the wheel), even the Marlboro Man as modern emblem of a devil-may-care attitude of the American West (not necessarily smart, but undaunted by risk). These and many other products, from the Model T to the Barbie doll to the PC and iPhone, have altered our lives and become handy reference points for thinking about the evolution of our society.

Many other physical products that affect us profoundly, however, are absorbed unnoted into our lives. Electricity, radio, refrigerators, washing machines, dryers, microwave ovens, the automatic starter (as opposed to the hand crank) on automobiles, vastly improved semiconductor chips—these all have enormous ripple effects on the way we live and work. What distinguishes the iconic products listed earlier is, more than anything else, their embodiment in music and movies and writing. That transformed them from useful products with benefits beyond their immediate functions to symbols of our culture.

34. By "spillovers" we mean the same thing as an economist would mean by saying externality. We use the term *cultural spillovers* to refer to cultural externalities. If a work of art or literature produced two hundred years ago serves as a reference point that enables us to better understand our current culture, then it has clearly provided a spillover benefit to the existing generation. On general considerations of spillovers and copyright law, see Brett Frischmann, *Spillovers Theory and Its Conceptual Boundaries*, 51 Wm. & Mary L. Rev. 801 (2009).

35. See e.g., Daly v. Palmer, 6 F.Cas. 1132 (S.D.N.Y. 1868).

36. Derivative rights were originally granted in the 1909 copyright act section 1(6); they are now codified in 17 USC § 106(2).

37. In 2008, international box office earnings made up 65 percent of the worldwide total take from theatre showings of feature films, while domestic sales (both the United States and Canada) made up 35 percent. See Motion Picture Association of America. Theatrical Market Statistics, available at www.mpaa.org/2008_Theat_Stats.pdf. Physical media (such as DVD) sales account for more than 50 percent of total film revenue. See, e.g., http://www.allbusiness.com/media-telecommunications/movies-sound-recording/10512814-1.html.

38. For a special case in which a work is taken whole without violating copyright, see Lee v. A.R.T. Co., 125 F.3d 580 (7th Cir. 1997) (physical copies of a work,

purchased individually, were resold in slightly altered form but in the particular case the use did not run afoul of the law's prohibition on producing unauthorized derivative works). Judge Frank Easterbrook, in an opinion of exceptional clarity, describes the economic and legal considerations that underlie treatment of derivative works.

39. Castle Rock Entm't Inc. v. Carol Publi'g Grp., 150 F.3d 132 (2d Cir. 1998).

40. *Id.* at 142.

41. Castle Rock Entm't v. Carol Publ'g Grp., Inc., 955 F. Supp. 260, 272 (S.D.N.Y. 1997).

42. Warner Bros. Entm't, Inc. v. RDR Books, 575 F.Supp. 2d 513 (S.D.N.Y. 2008).

43. *Id.* at 535.

44. 17 USC § 107.

45. 9 F. Cas. 342 (C.C.D. Mass. 1841). Justice Story's discussion was based on earlier holdings from English law.

46. Wendy J. Gordon, *Fair Use as Market Failure: A Structural and Economic Analysis of the Betamax Case,* 82 Colum. L. Rev. 1600 (1982); William M. Landes & Richard A. Posner; The Economic Structure of Intellectual Property Law 114–123 (Belknap Press 2003).

47. See e.g., Am. Geographical Union v. Texaco, Inc., 60 F.3d 913, 916 (2d Cir. 1994); Princeton Univ. Press v. Michigan Document Servs., Inc., 99 F.3d 1381 (6th Cir. 1996) (focusing heavily on the fourth factor of fair use: the effect on the market). The fact that the copyrighters had set up a system for licenses at a reasonable cost in these two cases meant that fair use was not a proper defense because the courts found no market failure. If there had not been a market set up to handle licensing, it would be more likely that fair use would have been a defense to the infringement.

48. See, e.g., Sony Corp. of Am. v. Universal City Studios, Inc., 464 U.S. 417 (1984); L.A. News Serv. v. KCAL-TV Channel 9, 108 F.3d 1119 (9th Cir. 1997); Monster Commc'ns, Inc. v. Turner Broad. Sys. Inc., 935 F. Supp. 490 (S.D.N.Y. 1996).

49. See, e.g., Harper & Row Publishers, Inc., v. Nation Enters., 471 U.S. 539 (1985) (Harper & Row brought a copyright infringement action against *The Nation* magazine for its unauthorized publication of verbatim quotes from former President Ford's memoirs. The court held that the publication was not fair use because, although there might be benefits to the public of publishing information about public political figures, there is a larger need for the author to be able to control first public appearance of the work. The court also looked at the effect of the market—Ford lost his contract because of the quotes, and the amount of the taking—the quotes including many substantial and important parts of the memoirs).

50. Courts have not proven terribly prescient in assessing such matters in the past. See, e.g., Kelo v. City of New London, 546 U.S. 807 (2005).

51. See Suntrust Bank v. Houghton-Mifflin Co., 268 F.3d 1257 (11th Cir. 2001).

52. 268 F.3d at 1266–67, *quoting* Suntrust Bank v. Houghton Mifflin Co., 136 F. Supp. 2d 1357, 1367 (N.D. Ga. 2001), *vacated,* 252 F.3d 1165 (11th Cir. 2001).

53. See discussion in Chapter 7.

54. 510 U.S. 569 (1994).

55. See, e.g., Liebowitz v. Paramount Pictures Corp., 137 F.3d 109 (2d Cir. 1998); Eugene Volokh, *Freedom of Speech and Independent Judgment Review in Copyright Cases,* 107 Yale L. J. 2431, 2461–62 (1998); Lisa Babiskin, *Oh, Pretty Parody:* Campbell v. Acuff-Rose Music, Inc., 8 Harvard J. L. & Tech. 193 (1994).

56. For discussion of a similar problem (arising from the ways in which particular personal views, such as enmity between two neighbors, can affect the sorts of bargains that will be reached in negotiation and litigation), see, e.g., Ward Farnsworth, *Do Parties to Nuisance Cases Bargain After Judgment? A Glimpse Inside the Cathedral,* 66 U. Chi. L. Rev. 373, 407 (1999). In our view, it is easy to appreciate Professor Farnsworth's observations about the ways in which responses such as enmity can prevent the operation of ordinary assumptions about market forces; it is less easy, however, to draw strong conclusions about whether those responses do or do not reflect broader social values.

57. 464 U.S. 417 (1984).

58. 239 F.3d 1004 (9th Cir. 2001).

59. 545 U.S. 913 (2005).

60. See Digital Millennium Copyright Act, 17 U.S.C. § 512(c)(1) (actual knowledge not required; if the enterprise knows or has reason to know that infringing activity is occurring or is profiting directly from it, the enterprise will be held liable). See, e.g., In re Aimster Copyright Litig., 334 F.3d 643 (7th Cir. 2003).

61. [1913] A. C. 263 (P.C.) (appeal taken from Australia).

62. See Keith N. Hylton, *Property Rules, Liability Rules, and Immunity: An Application to Cyberspace,* 87 B. U. L. Rev. 1, 12–13 (2007).

63. See Digital Millennium Copyright Act, 17 U.S.C. § 512(c)(1).

64. See Pub. L. 94–553, 90 Stat. 2541, codified at 17 U.S.C. § 101 et seq. (finally coming into conformity with the Berlin Act of 1908, which had modified the initial Berne Convention on Copyright).

65. Pub. L. 105–298, 112 Stat. 2827, codified at 17 U.S.C. §§ 302, 304.

66. 537 U.S. 186 (2003) (holding that the Copyright Term Extension Act did not violate constitutional limit on copyright terms, nor did it create a perpetual copyright).

67. See, e.g., Arthur De Vany, Hollywood Economics: How Extreme Uncertainty Shapes the Film Industry (Routledge 2004).

68. See, e.g., John Duffy, *Intellectual Property Isolationism and the Average Cost Thesis,* 83 Tex. L. Rev. 1077–1095 (2005). But see Mark Lemley, *Ex Ante versus Ex Post Justifications for Intellectual Property,* 71 U. Chi. L. Rev. 129 (2004).

69. The rationale for this argument is rooted in the same insight that informed Ed Kitch's analysis of patent law. See Edmund W. Kitch, *The Nature and Function of the Patent System*, 20 J.L. & Econ. 265 (1977). See also Duffy, *supra* note 67; F. Scott Kieff, *Propery Rights and Property Rules for Commercializing Inventions*, 85 Minn. L. Rev. 697 (2001).

70. For an insightful discussion of the consequences of such control, see Olufunmilayo Arewa, *Copyright on Catfish Row: Musical Borrowing*, Porgy and Bess, *and Unfair Use*, 38 Rutgers L. J. 277–353 (2006).

7. Trademark Law

1. There are not many comprehensive treatments of the economics of trademark law. Of those that we have found, the two most impressive are Robert G. Bone, *Enforcement Costs and Trademark Puzzles*, 90 Va. L. Rev.2099 (2004) and William M. Landes & Richard A. Posner, The Economic Structure of Intellectual Property Law 166–209 (2003). Our approach differs from these works in some important respects. We focus on the functions of trademark and only lightly touch the case law. Bone provides a very thorough discussion of the case law from an economic perspective. Landes and Posner put more emphasis on the general function of trademark. Unlike Bone, we find the justification for some modern expansions (e.g., dilution doctrine) defensible in light of the functions of trademark and find no need to consider enforcement costs (though one exception we recognize is trade dress doctrine, where Bone's enforcement-cost model appears to be the best approach to making sense of the case law). In comparison to Landes and Posner, we present a more detailed microanalysis of the functions of trademark.

2. Mark A. Lemley, *The Modem Lanham Act and the Death of Common Sense*, 108 Yale L.J. 1687 (1999); Glynn S. Lunney, Jr., *Trademark Monopolies*, 48 Emory L.J. 367 (1999).

3. See Robert G. Bone, *A New Look at Trade Secret Law: Doctrine in Search of Justification*, 86 Cal. L. Rev. 241, 265 (1998).

4. Unless one seller has a large market share and is therefore able to internalize most of the benefits from the investment. Although concentrated market structures are often viewed as inferior to competitive market structures, this is not necessarily so when one considers incentives to invest in promotion and quality. In a market, such as that for airline service, where firms are viewed as interchangeable, quality investment may depend on the existence of dominant firms.

5. Benjamin Klein & Keith B. Leffler, *The Role of Market Forces in Assuring Contractual Performance*, 89 J. Pol. Econ. 615 (1981); Ivan P. L. Png & David Reitman, *Why Are Some Products Branded and Others Not?*, 38 J. L. & Econ. 207–24 (1995).

6. Paul Milgrom & John Roberts, *Price and Advertising Signals of Product Quality*, 94 J. Pol. Econ. 796 (1986).

7. Collected Works of Abraham Lincoln, Vol. 3, at 81 (Roy P. Basler ed., Rutgers Univ. Press 1953).

8. E.g., Qualitex Co. v. Jacobson Prods. Co., Inc., 514 U.S. 159, 163–164 (1995); 1 J. Thomas McCarthy, McCarthy on Trademarks and Unfair Competition, § 2:5 (4th ed. 2002) [hereinafter McCarthy on Trademarks].

9. 537 F.2d 4 (2d Cir. 1976).

10. See Harold Hotelling, *Stability in Competition,* 39 Econ. J. 41, 41–57 (1929).

11. Landes & Posner, *supra* note 1, at 175; see also Stacey L. Dogan & Mark A. Lemley, *A Search-Costs Theory of Limiting Doctrines in Trademark Law,* 97 Trademark Rep. 1223–1251 (2007):

12. More precisely, the high price reflects a rent earned on the special location controlled by the owner of the generic mark. But since the generic mark should be available to all sellers, society loses welfare by permitting one seller to control the generic mark.

13. The static cost in this scenario is the reduction in society's welfare that results from the loss in output. If the firm that gains control of the term *orange* imposes a ninety-nine cent surcharge in order to take advantage of its legally protected brand advantage, that surcharge is a transfer of wealth from consumers to the protected firm.

14. Over time, this has the dynamic consequence mentioned earlier of shrinking the market down to only low-quality sellers. But we are discussing only static costs here.

15. John Henry Wigmore, Select Cases on the Law of Torts, with Notes and a Summary of Principles 318–368 (Little, Brown 1912).

16. 15 U.S.C. §§ 1051–1141n (2006).

17. Popham 143, 79 Eng. Rep. 1243 (K.B. 1618); for reprint see Wigmore on Torts, *supra* note 12, at 318.

18. E.g., 4 McCarthy on Trademarks, *supra* note 8, § 23:1.

19. *Id.,* § 23:20.

20. 66 Ill. App. 571 (1896).

21. *Id.* at *3.

22. See, e.g., Utah Lighthouse Ministry v. Found. of Apologetic Infor. & Research, 527 F.3d 1045, 1056 (10th Cir. 2008); Goto.Com, Inc. v. Walt Disney Co., 202 F.3d 1199, 1209 (9th Cir. 2000).

23. Crystal Corp. v. Manhattan Chem. Mfg. Co., 75 F. (2d) 506, 508 (C. C. P. A. 1935) (difficulty of remembering letter combinations); Ty Inc. v. Perryman, 306 F.3d 509 (7th Cir. 2002) (cognitive limitations as defense for diminution theory); Rebecca Tushnet, *Gone in Sixty Milliseconds: Trademark Law and Cognitive Science,* 86 Tex. L. Rev. 507 (2008).

24. See, e.g., Brennan's, Inc. v. Brennan's Rest., L.L.C., 360 F.3d 125 (2d Cir. 2004) (sophistication and geographic market differences despite similarity of mark avoided a finding of confusion); AMF Inc. v. Sleekcraft Boats, 599 F.2d 341, 353 (9th cir. 1979) (sophistication of consumers is an important factor in finding confusion);

Elec. Design and Sales Inc. v. Elec. Data Sys. Corp, 954 F.2d 713 (Fed.Cir.1992) (experienced sophisticated corporate officials did not risk confusion between E.D.S. computer services and E.D.S. power supplies).

25. 113 Mich. 133, 71 N. W. 470 (1897).

26. See, e.g., Kellogg Co. v. Nat'l Biscuit Co., 305 U.S. 111, 116–117 (1938); 2 McCarthy on Trademarks, *supra* note 8, § 12:1.

27. Delaware & Hudson Canal Co. v. Clark, 80 U.S. (13 Wall.) 311, 323 (1872).

28. See, e.g., 2 McCarthy on Trademarks, *supra* note 8, § 15:1.

29. *Id.,* § 15:5.

30. Zazu Designs v. L'Oreal, S.A., 979 F.2d 499, 503 (7th Cir. 1992); Blue Bell, Inc. v. Farah Mfg. Co., Inc., 508 F.2d 1260, 1264–1265 (5th Cir. 1975).

31. For a discussion and critique of the propertization argument, see Bone, *supra* note 1, at 212–2123. For the arguments of the critics of propertization, see Lemley, *supra* note 2; Lunney, *supra* note 2; Jessica Litman, *Breakfast with Batman: The Public Interest in the Advertising Age,* 108 Yale L.J. 1717 (1999); Harvey S. Perlman, *Taking the Protection-Access Tradeoff Seriously,* 53 Vand. L. Rev. 1831 (2000).

32. Dilution doctrine has developed in the common law of trademarks, and as the result of statutory law. The statutory law development, unlike the common law development, reflects in part the outcome of legislative lobbying by concentrated interest groups. Although interest groups and investments favoring particular stakeholders play some role in litigation, it is filtered through institutional mechanisms that are very different and produce very different effects on decision outcomes. For that reason, we are inclined to take a more wary (but not necessarily an opposed) view of the desirability of dilution protection that results from legislation. On the lobbying process and dilution, see Clarissa Long, *The Political Economy of Trademark Dilution, in* Trademark Law and Theory: A Handbook of Contemporary Research 132–147 (Graeme Dinwoodie & Mark Janis eds., Edward Elgar Publishing 2008).

33. See JC Penney Co. v. Sec. Tire and Rubber Co., 382 F.Supp. 1342 (E.D.Va.1974); 4 McCarthy on Trademarks, *supra* note 8, § 24:18.

34. See, e.g., Octocom Sys., Inc. v. Houston Computer Servs. Inc., 918 F.2d 937 (Fed.Cir.1990) (modem software and computer programming software risk confusion despite not directly competing because they are technologically related and might be used alongside one another).

35. This is similar to Judge Posner's argument that in the absence of the protection provided by dilution doctrine, consumers would suffer the mental search costs of trying to retrieve the meaning of the first user's mark. The effect is a dilution in the value of the mark to the first user. See Ty, Inc. v. Perryman, 306 F.3d 509 (7th Cir. 2002).

36. 15 U.S.C. § 1125 (c).

37. See, e.g., Long, *supra* note 19, at 144–145.

38. See, e.g., Dr. S. A. Richmond Nervine Co. v. Richmond, 159 U.S. 293 (1895).

39. See, e.g., Regis v. Jaynes, 77 N.E. 774 (Mass. 1906).

40. See, e.g., Maye v. Yappen, 23 Cal. 306 (1863).

41. See, e.g., Quick Technologies Inc. v. Sage Grp. PLC, 313 F.3d 338, 349 (5th Cir. 2002); Banjo Buddies Inc. v. Renovsky, 339 F.3d 168 (3d Cir. 2005).

42. On the economics of compensatory and gain-stripping remedies, see Keith N. Hylton, *Property Rules and Liability Rules, Once Again,* 2 Rev. Law & Econ. 137 (2006); Guido Calabresi & A. Douglas Melamed, *Property Rules, Liability Rules, and Inalienability: One View of the Cathedral,* 85 Harv. L. Rev. 1089 (1972).

43. 547 U.S. 388 (2006) (holding that traditional equity principles apply to patent injunctions, with no general presumption of an injunction issuing). On the economics of patent injunctions, see John M. Golden, *Principles for Patent Remedies,* 88 Tex. L. Rev. 505 (2010); Paul J. Heald, *Optimal Remedies for Patent Infringement: A Transactional Model,* 45. Hous. L. Rev. 1165 (2008); Henry E. Smith, *Institutions and Indirectness in Intellectual Property,* 157 U. Pa. L. Rev. 2083, 2125–32 (2009). See discussion, *infra,* Chapter 8.

44. Best Lock Corp. v. Schlage Lock Co., 413 F.2d 1195, 1199–1200 (C.C.P.A. 1969); Qualitex Co. v. Jacobson Products Co., Inc., 514 U.S. 159, 164–165 (1995).

45. Bone, *supra* note 1, at 2180–81, suggests that the law's protection is broader than this norm would imply because judges use broad intuitive notions of the relevant market for the challenged products. He argues that the case law is largely defensible because of the litigation costs that would be required if courts were to attempt to define the relevant market more rigorously.

46. On the consequences of licensing in India, see Clive Crook, "India: Plain Tales of the License Raj," 319 Economist S9-S14 (May 4, 1991); on Africa, see Peter T. Bauer, Reality and Rhetoric: Studies in the Economics of Development 90–105 (Harvard Univ. Press 1984).

47. 77 Eng. Rep. 1260 (K.B. 1603).

8. Making International Property Rights Work—Or Not

1. 45 F.2d 191, 121 (2d Cir. 1930), cert. denied, 282 U.S. 902 (1931).

2. See, e.g., Roger Bate, *Stopping Killer Counterfeits,* The Wash. Post, July 18, 2008; WHO report World Health Organization, *Counterfeit Drugs Kill!* (2008) (Last visited Aug 11. 2010) http://www.who.int/impact/FinalBrochureWHA2008a.pdf.

3. *FDA Thinks it has trigger in Heparin Deaths,* CNN, April 21 2008, http://www.cnn.com/2008/HEALTH/04/21/fda.heparin/ ; see also Bate, *supra* note 2.

4. See, e.g., American Council on Science and Health, Counterfeit Drugs 2 (2009), available at http://www.acsh.org/docLib/20090202_counterfeitdrug09.pdf.

5. Laurie J. Flynn, "U.S. Discloses Moves to Stop Piracy of Intellectual Property," N.Y. Times, Sept. 21, 2005, at C1 (citing 2004 figures from the World Customs Organization and Interpol); see also *Counterfeiting Intelligence Bureau,* International Chamber of Commerce Commercial Crime Services, http://www.icc-ccs.org/home/cib/ (last visited Aug. 20, 2011) (counterfeiting totals $600 billion per year, or

between 5–7 percent of world trade); Moises Naim, "Broken Borders," Newsweek, Oct. 24, 2005, at 57 (counterfeiting totals $630 billion per year); compare Organisation for Economic Co-Operation and Development, *Magnitude of Counterfeiting and Piracy of Tangible Products* 1 (2009), available at http://www.oecd.org/dataoecd/57/27/44088872.pdf (counterfeit and pirated products, not including domestic or non-tangible goods, worth $250 billion—or roughly 2 percent of world trade—in 2007).

6. Connie Neigel, *Piracy in Russia and China: A Different U.S. Reaction,* 63 L. & Contemp. Probs. 179, 187 (Autumn 2000).

7. "China's Software Piracy Hits Snag," L.A. Times, July 12, 1995, at D9.

8. See, e.g., Diane Bartz, Study Finds Software Piracy Growing, Reuters, May 12, 2009, available at http://www.reuters.com/article/technologyNews/idUSTRE54B0UD20090512.

9. See Business Software Alliance & IDC, *Sixth Annual Business Software Alliance-IDC Global Piracy Study* 1, 6, 8 (May 2009).

10. *Id.* at 8. The study also estimated that losses from illegally appropriated software worldwide amounted to approximately 70 percent of the value of the legitimate software market, including the value of freely available software. *Id.* at 2–3, 7–8.

11. The Paris Convention gave rise to WIPO, and it still plays an important role in regulating the interactions among developed nations' patent and trademark regimes.

12. Berne Convention for the Protection of Literary and Artistic Works, September 9, 1886, as revised at Paris on July 24, 1971 and amended in 1979, art. 2(1) S. Treaty Doc. No. 99–27, 99th Cong., 2d Sess. 1 (1985), 828 U.N.T.S. 221, 221.

13. "Abbot to Stop Launching New Drugs in Thailand in Response to Country's Compulsory License for Antiretrovira Kaletra," Medical News Today, Mar. 16, 2007, http://www.medicalnewstoday.com/articles/65274.php. Ironically, the nations that have greatest likelihood of gaining foreign investment—because they have large populations, rapidly growing economies, etc.—have less need to adopt measures specifically targeted to attract foreign investment. For that reason, some studies that assessed levels of protection for intellectual property rights and levels of investment (without endeavoring to ask the *ceteris paribus* question in a serious way) found inverse correlations. Later studies, correcting for that concern, found positive correlations. See generally Anup Tikku, *Indian Inflow: The Interplay of Foreign Investment and Intellectual Property,* 19 Third World Q. 87 (1998); Catherine Y. Co, John A. List & Larry D. Qui, *Intellectual Property Rights, Environmental Regulations, and Foreign Direct Investment,* 80 Land Economics 153 (2004).

14. Professor Pamela Samuelson raises the possibility that nations with low production of domestic intellectual property may benefit from "intellectual property arbitrage"—by holding protection levels low, they may under certain conditions force world protections toward a lower level as sales into the lower-level markets inevitably compromise protection worldwide. Pamela Samuelson, *Intellectual*

Property Arbitrage: How Foreign Rules can Affect Domestic Protections, 71 U. Chi. L. Rev. 223 (2004). We do not believe that this is as much of a problem as Professor Samuelson; our expectation is that, under most circumstances, enterprises with high-value intellectual property embedded in their products are more likely to forgo sales in a suspect market than to risk that investment.

15. See, e.g., James M. Buchanan & Gordon Tullock, The Calculus of Consent, Logical Foundations of Constitutional Democracy (Univ. of Michigan Press 1962); James M. Buchanan & Robert D. Tollison, The Theory of Public Choice (Univ. of Michigan Press 1972); Anthony Downs, An Economic Theory of Democracy (Harper 1957); Mancur Olson, The Logic of Collective Action (Harvard Univ. Press 1965).

16. The reduction in overall welfare is a standard result from efforts to handicap more successful competitors, whether through trade barriers, domestic regulation, or taxes. See, e.g., Z. Clark Dickinson, *Incentive Problems in Regulation Capitalism,* 34 Am. Econ. Rev. Part 2, Supplement 151, 160 (Mar. 1994); Jong-Wha Lee & Phillip Swagel, *Trade Barriers and Trade Flows Across Countries and Industries,* 79 Rev. Econ. & Stat. 372 (Aug 1997).

17. This has been a standard conclusion of economists dating back to Adam Smith's *Wealth of Nations* and David Ricardo's explanation of comparative advantage. Adam Smith, The Wealth of Nations (Edwin Cannan ed., Bantam Dell 2003) (1776); David Ricardo, Principles of Political Economy and Taxation (E. C. K. Gonner ed., G. Bell & Sons 1919) (1817). Indeed, despite a few notable qualifications and some possibilities that are heavily dependent on peculiar factual assumptions, that remains perhaps the most widely and thoroughly endorsed economic thesis. Steven E. Landsburg, Price Theory and Applications 263 (8th ed., South-Western College Pub. 2010).

18. See, e.g., Robert E. Baldwin, The Political Economy of U.S. Import Policy (MIT Press 1985); Jagdish N. Bhagwati, Protectionism (MIT Press 1988); Jan Tumlir, Protectionism: Trade Protection in Democratic Societies (American Enterprise Institute 1985).

19. The first explication of this is credited to Elmer Schattschneider. See E. E. Schattschneider, Politics, Pressures, and the Tariff: A Study of Free Private Enterprise in Pressure Politics, as Shown in the 1929–1930 Revision of the Tariff (Prentice-Hall 1935).

20. For example, the Madrid Agreement on implementing key features of the Paris Convention was negotiated and concluded in 1891, but the United States did not accede until 2003, after the agreement had been modified as what is commonly called the Madrid Protocol.

21. Paul Steidlmeier, *The Moral Legitimacy of Intellectual Property Claims: American Business and Developing Country Perspectives,* 12 J. Bus. Ethics 157, 160–62 (Feb. 1993).

22. See, e.g., Ronald A. Cass, *The Rule of Law and Implementation of International Norms,* Hague Conference (Oct. 2007).

23. Medellín v. Texas, 552 U.S. 491 (2008).

24. See Avena and Other Mexican Nationals (Mexico v. U.S.), 2004 I.C.J. 12 (Mar. 31, 2004).

25. A well-known example is the effect of the U.S. "Special 301" law.

26. Agreement on Trade-Related Aspects of Intellectual Property Rights, Apr. 15, 1994, Marrakesh Agreement Establishing the World Trade Organization, Annex 1C, in Legal Instruments—Results of The Uruguay Round, vol. 31, 33 I.L.M. 81 (1994).

27. See Rochelle Cooper Dreyfuss & Andreas F. Lowenfeld, *Two Achievements of the Uruguay Round: Putting TRIPS and Dispute Settlement Together,* 37 Va. J. Int'l L. 275 (1997).

28. *North American Free Trade Agreement, U.S.-Canada-Mexico, arts. 1102–03, Dec. 17, 1992, 32 I.L.M. 289;* Convention on the Settlement of Investment Disputes Between States and Nationals of Other States, opened for signature *Mar. 18, 1965, 17 U.S.T. 1270, 575 U.N.T.S. 159.*

29. See Lawrence Lessig, Free Culture: How Big Media Uses Technology and the Law to Lock Down Culture and Control Creativity (Penguin Press 2004).

30. The collective action problem that entities like ASCAP can help solve is discussed, *infra,* at 29. See also Comment, *Ascap and the Antitrust Laws: The Story of a Reasonable Compromise,* 1959 Duke L. J. l 258 (1959). Robert P. Merges, *Contracting into Liability Rules: Intellectual Property Rights and Collective Rights Organizations,* 84 Cal. L. Rev. 1293 (1996).

31. NTP, Inc. v. Research In Motion, Ltd., 397 F.Supp 2d 785 (E.D. Va. 2005); Tim Wu, *Weapons of Business Destruction: How a Tiny Little "Patent Troll" Got Black-Berry in a Headlock,* Slate, Feb. 6, 2006, http://slate.msn.com/id/2135559/.

32. Questions respecting NTP's patents' validity are still being contested in the PTO at this writing.

33. 547 U.S. 388 (2006).

34. 547 U.S. at 391.

35. For a brief defense of the historic inclination to use injunctions in patent cases, but not of a formal, categorical presumption, see Chief Justice Roberts' concurring opinion in *e-Bay v. MercExchange,* joined by Justices Scalia and Ginsburg, 347 U.S. at 394–395.

36. Justice Anthony Kennedy's concurrence, joined by Justices Stevens, Souter, and Breyer, noted both the problem associated with injunctions when the patent is for lesser-value component parts of a larger, complex product and the problem with use of injunctions for infringement of business method patents. See 547 U.S. at 395, 396–397.

37. Customer Identification and Marketing Analysis Systems, U.S. Patent No. 6070147 (issued May 30, 2000).

38. See discussion in Chapter 4.

39. eBay v. MercExchange, 547 U.S. 388 (2006); Bilski v. Kappos, 130 S. Ct. 3218 (2010).

40. In re Bilski, 545 F.3d 943 (Fed. Cir. 2008).

41. Bilski v. Kappos, 130 S.Ct. 3218 (2010).

42. Spansion, Inc. v. Int'l Trade Comm'n, 629 F.3d 1331 (Fed. Cir. 2010).

43. Peter Lewin, *Creativity or Coercion: Alternative Perspectives on Rights to Intellectual Property,* 71 J. Bus. Ethics 441, 446–448 (Apr. 2007).

44. See, e.g., Michael Abramowicz, *Perfecting Patent Prizes,* 56 Vand. L. Rev. 115 (2003); Michael Kremer, *Patent Buyouts: A Mechanism for Encouraging Innovation,* 113 Q.J. Econ. 1137 (1998); Steven Shavell & Tanguy van Ypersle, *Rewards versus Intellectual Property Rights,* 44 J.L. & Econ. 525 (2001).

45. See John F. Duffy, *The Marginal Cost Controversy in Intellectual Property,* 71 U. Chi. L. Rev. 21 (2004).

46. See Duffy, *supra.*

47. See Anatol Rapoport, *Prisoner's Dilemma,* in The New Palgrave: Game Theory 199 (John Eatwell, Murray Milgate & Peter Newman eds., W.W. Norton 1989). The original hypothetical is credited to Albert W. Tucker.

48. Carl Shapiro, *Navigating the Patent Thicket: Cross Licenses, Patent Pools, and Standard Setting,* 1 Innovation Pol'y & Econ. 119, 124–125 (2000).

49. This section is taken in part from Ronald A. Cass, *Compulsory Licensing of Intellectual Property: The Exception that Ate the Rule?* Washington Legal Foundation, Critical Legal Issues Series, Working Paper No. 150 (September 2007), available at available at http://www.wlf.org/upload/casswpCover.pdf.

50. See, e.g., Richard A. Epstein, Takings: Private Property and the Power of Eminent Domain (Harvard Univ. Press 1985).

51. In the United States, the requirement of just compensation is embedded in the Constitution's "takings clause." U.S. Const., Amend. V, cl. 4. The Constitution also imposes restraints on another type of taking of property, prohibiting governments from quartering troops in private homes without the consent of the owner when the nation is at peace and strictly limiting the circumstances under which this can be done in wartime. U.S. Const., Amend. III.

52. See, e.g., Thomas W. Merrill, *The Economics of Public Use,* 72 Cornell L. Rev. 61 (1986).

53. See, e.g., Lucas v. South Carolina Coastal Council, 505 U.S. 1003 (1992).

54. We refer to Kelo v. City of New London, 545 U.S. 469 (2005) and its aftermath.

55. See, e.g., Kurt M. Saunders, *Patent Nonuse and the Role of Public Interest as a Deterrent to Technology Suppression,* 15 Harv. J.L. & Tech. 389 (2002).

56. 42 U.S.C. § 2183 (2006).

57. 45 U.S.C. § 7608 (2006).

58. See 17 U.S.C. § 115 (2006) (compulsory license for phono-recordings of non-dramatic works); 17 U.S.C. § 115 (2006) (statutory license for cable transmission of broadcast programming).

59. Paris Convention for the Protection of Industrial Property, Mar. 20, 1883 (as revised at Stockholm, July 14, 1967), *21 U.S.T. 1583,* 828 U.N.T.S. 305.

60. TRIPS Article 21.

61. See, e.g., Rochelle Cooper Dreyfuss, *Coming of Age with TRIPS: A Comment on J. H. Reichman, The TRIPS Agreement Comes of Age: Conflict or Cooperation with the Developing Countries?* 33 Case W. Res. J. Int'l L. 179 (2001).

62. Cass, *supra* note 49.

63. See, e.g., Frederick M. Abbott, *The WTO TRIPS Agreement and Global Economic Development,* in Public Policy and Global Technological Intergration 39 (Frederick M. Abbott & David J.Gerber eds. 1997).

64. Anna Lanoszka, *The Global Politics of Intellectual Property Rights and Pharmaceutical Drug Policies in Developing Countries,* 24 Int'l. Pol. Sci. Rev. 181 (2003).

65. Later ministerial declarations, in 2003 and 2005, provided (first on a temporary and then, subject to approval by the requisite number of WTO members, a permanent basis) greater freedom for less developed nations to use compulsory licenses in the absence of domestic production of the licensed product or process.

66. See, e.g., James Love, *Measures to Enhance Access to Medical Technologies and New Methods of Stimulating Medical R&D,* 40 U.C. Davis L. Rev. 679 (2007).

67. *See* World Bank, Data and Statistics (2007), available at http://siteresources .worldbank.org/DATASTATISTICS/Resources/GDP.pdf. Thailand ranks far higher (nineteenth) on a purchasing-power-parity basis, which removes distortion caused by disparities between nominal exchange rates and effective market rates for currency. See World Bank, Data and Statistics (2007), available at http://siteresources .worldbank.org/DATASTATISTICS/Resources/GDP_PPP.pdf.

68. See USAID, *Health Profile: Thailand– HIV/AIDS,* available at http://www .usaid.gov/our_work/global_health/aids/Countries/ane/thailand_05.pdf. See also UNAIDS, *Report on the Global AIDS Epidemic* (2006), at 6, available at http://data .unaids.org/pub/globalreport/2006/2006_GR-ExecutiveSummary_en.pdf. Prior to its compulsory licensing announcement, Brazil also had substantially reduced HIV/ AIDS-related deaths and, like Thailand, lowered its rate of new infections as well. See Kaiser Family Foundation, *Proven HIV Prevention Strategies—Real-World Evidence of Effectiveness,* available at http://www.kff.org/hivaids/upload/050106_ HIVPreventionStrategies.pdf.

9. Antitrust and Intellectual Property

1. See, e.g., Phillip Areeda, Louis Kaplow, & Aaron Edlin, Antitrust Analysis: Problems, Text, and Cases 343 (6th ed. 2004).

2. See Ernest Gellhorn & William E. Kovacic, Antitrust Law and Economics in a Nutshell 410–11 (4th ed., West Group Publishing 1994). We apologize to readers who believe that a law "nutshell" should not be used as a serious source of information on the law. However, the Gellhorn-Kovacic nutshell is authored by two first-rate antitrust scholars. It is a richer treatment of antitrust law than many of the existing hornbooks and treatises.

3. See, e.g., Keith N. Hylton, *The Law and Economics of Monopolization Standards, in* Antitrust Law and Economics (K. N. Hylton ed., Edward Elgar Publishers 2010).

4. For earlier discussions of the economics of intellectual property law and antitrust law, see Louis Kaplow, *The Patent-Antitrust Intersection: A Reappraisal*, 97 Harv. L. Rev. 1813 (1984); William M. Landes and Richard A. Posner, The Economic Structure of Intellectual Property Law 372–402 (Harvard Univ. Press 2003); Dennis W. Carleton & Robert Gertner, Intellectual Property, Antitrust and Strategic Behavior, in 3 National Bureau of Economic Research, Innovation Policy and the Economy (Adam B. Jaffee, Joshua Lerner & Scott Stern eds., MIT Press 2003). For an exhaustive treatment of the law, see Herbert Hovenkamp, Mark D. Janis, & Mark A. Lemley, IP and Antitrust: An Analysis of Antitrust Principles Applied to Intellectual Property Law (2003).

5. The market outcome in this example is shown in the figure immediately below, where the horizontal axis measures the number of widgets (per week). The demand schedule for widgets, which shows the relationship between the quantity of widgets demanded each week and the price of a widget, is shown as a downward sloping line. The demand schedule shown assumes that as the price of the widget increases, consumers will buy fewer of them—which is a sensible assumption.

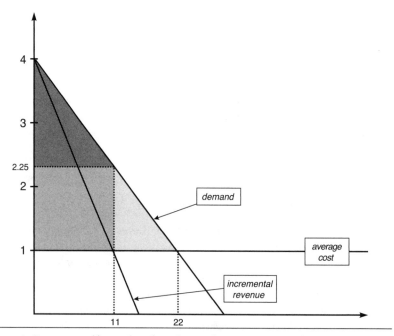

Figure 1: Consumer welfare and profit under a widget-patent monopoly

6. It is shown in Figure 1, *supra* note 5, by the downward-sloped line below the demand schedule, labeled *incremental revenue.*

7. The rectangle shaded in gray, in Figure 1, *supra* note 5, shows the firm's profit amount.

8. See the dark gray shaded triangle at the top of Figure 1, *supra* note 5.

9. See Figure 1, supra note 5, the light gray shaded triangle.

10. See Figure 1. The surplus to consumers when the widget price is set at $1 is equal to the entire shaded area in the figure, which is ($3x22)/2 = $33.

11. If we continue to assume that the rate of interest is 5 percent, then the dynamic benefit is worth $2372.66 and the present value of the static cost (for the years five to twenty) is $3175.86. So at 5 percent, the benefit is less than the cost. But if the interest rate were sufficiently high, the benefit would exceed the cost. For example, if the interest rate is 10 percent, the benefit would be $2049.11, and the cost would be $1894.80. So, in this example, the benefit is less than the cost if the interest rate is 5 percent, and it is greater than the cost if the interest rate is 10 percent.

12. See, e.g., Keith N. Hylton, Antitrust Law: Economic Theory and Common Law Evolution 233 (Cambridge Univ. Press 2003).

13. FTC v. Staples, Inc., 970 F. Supp. 1066 (D.D.C. 1997).

14. Illinois Tool Works Inc. v. Indep. Ink Inc., 547 U.S. 28 (2006).

15. Walker Process Equip. v. Food Mach. & Chem. Corp. 382 U.S. 172, 175–177 (1965).

16. Microsoft v. Commission, Case T-201/04, available at http://curia.europa.eu/jurisp/cgi-bin/gettext.pl?lang=en&num=79929082T19040201&doc=T&ouvert=T&seance=ARRET.

17. The Court of First Instance upheld the Commission's finding that Microsoft had abused its dominant position under Article 82 of the EC by refusing to license interoperability information to rivals. Microsoft v. Commission (T-201/04) [2007] 5 C.M.L.R. 11 at [319]. The court found the Microsoft did not present an "objective justification" for its refusal to disclose the interoperability information, Microsoft [2007] 5 C.M.L.R. 11 at [711], or to support a finding that disclosure "would have a significant negative impact on its incentives to innovate," Microsoft [2007] 5 C.M.L.R. 11 at [697].

18. Daniel F. Spulber, *Competition Policy and the Incentive to Innovate: The Dynamic Effects of* Microsoft v. Commission, 25 Yale J. Reg. 247, 257–261 (Summer 2008); Bo Vesterdorf, *Article 82 EC: Where Do We Stand after the Microsoft Judgment,* 1 Global Antitrust Rev. (2008), available at http://www.icc.qmul.ac.uk/GAR/Vesterdorf.pdf.

19. It is notable that the European Commission has begun using extraordinarily large fines to deter firms from conduct that might contravene its interpretation of European competition laws, especially in single firm (dominance) cases. Dynamic effects of this change in law enforcement could be as important as the changes in the underlying law respecting competition by firms whose market position rests on

particularly successful innovations. It is notable as well that these effects are unlikely to be confined to Europe, among other reasons because there will be competition among antitrust/competition authorities in the application of their legal regimes. See Ronald A. Cass, *Competition in Antitrust Regulation: Law Beyond* Limits, 6 J. Comp. L. & Econ. 119 (2010).

20. Cont'l Paper Bag Co. v. E. Paper Bag Co., 210 U.S. 405 (1908); Dawson Chem. Co. v. Rohm & Haas Co., 448 U.S. 176 (1980).

21. Verizon Commc'ns, Inc., v. Law Offices of Curtis V. Trinko, LLP, 540 U.S. 398 (2004).

22. Pacific Bell Tel. Co. v. Linkline Commc'ns, Inc., 555 U.S. 1109, 129 S. Ct. (2009).

23. 379 U.S. 29 (1964).

24. See, e.g., Frank H. Easterbrook, *Contract and Copyright,* 42 Hous. L. Rev. 953, 955 (2005).

25. E.g., Scheiber v. Dolby Labs Inc., 293 F.3d 1014, 1017 (7th Cir. 2002) (Posner, J., "If royalties are calculated on post-patent term sales, the calculation is simply a risk-shifting credit arrangement between patentee and licensee.")

26. Morton Salt Co. V. G.S. Suppiger Co., 314 U.S. 488, 491 (1942). The patent misuse theory of *Morton Salt* has been limited by more recent statutory and case law developments.

27. *Id.*

28. See, e.g., *Independent Ink* for a discussion of the changing views within the Court on tying law. For a critique of one application of the law especially hostile to any form of tying, technological as well as contractual, see Ronald A. Cass *No Harm in Tying: A Misconceived Case Misunderstood by Its Judge,* in Trial and Error: United States v. Microsoft 53–61 (Paul Beckner and Erick R. Gustafson eds., Citizens for a Sound Economy Foundation 2000).

29. Independent Ink, 547 U.S. at 46.

30. On the narrowing in the case law, see, e.g., Gellhorn & Kovacic, *supra* note 2, at 422–23.

31. 35 U.S.C. §271(d)(5).

32. Perhaps one sign of the movement toward reconciliation is Princo Corp. v. ITC, 616 F.3d 1318 (Fed. Cir. 2010). The court rejected a patent misuse claim based on the theory that the licensing patent holder and another firm had entered into an agreement to refuse to license a competing technology. The court's opinion draws heavily on rule-of-reason arguments in antitrust law.

33. See, e.g., Hylton, *supra* note 6, at xiv–xv.

34. For a discussion of recent legislative incursions into intellectual property law, with a focus on trademark, see Clarissa Long, *The Political Economy of Trademark Dilution,* 132–147, *in* Trademark Law and Theory: A Handbook of Contemporary Research (Graeme B. Dinwoodie & Mark D. Janis eds., Edward Elgar Publishing 2008). Administrative agencies such as the Patent and Trademark Office or the

Registrar of Copyrights play roles in the administration of the intellectual property laws and to some degree in shaping the laws; those agencies play a less visible and important role in the litigation of intellectual property cases. The intellectual property agencies also are not involved in selecting the cases that come before the courts, which is itself a substantial input into the evolution of other areas of law. On case selection and common law evolution, see George L. Priest & Benjamin Klein, *The Selection of Disputes for Litigation*, 13 J. Legal Stud. 1 (1984); Keith N. Hylton, *Information, Litigation, and Common Law Evolution*, 8 Am. L. Econ. Rev. 33 (2006).

35. We disagree with the view expressed by Landes and Posner that intellectual property law can be distinguished from common law subjects (such as torts) because it is "an amalgam of frequently amended federal statutes, . . .", William M. Landes & Richard A. Posner, The Economic Structure of Intellectual Property Law 10 (Harvard Univ. Press 2003). While this is a valid description of the current state of intellectual property law, it overlooks its developmental stage, which was largely driven by common law decisions.

36. 11 Coke 84, 77 Eng. Rep. 1260 (K.B. 1603).

37. On the movement toward rule-of-reason analysis in tying, see Hylton, *supra* note 6, at 292–302.

38. 433 U.S. 36 (1977).

39. The case law is generally favorable toward reverse payment settlements, but there are exceptions. On the side of legality, see, e.g., In re Tamoxifen Citrate Antitrust Litig., 466 F.3d 187, 190 (2d Cir. 2006) (refusing to impose antitrust liability where generic accepted payment in exchange for agreement to delay entry); Schering-Plough Corp. v. FTC, 402 F.3d 1056, 1076 (11th Cir. 2005) (same); see also In re Ciprofloxacin Hydrochloride Antitrust Litig., No. 08–1097 (Fed. Cir. Oct. 15, 2008) available at http://www.cafc.uscourts.gov/opinions/08-1097.pdf (same). Opposing legality, see, e.g., In re Cardizem CD Antitrust Litig., 332 F.3d 896, 908 (6th Cir. 2003) (finding per se antitrust violation in agreement to delay generic entry); Andrx Pharm., Inc., v. Biovail Corp. Int'l, 256 F.3d 799 (D.C. Cir. 2001) (same). For influential views opposing legality, see Herbert Hovenkamp, Mark Janis & Mark A. Lemley, *Anticompetitive Settlement of Intellectual Property Disputes*, 87 Minn. L. Rev. 1719 (2003); Scott C. Hemphill, *Paying for Delay: Pharmaceutical Patent Settlement as a Regulatory Design Problem*, 81 N.Y.U. L. Rev. 1553 (2006); Carl Shapiro, *Antitrust Limits to Patent Settlements* 34 Rand. J. Econ. 391 (2003).

40. Keith N. Hylton and Sungjoon Cho, *The Economics of Injunctive and Reverse Settlements,* 12 Am. Law & Econ. Rev. 181 (2010).

41. See, e.g., Ronald A. Cass & Richard Boltuck, *Antidumping and Countervailing Duty Law: The Mirage of Equitable Competition,* in Fair Trade and Harmonization: Prerequisites for Free Trade? vol. II 351–414 (Jagdish N. Bhagwati & Robert E. Hudec eds., MIT Press 1996).

42. The antidumping complainant may be right in asserting that firms exporting to the affected nation are benefiting from trade barriers that permit market segmentation

(permitting a lower price for exports that does not reflect greater efficiencies). That gives rise to the argument that enforcement of antidumping laws can facilitate an improvement in open trade and a move toward greater global efficiency, though the argument only works if the exporting nation is more sensitive to preserving export markets than it is to protecting the domestic market against competition. The initial work on antidumping as a reflection of market segmentation (an essential prerequisite to differential pricing) is Gottfried von Haberler, The Theory of International Trade with its Application to Commercial Policy, chapter 18 (Wm. Hodge & Co., Ltd. 1936).

43. For a discussion of these issues by Judge Posner, see Asahi Glass v. Pentech Pharm. 289 F.Supp. 2d 986 (2003).

44. On one alternative that might be consistent with the experience and training of judges, see Daniel A. Crane, *Exit Payments in Settlement of Patent Infringement Lawsuits: Antitrust Rules and Economic Implications,* 54 Fla. L. Rev. 747 (2002) (arguing for per se prohibition of reverse payment settlement only after a determination that the likelihood of patent infringement was low).

45. Interestingly, no legislators have proposed banning the settlement of antidumping prosecutions, even though settlements in the antidumping context are more likely to have harmful effects on consumer welfare than will settlements in the pharmaceutical patent cases. The reason for legislative apathy is straightforward. The interest groups that support antidumping legislation are concentrated and have enormous influence in Congress.

46. E.g., Michael Kades, *Whistling Past the Graveyard: The Problem with the Per Se Legality Treatment of Pay-for-Delay Settlements,* 5 Comp. Pol'y Int'l 143 (2009).

47. James Bessen & Michael J. Meurer, Patent Failure: How Judges, Bureaucrats, and Lawyers Put Innovators at Risk 138–147 (Princeton Univ. Press 2008).

48. The Drug Price Competition and Patent Term Restoration Act of 1984, Public law 98–417.

49. 21 U.S.C. § 355(j).

50. 21 U.S.C. § 355(b)(2)(A)(iv).

51. 21 U.S.C. § 355(c)(3)(C).

52. *Id.*

53. 21 U.S.C. § 355(j)(5)(B)(iii)(IV).

54. *Id.*

55. See, e.g., Generic Drug Entry Prior to Patent Expiration: An FTC Study, 2002, available at: http://books.google.com/books?id=9sDK5QQnGQQC&printsec=frontcover&source=gbs_navlinks_s#v=onepage&q=&f=false.

56. 186 U.S. 70 (1902).

57. U.S. Phillips Corp. v. International Trade Commission, 424 F.3d 1179 (Fed. Cir. 2005).

58. U.S. v. New Wrinkle, Inc., 341 United States 371 (1952).

10. Understanding Intellectual Property Law

1. We refer to the influential writings of Lessig, Stallman, and others discussed in Chapter 1.

2. 9 F. Cas. 342 (C.C.D. Mass. 1841).

3. The Venetian patent law of 1474 and Statute of Anne (1710) (copyright) are examples of such statutory innovations. In the case of the Statute of Anne, however, the law simply formalized a set of norms that had developed within the early publishing industry.

4. John Henry Wigmore, Select Cases on the Law of Torts, with Notes and a Summary of Principles 318–368 (Little, Brown & Co. 1912).

5. Ronald H. Coase, *The Problem of Social Cost,* 3 J.L. & Econ. 1 (1960).

6. James Bessen & Michael J. Meurer, Patent Failure 32 (Princeton Univ. Press 2008).

7. 537 U.S. 186 (2003).

8. Michele Boldrin & David K. Levine, Against Intellectual Monopoly 100 (Cambridge Univ. Press 2008). More generally, scholars have argued that the process of lawmaking has been captured by entrenched rights-holders, see Lawrence Lessig, Free Culture: How Big Media Uses Technology and the Law to Lock Down Culture and Control Creativity (Penguin Press 2004).

9. On the public choice theory of interest group legislation see, e.g., Mancur Olson, The Logic of Collective Action: Public Goods and the Theory of Groups (Harvard Univ. Press 1965). In the copyright setting, however, there may be countervailing concentrated interests going against rights-holders. Users of intellectual property rights also can form small, intensely interested groups opposed to strong rights. Those groups at times can be more concentrated and more influential in the legislative process than rights-holders.

10. L. Ray Patterson & Stanley Lindberg, The Nature of Copyright: A Law of Users' Rights 102–106 (Univ. of Georgia Press 1991).

11. 130 S. Ct. 3218 (2010).

Acknowledgments

As with any project that, like this book, has been in the works for a long time, there is a long list of people who should be thanked, both for their direct contributions to the project and for their help in advancing our understanding of the practical, legal, and economic issues that affect the subject of this book. We are unlikely to remember to include the names of all of those people in this section, having had too many conversations with too many people about this book to acknowledge all of the sources of useful suggestions here. For those whose names should be here and are not, we apologize and plead fading memories.

Fortunately, our memories are working well enough to recall some of the people who have helped us with this project. We have benefited from many, detailed comments on the whole manuscript from Robert Merges and Henry Smith. We have also received comments on specific parts from Olufunmilayo Arewa, Scott Baker, Barton Beebe, Tom Bell, Susan Cass, Andrew Chin, Ben DePoorter, Peter DiCola, Frank Easterbrook, Paul Heald, Sonia Katyal, Jay Kesan, Scott Kieff, Jessica Litman, Fred McChesney, Adam Mossoff, Sean Seymore, and Katherine Strandburg. In addition, Henry Butler helped us enormously by holding a conference on our manuscript, while it was still in progress, at Northwestern University's Searle Institute (since then decamped to George Mason University). The conference helped us see some of the ways in which we could better address the diverse issues in current intellectual property law scholarship. Early in the project's life, David Evans and Bob Bone offered helpful ideas, comments and encouragement. Research support was provided by Boston University, the Center for the Rule of Law, the International Centre for Economic Research, and the Searle Institute. For research assistance we thank James Odell, Avantika Kulkarni, Crelea Henderson, and especially Matt Saldana, who scoured the entire manuscript for omissions. We take responsibility, of course, for the errors and omissions that remain.

Index